Creating Constructive Cultures

Creating Constructive Cultures

Leading People and Organizations to Effectively Solve Problems and Achieve Goals

Janet L. Szumal, PhD with Robert A. Cooke, PhD

2019

Human Synergistics International

Human Synergistics International
39819 Plymouth Road
Plymouth, MI 48170
United States of America

Copyright © 2019 by Human Synergistics International.

All rights reserved. No part of this work may be reproduced, stored in a retrieval system, transcribed in any form or by any means, including but not limited to electronic, mechanical, photocopying, recording, or other means, without prior written permission. *While we're not vengeful, we are provokable.*®

Library of Congress Control Number: 2019917419

ISBN 9780578544052

Printed in the United States of America.

Production credit: Studio 20/20.

Dedicated to Clay Lafferty, whose ingenuity and insights continue to inspire us and our work.

Contents

Illustrations viii
Acknowledgements xi

Introduction: A Different Way of Looking at Your Impact 1

Part I. Why and How Leaders Create Constructive Cultures

Chapter 1. Why Create a Constructive Culture? 21
Chapter 2. How Leaders Directly and Indirectly Influence and Change Culture 65

Part II. Examples from Different Countries and Key Learnings

Chapter 3. Launching—and Relaunching—Constructive Cultural Change (USA) 109
Chapter 4. Using a Shared Language to Increase Self-Awareness
and Reduce Conflict (Germany) 121
Chapter 5. Making Culture a Strategic Priority to Become More Ambidextrous
and Overcome Market Disruption (Switzerland) 141
Chapter 6. Deploying Levers for Cultural Change
to Expedite Strategy Implementation (Mexico) 161
Chapter 7. Trading Command and Control for Expansion and Growth (Serbia) 179
Chapter 8. Leveraging the Capacity of HR Directors and Middle Managers
to Effect Culture Change (Hungary) 197
Chapter 9. Leading People to Think Outside the Box
and Move the Organization onto the Fast Track (Australia) 215
Chapter 10. Sustaining Constructive Cultures through
Continuous Monitoring, Coaching, and Support (Canada) 233
Chapter 11. From the Middle to the Top of the Organization:
Making Culture a Habit of Grace (USA) 249

Part III. Taking the Next Step

Chapter 12. Leading Your Organization's Culture Journey 271

Learn More 293
Notes 295
Bibliography 305
About the Authors 323

Illustrations

Figures

I.1.	The Reciprocal Relationship between Culture and Leadership	7
I.2.	The Human Synergistics Circumplex	9
I.3.	The Human Synergistics Integrated Diagnostic System	15
1.1.	Effectiveness of Most and Least Constructive Organizations	22
1.2.	Composite Operating Culture Profile of the "Best of the Best"	24
1.3.	The Electronic Disintegration of Interpersonal Processes	29
1.4.	Subcultures of Average Performers versus Top Performers	33
1.5.	Cultural Norms and Sales Growth	40
1.6.	Cultural Norms and Share Price	41
1.7.	Typical Ideal Culture Profile	47
1.8.	Ideal Organizational Culture Profiles across the Globe	49
1.9.	Ideal Cultures Described by Different Age Groups	57
1.10.	Ideal Cultures Described by Females versus Males	60
2.1.	Operating Culture at Different Levels	67
2.2.	How Culture Works	68
3.1.	Shift in Port of San Diego's Operating Culture	113
4.1.	Leaders' Composite Ideal Impact Profile (2015)	129
4.2.	Leaders' Composite Actual Impact Profiles (2015)	130
4.3.	Spreadshirt's Revenues Over Time	138
5.1.	Straumann's Share Price Development: 2008 to 2012	143
5.2.	Straumann's Ideal and Operating Culture Profiles (2014)	150
5.3.	Operating Culture of Packaging Group (2016)	153
5.4.	Straumann's Share Price Development: 2012 to 2016	157
6.1.	Agroenzymas' Ideal and Operating Culture Profiles (2014)	168
6.2.	Agroenzymas' Operating Culture and Gross Revenue Over Time	175
7.1.	Serbian Organizational Culture Research Results and Pons Culture Results	185
7.2.	Pons's 2014 Results for Causal Factors	188
7.3.	Shift in Top Team's Group Styles (based on the *Group Styles Inventory*)	191
7.4.	Goran's Impact on Others	192
8.1.	Dreher's Cultural Ambition	204

8.2.	Dreher's Culture Journey: 2012 to 2016	209
9.1.	Senior Leaders' Composite *Life Styles Inventory* Profiles	220
9.2.	Sanitarium's Operating Culture Over Time	225
9.3.	Senior Leaders' Composite *Life Styles Inventory* Profiles Over Time	226
9.4.	Senior Leaders' Composite *Leadership/Impact* Results (2014)	226
9.5.	Changes in Senior Leaders' Thinking Styles Create Ripple Effect on Operating Culture	227
10.1.	SaskCentral's Operating Culture and Ideal Culture (1996)	237
10.2.	SaskCentral's Operating Culture Over Time	241
11.1.	Diocese of Chicago's Operating and Ideal Culture Profiles (2011)	254
11.2.	Culture Shift at the Diocese of Chicago	261
11.3.	Church Center's Operating and Ideal Profiles (2016)	264
11.4.	Shift in Church Center's Operating Culture	267
12.1.	A Four-Phase Process for Strengthening Constructive Cultures	275
12.2.	Example Culture Profiles with Equivalent Single Number Index Scores	281

Tables

I.1.	How Personal Orientations Relate to Effectiveness and Personal Success	5
I.2.	The Twelve Cultural Norms Based on the *Organizational Culture Inventory*	13
I.3.	The Twelve Thinking and Behavioral Styles Based on the *Life Styles Inventory*	14
1.1.	Ideal Organizational Cultures and Societal Values	50
1.2.	Ideal Cultures and World Competitiveness Rankings Five and Ten Years Later	54
2.1.	Causal Factors Related to Constructive and Defensive Behavioral Norms (Summary of Findings)	70
2.2.	Examples of Prescriptive and Restrictive Leadership Strategies	98
2.3.	Leadership Activities to Target for Change	100
2.4.	Examples of Facilitating and Inhibiting Management Approaches	103
2.5.	Management Activities to Target for Change	104
5.1.	Straumann's Financial Performance: 2012 to 2016	156
8.1.	Sales Force New Hire Departures: 2012 versus 2017	211
9.1.	Leadership and Management Responsibilities	219
12.1.	Recent *Life Styles Inventory* Findings	273

Acknowledgements

We want to express our deepest appreciation to all the leaders, managers, and consultants highlighted in the chapters in this book, without whom these inspirational examples would not exist. It is an honor to share their stories and insights about creating Constructive cultures.

We acknowledge and thank the following colleagues for introducing us to the leaders of the organizations featured in this book, providing us with invaluable background information, and/or reviewing early versions of specific cases:

- Tim Kuppler, Director of Culture and Leadership at Human Synergistics, Inc., and consultant to Port of San Diego and the Episcopal Church;
- John van Etten, Managing Director of Human Synergistics InterConnext GmbH (chapters on Spreadshirt and Straumann);
- Jochen Grotenhöfer, owner of Transition Consult and consultant to Spreadshirt;
- Guy Kempfert, previously Head of People and Organizational Development at Straumann, now owner and Managing Director of Culture Works; Kimberly Keating-Posco, Director of Learning and Organizational Development, Straumann Group; and Pieter van der Veen, founder and owner of Room to Act and consultant to Straumann;
- Marcela Hurtado, founder of Blue Sector Group and Jose Eusebio Lopez, cofounder of Blue Sector Group and consultant to Agroenzymas;
- Ivan Dmitrić, Managing Director of Human Synergistics Serbia and consultant to Pons Bakery;
- Gábor Zsikla, Dr. Ildikó Magura, and Péter Kalmár of Human Synergistics Hungary Kft and The Flow Group and consultants to Dreher Brewery;

- Shaun McCarthy, Chairman and Director of Human Synergistics New Zealand/Australia; David Byrum, Managing Director of Human Synergistics Australia; and Matthew Croxford, formerly senior consultant with Human Synergistics Australia, now Partner and National Head of Human Capital at Grant Thornton in Sydney (chapter on Sanitarium); and
- Greg Fieger and Ken Curtis, who, back in the 1990s when both were with Ernst and Young, introduced us to the leaders of SaskCentral.

Special thanks to Dr. Liz Alexander for her work with Janet and her mentoring and guidance during the first few years of working on the case studies.

We are grateful to all the staff members at the Human Synergistics offices in the United States and abroad for their ongoing support throughout this project and their dedication to our collective mission: Changing the World—One Organization at a Time.® It is a privilege to work with each and every one of you! We especially want to acknowledge the following for their tireless efforts, patience, and good humor while helping us make this book a reality:

- Meghan Oliver for the initial editing of chapters and formatting of graphics and Jason Bowes for his work on the tables and figures;
- Daryl Lynn O'Donnell and Mary Ayers for transcribing nearly all the interviews carried out for this book;
- Bonnie Battin and Dr. Cheryl Boglarsky for assembling the recent survey data that enabled us to carry out new analyses on organizational culture, leadership, levers for change, and outcomes; and
- Cathleen Cooke and Jessica Cooke for providing us with additional resources, suggestions, and assistance throughout this project.

Introduction

A Different Way of Looking at Your Impact

> Out of all the measures in my organization, the one I choose to measure my performance—to do my self-assessment—is culture.
> Rebecca Kardos, CEO, Aurora Energy[1]

During more than thirty years of research, I have never seen the idea of organizational culture in such a prominent position: leaders are more concerned now with the culture of their organizations than they have ever been. Back in the late 1970s when Drs. Robert A. Cooke (developer of the *Organizational Culture Inventory®*) and J. Clayton Lafferty (founder of Human Synergistics) began working together, the concept of organizations having cultures wasn't discussed beyond the spheres of organizational psychology and academic theory. Since I joined Human Synergistics in 1986, Rob Cooke and I have witnessed and contributed to the evolution of organizational culture to its current state as a widely acknowledged priority and source of competitive advantage. Certainly, some of the attention is due to the increased publicity about the damages caused by organizational cultures gone wrong. However, like Rebecca Kardos, whom we met at Human Synergistics Australia's Twentieth Annual Leadership and Culture Conference, most of the leaders we encounter are primarily interested not in crisis management or damage control but rather in evaluating and improving their organizations' cultures because of the distinct advantages associated with cultures that are Constructive. We focus on such leaders in this book, exploring their experiences as they move the cultures of their organizations in a more Constructive direction and highlighting the levers that you and your leadership team can use to improve the effectiveness and sustainability of your organization.

The Universal Value of Constructive Cultures

We define *organizational culture* as

> a system of shared values and beliefs that can lead to behavioral norms that, in turn, guide the way members of an organization approach their work, interact with one another, and solve problems.

Importantly, we distinguish an organization's *espoused* values, which are its stated values, from its *operating culture*, which is the set of norms and expectations that drives the behavior of all members, including leaders, on a day-to-day basis. As you'll see, although operating cultures are influenced by espoused values, the two are not necessarily aligned.

One of the things we've found by measuring and comparing the ideal and the actual operating cultures of thousands of organizations over the past several decades is that the cultures described by leaders and other members as optimal are remarkably similar across organizations and industries. Specifically, the ideal cultures they describe—which reflect their values—are consistent with what we call *Constructive cultures*.

A Constructive culture is one that that encourages members to work to their full potential, take initiative, think independently, participate without taking over, and voice unique perspectives and concerns while working toward consensus. In organizations with strong Constructive cultures, quality is valued over quantity; creativity and curiosity are fostered in place of conformity and indifference; collaboration and coordination are believed to lead to better results than competition and silos; the bigger picture is emphasized over minutiae; and doing good is viewed as more important than looking good or "being good."

Of course, you don't need to be a researcher to notice the similarity in the values that different organizations espouse, given that they are often published on their websites or in their annual reports. As we'll demonstrate in the first chapter of this book, there is a genre of behaviors in organizations that attracts and keeps talent, promotes adaptation and innovation, supports the creation and implementation of effective strategies and business models, and, more generally, increases the capability of people to independently and interactively solve problems and achieve goals. These behaviors, we have found, are strikingly similar across organizations, because all organizations are characterized by a common set of properties that give rise to the same set of problems, regardless of the industry or the country in which the organization operates. For instance, within all organizations there are interdependencies among members that lead to the universal problem of (and need for) coordination. As another example, all organizations are dependent on the external environment for resources, which gives rise to the familiar problem of adaptation. In addition, all organizations are characterized by partial inclusion of members (who also belong to other groups—such as families, professional associations, volunteer groups, community organizations, and societies) and therefore must address the problem of integrating members into the system.[2]

Yet knowing what types of cultures are effective and productive doesn't necessarily translate into acting on that knowledge or creating those kinds of cultures. Recent polls of managers, directors, and C-level executives show that over 80 percent feel their cultures are not properly "designed" or managed—and many feel a major overhaul is necessary.[3] Perhaps less widely recognized is the fact that senior leaders tend to have a more optimistic view of their organizations' operating cultures than do people at other levels. As we'll show in chapter 2, the behavioral norms that guide the ways in which members approach their work and interact with one another tend to stray further from the organization's values as one moves down the organizational hierarchy. While this tendency might seem to suggest that the origins of *culture disconnects*—where behavioral norms diverge from values—are at the lower levels of organizations, we find that the roots of such problems are usually embedded at the top.

Leaders Affect Culture…and Culture Affects Leaders

Our initial interest wasn't in how leaders affect culture but rather in how culture affects leaders. This interest came out of Rob's early research (he was teaching at the University of Michigan and working as an associate research scientist at its Survey Research Center) on the *Life Styles Inventory*™—a 240-item survey originally developed by J. Clayton Lafferty that measures twelve personal thinking and behavioral styles. Clay asked Rob to assess the reliability and validity of the *Life Styles Inventory* and suggest improvements. Rob analyzed data on thousands of individuals who had a) described their thinking styles using the *Self-Description* form of the *Inventory*, and b) received feedback on their behavioral styles from others who had completed the *Description by Others* form for them. Rob discovered that the twelve styles clustered into three general personal orientations, which he later labeled *Passive/Defensive*, *Aggressive/Defensive*, and *Constructive*. (We describe these sets of styles in more detail later in this introduction.) He then examined the relationship between these sets of styles and indicators of managerial success, health and well-being, and effectiveness.

Rob found that the Constructive styles were strongly correlated with managerial effectiveness, positive interpersonal relations, and interest in self-improvement as rated by others. With Clay and colleagues, Rob also found that teams with members who were more Constructive performed more effectively on group problem-solving simulations (such as Human Synergistics' *Desert Survival Situation*™, *Subarctic Survival Situation*™, and *Project Planning Situation*™) than those with members who were less Constructive. These positive and statistically significant relationships are indicated by the plus marks (+) in the first column of Table I.1.

Constructive ways of thinking tended to be related to organizational level. However, the correlation with salary was not significant (indicated by the zero in the first column of the table), suggesting Constructive styles were not necessarily being rewarded and reinforced by organizations. Instead, those who were rewarded with promotions and pay raises tended to be strongly oriented toward competing with, dominating, and controlling others; being critical of others; and remaining detached, impersonal, and focused on details (see the pluses in the last column of Table I.1). Despite the positive correlation between Aggressive/Defensive styles and material gain, these styles were not related to task effectiveness (indicated in the table by a zero). Additionally, these styles correlated negatively with both interpersonal relations and problem-solving effectiveness (indicated by the minuses in the last column of the table) and with health and well-being. Participants who tended to use Aggressive/Defensive styles showed psychological and physiological symptoms of strain, such as anxiety, ulcers, and heart attacks.

While certainly not mainstream findings at the time, these disconcerting results were consistent with the thesis of the 1975 article "On the Folly of Rewarding A, while Hoping for B." This classic work highlights the short-sighted focus of so many organizational policies and practices, including performance management and reward systems. Author Steven Kerr of Ohio State University noted:

> It is *hoped* that administrators will pay attention to long run costs and opportunities and will institute programs which

will bear fruit later on. However, many organizational reward systems pay off for short run sales and earnings only. Under such circumstances it is personally rational for officials to sacrifice long term growth and profit (by selling off equipment and property, or by stifling research and development) for short term advantages.[4]

Table I.1. How Personal Orientations Relate to Effectiveness and Personal Success

	Personal Orientation[a]		
	Constructive	Passive/ Defensive	Aggressive/ Defensive
Salary[a]	0	--	+
Organizational Level[a]	+	--	+
Managerial Effectiveness[b]	++	0	0
Quality of Interpersonal Relations[b]	+	++	--
Interest in Self-Improvement[b]	++	+	--
Psychological/Physiological Health[a]	++	-	--
Problem-Solving Effectiveness[c]	+	-	-

Table from the *Life Styles Inventory*™ Leader's Guide, Appendix D.
Copyright © Human Synergistics International.

Note. Results based on samples ranging from 500 to 1,000 focal individuals. Plusses and minuses denote statistically significant positive and negative relationships, respectively. Single plusses and minuses indicate $p<.05$; double plusses and minuses indicate $p<.01$. Zero indicates no statistically significant relationship.

[a] Based on Life Styles Inventory (LSI) Self Description.
[b] Based on LSI Descriptions by Others.
[c] Based on performance on problem-solving simulations.

Kerr reported a similar inconsistency around what we now call *Passive/Defensive* behaviors. During his interviews with managers, they complained about lower level members' tendencies toward "apple polishing" and conservatism. However, via brief surveys, he found that subordinates claimed that "always agreeing with the boss" and "going along with the majority" were the "most rational course(s) of action in light of the existing reward system."[5] Again, organizations were somehow reinforcing behaviors that were the opposite of what managers were hoping for. However, based on the results shown in the center column of Table I.1, promotions and pay raises apparently are not responsible for these passive behaviors. In fact, the data indicate that these styles are negatively related to these tangible rewards. It seems more likely that the leadership styles of the respondents' superiors—including their aggressive behaviors and the nature of the feedback they provided—produced passive responses.

Similarly, managers who participated in development programs based on the *Life Styles Inventory* made it clear that they were encouraged to behave aggressively by factors beyond just pay and promotion. They cited various forces within their organizations that signaled the need for these behaviors. As one of them said in a follow-up debrief (with a mix of humor and frustration), those at the top of the organization, along with his peers, would "simply chew me up and spit me out" if he engaged in less aggressive and more constructive behaviors on a day-to-day basis.

Rob felt it was important for organizations to understand the thinking and behavioral styles they were reinforcing. Though he began by writing a survey focusing on what they rewarded, it struck him that some of the forces leading to these behaviors were more subtle and pervasive—almost cultural. But the cultural forces at play were more at the organizational level rather than the societal level. At the same time, most of the writings on culture by anthropologists such as Edward T. Hall focused exclusively on societies and rarely mentioned organizations.[6]

Consequently, rather than developing a survey that focused just on what was being rewarded, Rob created the *Organizational Culture Inventory* to measure the extent to which members believed their organization expected or implicitly required the sets of styles assessed by the *Life Styles Inventory*. Rob's original intention was to use the *Organizational Culture Inventory* to provide organizations with a picture of their cultures to stimulate changes consistent with and supportive of the leadership development programs based on the *Life Styles Inventory*. The irony was that for an organization to support leaders in their efforts to think and behave in more effective ways, those leaders often had to redirect their organization's culture—a "which comes first, the chicken or the egg" conundrum. This is why Rob and I started working together to uncover the various ways in which leaders create cultures that are more strongly Constructive.

Clearly, leadership styles shape culture and, reciprocally, culture shapes the thinking and behavioral styles of leaders. This type of causality is consistent with the notion of *reciprocal determinism* proposed by psychologist Albert Bandura.[7] Instead of viewing the environment as a one-way determinant of behavior, Bandura pointed out that behavior also influences the environment, and both are influenced by the individual's cognitions and predispositions. Figure I.1 illustrates how this works with respect to leadership and culture. *Environment* includes the organization's operating culture in terms of shared behavioral norms and expectations, as well as the more tangible aspects of organizations such as their structures and systems. *Behaviors* refer to the leader's behavioral styles (such as those measured by the *Life Styles Inventory Description by Others*). *Thinking* includes the leader's task-oriented versus people-oriented patterns of thinking, which are driven by higher-order versus lower-order needs, as measured by the *Life Styles Inventory Self-Description*.

Figure I.1. The Reciprocal Relationship between Culture and Leadership

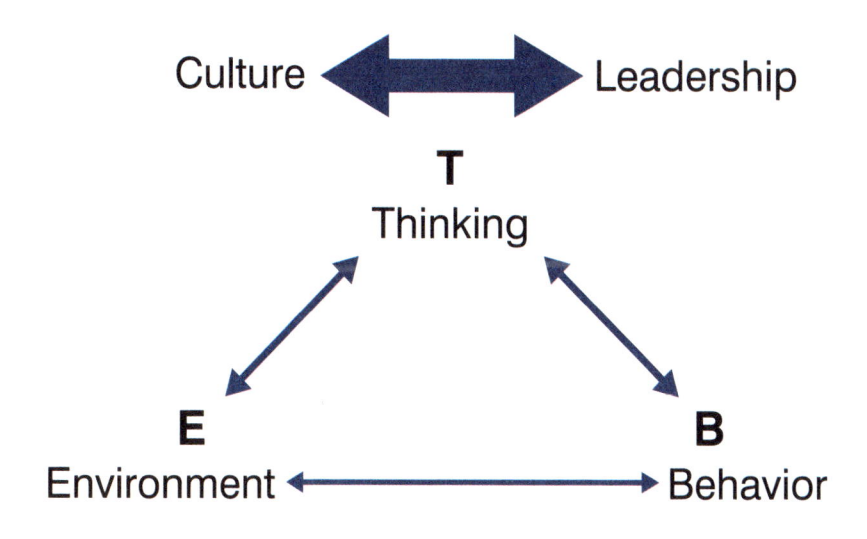

Adapted from Albert Bandura, The Self System in Reciprocal Determinism, American Psychologist, April 1978, pp. 344-358.

Bandura's work is instructive in understanding the complexity of culture transformation and the difficulty of effecting sustained change. Leaders can change their own behaviors, but such changes are fragile if: a) their thinking doesn't change (such as when leaders are just "going through the motions" or giving "lip service" to change efforts) or b) environmental factors are nonsupportive or point in another direction (such as when leaders are criticized when they're trying to practice something new—for example, behaving in a more Constructive manner). As noted in a recent *Harvard Business Review* article, many leadership development programs today do not have a significant impact on their target organizations because of deficiencies "in the policies and practices created by top management"[8]—who in many cases are the same leaders who initiated the development programs.

Such behavioral and environmental factors include not only the *skills and qualities* of leaders but also *systems*, such as those around reinforcement, performance management, and goal setting; *structural features*, such as empowerment and the distribution of influence; and *technological factors* influencing the design of jobs. All these factors send signals that translate into the shared beliefs held by members of an organization regarding what's actually expected (i.e., the operating culture). The emergent behavioral norms and expectations may be inconsistent with the organization's stated values and preferred culture and stand in the way of even elegant programs designed to change leaders' behaviors. Consequently, to effectively and sustainably achieve improvements in performance, development initiatives must simultaneously address leaders and members as individuals and the organization as a system in a way that is consistent with the organization's stated values and preferred culture. This doesn't imply that everything has to be changed all at once and right away. Rather, the members of an organization need to see from a leader's initial changes that a different set of behaviors is truly expected and will be supported. This is much easier said than done, particularly when leaders are unaware of their own thinking and behavior and how they affect—and are affected by—the organization's current culture.

A Framework and Language for Describing Leadership and Culture

The language used throughout this book to describe an organization's current and ideal culture, leaders' thinking and behavioral styles, and the impact of leaders on others is based on the Human Synergistics Circumplex (see Figure I.2), as developed by J. Clayton Lafferty in the 1970s and revised and validated by Rob in the 1980s.

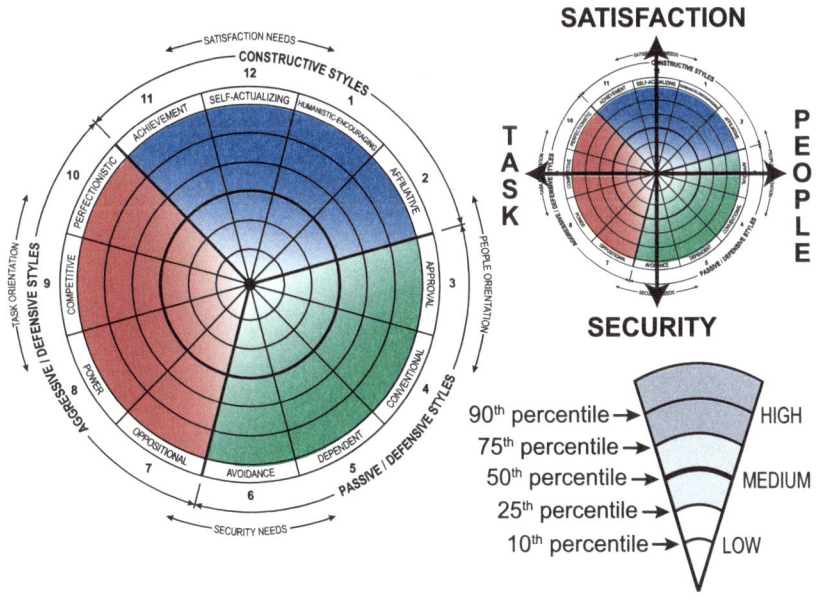

Figure I.2. The Human Synergistics Circumplex

Research and development by Robert A. Cooke, Ph.D. and J. Clayton Lafferty, Ph.D.
Copyright © 1987 by Human Synergistics International. All Rights Reserved

The Circumplex identifies twelve styles that are grouped into three general clusters—Constructive, Passive/Defensive, and Aggressive/Defensive. Styles at the top of the Circumplex are driven by higher-order *satisfaction* needs for growth, development, relationships with others, and achievement; styles at the bottom are triggered by lower-order needs for protecting and maintaining one's own *security*, interests, position, and status. Styles on the right side of the Circumplex reflect a concern for *people* while those on the left side are oriented toward *tasks*. The specific placement of the styles around the Circumplex indicates their degree of similarity to one another. Styles that are more similar and that covary are placed closer to one another on the Circumplex, while those that are less similar or even opposing are placed farther apart.[9]

Throughout this book, you'll see various Circumplex profiles showing results for different leaders and organizations that have used our surveys.

The extent to which each section of the Circumplex is filled with blue, green, or red depicts the extent to which each style describes the focal individual, group, or organization based on comparisons to others who previously completed our surveys. Long extensions represent relatively strong tendencies along a style; short extensions indicate that the style is not characteristic of the individual, group, or organization represented in the profile. In other words, the Circumplex is used to transform raw scores on style measures to percentile scores.

CONSTRUCTIVE (BLUE) STYLES are labeled Achievement, Self-Actualizing, Humanistic-Encouraging and Affiliative and are located—using the analogy of a clock—in the eleven to two o'clock positions on the Circumplex. We use the word *constructive* as consistent with its dictionary definition, "relating to construction or creation" and "promoting improvement or development."[10]

Leaders and organizational cultures that promote and reinforce Constructive styles motivate members toward *self-development* and *doing good*. They also encourage members to pay attention to the development of others and the organization, and to take initiative in solving problems, accomplishing objectives, and building effective work relationships with others. Members are expected to strike a balance between prioritizing tasks and prioritizing people, as well as to balance their own needs and interests with those of their group or organization. More generally, many of the ways of thinking and the behaviors that are activated in Constructive cultures are associated with classic research on higher-order needs and motivation[11] and have since been identified as components of *emotional intelligence* and *positive mindsets*. As described in the next chapter and illustrated by the cases that make up the bulk of this book, when Constructive styles are strongly (rather than weakly) supported by an organization's operating culture, members tend to be more satisfied and engaged; teamwork and synergy are more evident; and individuals, groups, and the overall organization perform more effectively.

PASSIVE/DEFENSIVE (GREEN) STYLES—labeled Approval, Conventional, Dependent, and Avoidance—are found in the three to six o'clock positions of the Circumplex. The word *passive*—defined as "lacking in energy or will," "lethargic," "not active," and "submissive"—and the word *defensive*—defined as "serving to defend or protect"—together capture the essence of the underlying orientation shared by these styles.

Passive/Defensive ways of thinking and behaving are driven by the need to maintain personal security and safety via interactions with *people*. While the underlying motivation is for *self-protection* and *being good*, these styles reflect a tendency to subordinate personal interests to those of the group or organization. Leaders and organizational cultures that implicitly require and activate these styles promote the belief that fitting in, being accepted, following orders (even if they are wrong), and avoiding blame take priority over effectively solving problems or accomplishing tasks. Consequently, regardless of whether the Passive/Defensive styles are intentionally or inadvertently reinforced by leaders or by the cultures they create, these behaviors stifle diversity, creativity, and initiative and allow individual members as well as the overall organization to stagnate.

AGGRESSIVE/DEFENSIVE (RED) STYLES—which include Oppositional, Power, Competitive, and Perfectionistic—are shown in the seven to ten o'clock positions on the Circumplex. These behaviors are characterized by *aggression*, which is defined as "a forceful action or procedure (such as an unprovoked attack) especially when intended to dominate and master" and "hostile, injurious, or destructive behavior, especially when caused by frustration." Like the passive styles described above, the aggressive styles are driven by the perceived need to defend and maintain a personal sense of security.

While the results of Aggressive/Defensive norms and expectations can be destructive and counterproductive, the underlying intentions are more benign. Leaders in Aggressive/Defensive cultures are motivated by the desire to *look good*. Their priority is *self-promotion*, and, more generally, the protection of their own security and status via task-related behaviors. Individuals who are encouraged by leaders or their organization's culture to think and behave in these ways tend to place their own interests above those of the group or organization and, in certain ways, use the group or organization as a vehicle or arena for meeting their own needs.

As described in the next chapter and illustrated by some of the cases, organizations with strong Aggressive/Defensive cultures have a more difficult time attracting and retaining talent; they experience more conflicts within as well as between teams; they are more likely to break into silos; and they tend to perform more unevenly or inconsistently than organizations in which these styles are not emphasized.

Brief descriptions of the twelve specific cultural norms measured by the *Organizational Culture Inventory* are provided in Table I.2. As you review the descriptions, consider the extent to which your organization's day-to-day operating culture currently embodies the characteristics listed.

As noted earlier, the Circumplex framework and terminology are relevant not only to describing an organization's current and ideal culture (measured by the *Organizational Culture Inventory* and *Organizational Culture Inventory—Ideal*, respectively) but also the thinking and behavior of individuals as measured by the *Life Styles Inventory* as well as ACUMEN® Leadership Work*Styles*™ (a derivative of the *Life Styles Inventory*). Descriptions of the twelve personal thinking and behavioral styles are provided in Table I.3. As you read the descriptions, consider the extent to which they: a) describe your own thinking and b) reflect how others would describe your behavior.

These inventories provide a structured, quantitative, and comprehensive means of assessing your organization's culture and your personal styles. You may have already noticed some parallels between your own thinking and behavioral styles and the culture of your organization simply by reading these brief descriptions and reflecting on what you have observed in your organization and in your own thinking and behavior. More generally, using the same language and framework to describe what is happening at the individual, group/team, and organizational levels can be pivotal in helping leaders connect their own thinking, behavior, and impact to the interactions within their groups and to the broader culture of their organizations.

The full diagnostic system based on the Circumplex is summarized in the diagram in Figure I.3. In addition to personal styles and cultural norms, the framework and terminology are used to identify the personal impact of leaders and managers on the behavior of other people and the culture (measured by *Leadership/Impact®* and *Management/Impact®*). The framework and terminology are also used to describe members' interaction within groups (measured using the *Group Styles Inventory*™) and with customers (measured by Customer Service*Styles*™). Thus, the Circumplex helps leaders to understand how their own thinking and behavior are affected by as well as affect other members, groups and teams, and the organization's culture in terms of styles. Possibly more importantly, the use of a single shared framework and terminology facilitates multilevel change and development that are integrated and mutually reinforcing rather than unrelated, inconsistent, or even mutually exclusive.

Introduction

Table I.2. The Twelve Cultural Norms Based on the *Organizational Culture Inventory*

Constructive Styles

	An **Achievement** culture characterizes organizations that do things well and value members who set and accomplish their own goals. Members are expected to set challenging but realistic goals, establish plans to reach these goals, and pursue them with enthusiasm.
	A **Self-Actualizing** culture characterizes organizations that value creativity, quality over quantity, and both task accomplishment and individual growth. Members are encouraged to gain enjoyment from their work, develop themselves, and take on new and interesting activities.
	A **Humanistic-Encouraging** culture characterizes organizations that are managed in a participative and person-centered way. Members are expected to be supportive, developmental, and open to influence in their dealings with one another.
	An **Affiliative** culture characterizes organizations that place a high priority on positive interpersonal relationships. Members are expected to share thoughts and feelings and be friendly, open, and sensitive to the satisfaction of work group members.

Passive/Defensive Styles

	An **Approval** culture describes organizations in which conflicts are avoided and interpersonal relationships are pleasant—at least superficially. Members feel that they should agree with, gain the acceptance of, and be liked by others.
	A **Conventional** culture is descriptive of organizations that are conservative, traditional, and bureaucratically controlled. Members are expected to conform, follow the rules, make a good impression, and always follow policies and practices.
	A **Dependent** culture is descriptive of organizations that are hierarchically controlled and fail to empower their members. Members are expected to do only what they are told, clear all decisions with superiors, and please their superiors.
	An **Avoidance** culture characterizes organizations that fail to reward success but nevertheless punish mistakes. Members believe they must shift responsibilities to others, take few chances, and guard against any possibility of being blamed for a problem.

Aggressive/Defensive Styles

	An **Oppositional** culture describes organizations in which confrontation prevails and negativism is rewarded. Members believe they can gain status and influence by being critical, opposing the ideas of others, and making safe (but ineffectual) decisions.
	A **Power** culture is descriptive of nonparticipative organizations structured on the basis of the authority inherent in members' positions. Members believe they are expected to take charge, control subordinates and, at the same time, be responsive to the demands of superiors.
	A **Competitive** culture is one in which winning is valued and members are rewarded for outperforming one another. Members operate in a "win-lose" framework and believe they must turn the job into a contest and work against (rather than with) their peers to be noticed.
	A **Perfectionistic** culture characterizes organizations in which perfectionism, persistence, and hard work are valued. Members feel they must avoid any mistakes, keep track of everything, and work long hours to attain narrowly defined objectives.

From the *Organizational Culture Inventory*®(OCI®) by Robert A. Cooke Ph.D. and J. Clayton Lafferty, Ph.D. Copyright © 1989, 1987, 1983 by Human Synergistics International. All Rights Reserved.

Table I.3. The Twelve Thinking and Behavioral Styles Based on the *Life Styles Inventory* Styles

Constructive Styles

	The **Achievement** style reflects a strong motivation to solve problems and to attain high-quality results. Characteristics include a focus on accomplishment, ambition, enjoyment of challenges, and the ability to set realistic, attainable goals.
	The **Self-Actualizing** style reflects a way of thinking that results in the highest form of personal fulfillment. Characteristics include concern for self-development, an energetic, interested approach to life, and a desire to know about and experience things directly.
	The **Humanistic-Encouraging** style reflects a concern for the growth and development of people. Characteristics include the ability to inspire and motivate others, thoughtfulness, and a willingness to help.
	The **Affiliative** style reflects one's commitment to forming and sustaining satisfying relationships. Characteristics include strong, well-developed interpersonal skills, diplomacy, and a need to build relationships that are meaningful and reciprocal.

Passive/Defensive Styles

	The **Approval** style reflects one's need to be accepted by others to increase feelings of self-worth. Characteristics include low self-esteem, a preoccupation with the opinions of others, and an over-concern with being well-liked.
	The **Conventional** style reflects the tendency to act in a conforming way to avoid calling attention to one's self. Characteristics include a tendency to view rules as a source of security, reduced initiative, and obedience to authority figures.
	The **Dependent** style reflects the need to rely on the guidance and direction of others in order to feel secure and protected. Characteristics include passivity, eagerness to please, compliance, respect for others, and a tendency to be easily influenced.
	The **Avoidance** style reflects use of the defensive strategy of withdrawal to avoid what is personally threatening. Characteristics include feelings of self-doubt, tension, and avoidance of risks and decisions.

Aggressive/Defensive Styles

	The **Oppositional** style reflects the need to seek attention and recognition by disagreeing with others and being overly critical. Characteristics include suspicion, a need to look for flaws in everything, and a negative, cynical attitude.
	The **Power** style reflects a high need for status, influence, and control. Characteristics include narrow and rigid thinking, abruptness, and a lack of confidence in others.
	The **Competitive** style reflects the need to establish feelings of self-worth through competing against and comparing one's self to others. Characteristics include a preoccupation with winning, a desire to be seen as "the best," an extreme fear of failure, and a strong need to impress others.
	The **Perfectionistic** style reflects a driven need to be "perfect" by attaching feelings of self-worth to task accomplishment. Characteristics include a preoccupation with detail and an excessive concern with avoiding mistakes.

From the *Life Styles Inventory*™ *Description by Others Self-Development Guide* by J. Clayton Lafferty, Ph.D. Copyright © 2004, 1990 by Human Synergistics International. All Rights Reserved.

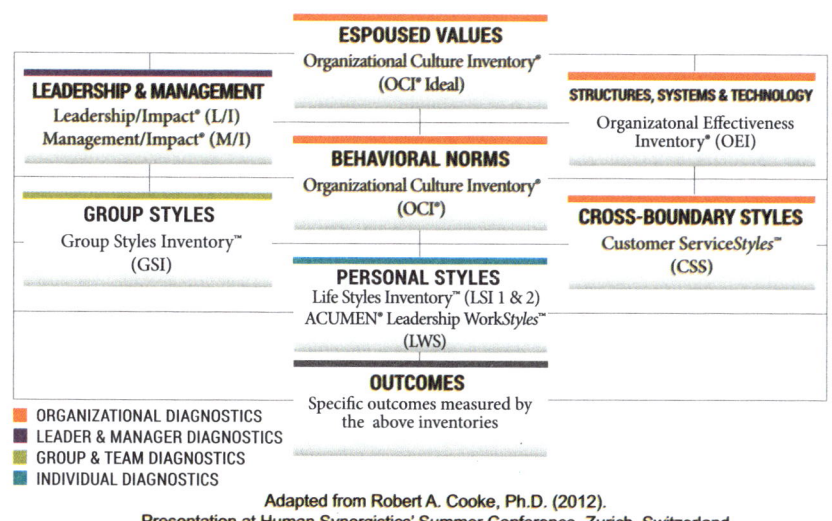

Figure I.3. The Human Synergistics Integrated Diagnostic System

```
                          ESPOUSED VALUES
                     Organizational Culture Inventory®
 LEADERSHIP & MANAGEMENT        (OCI® Ideal)           STRUCTURES, SYSTEMS & TECHNOLOGY
  Leadership/Impact® (L/I)                              Organizatonal Effectiveness
  Management/Impact® (M/I)                                  Inventory® (OEI)
                           BEHAVIORAL NORMS
                     Organizational Culture Inventory®
      GROUP STYLES             (OCI®)                    CROSS-BOUNDARY STYLES
   Group Styles Inventory™                                 Customer ServiceStyles™
          (GSI)                                                   (CSS)
                           PERSONAL STYLES
                     Life Styles Inventory™ (LSI 1 & 2)
                     ACUMEN® Leadership WorkStyles™
                                (LWS)

                              OUTCOMES
                      Specific outcomes measured by
 ■ ORGANIZATIONAL DIAGNOSTICS     the above inventories
 ■ LEADER & MANAGER DIAGNOSTICS
 ■ GROUP & TEAM DIAGNOSTICS
 ■ INDIVIDUAL DIAGNOSTICS
```

Adapted from Robert A. Cooke, Ph.D. (2012).
Presentation at Human Synergistics' Summer Conference, Zurich, Switzerland.
Copyright © 2012-2019 by Human Synergistics International. All Rights Reserved.

Overview of This Book

Throughout this book you'll be presented with a variety of examples of how the Circumplex framework and language have been used by organizations as well as researchers around the world to a) understand the relationship between Constructive styles and outcomes, b) uncover misalignments between cultural values and norms, and c) identify how leaders can and do create more Constructive cultures within their organizations.

In chapter 1, we'll review research and highlight some case examples that together demonstrate how important Constructive cultures are to effectiveness and performance. We'll also show how Constructive cultural norms relate to the values espoused by various organizations and to the ideal cultures described by men and women, people of different ages, and organizational leaders in different countries.

Starting in chapter 2, we'll address the question of how leaders directly and indirectly affect and change culture by sharing our findings on how culture works. Through our research and early case studies, we've uncovered more than thirty enablers of operating cultures. For many leaders, this section can be a real eye-opener to the inadvertent impact they have been having on culture and the many potentially constructive changes they have the power to make.

Beginning with chapter 3, we'll share the recent stories of nine different organizations around the globe that illustrate some of the ways in which leaders have used the Circumplex language and framework to a) identify the prevalence of the different styles within their organization, b) define what's ideal, and c) address culture disconnects to strengthen their organizations' capacity to tackle universal business challenges and achieve organizational goals. The leaders, managers, and change agents featured in this book were open and generous in sharing their experiences and the insights they've gained thus far from their organization's culture change journey. They were also courageous in that they resisted approaching change in the manner that one would have predicted, given their organizations' operating cultures at the time they began their journeys. Rather than going through the motions, they chose to change their own thinking and behavior, to actively engage others in the process, and even to implement complementary changes (for instance, to structures, systems, technology, and skills/qualities) to shift the operating cultures of their organizations in a more productive direction. Many organizations and leaders underestimate the value of this kind of integrated multilevel approach.

The most senior-level leaders we interviewed were a diverse group that included

- the first female CEO of the fourth-largest port in the state of California;
- the CEO of an internationally based privately held online retail company headquartered in Germany;
- the CEO of a publicly traded global organization in the dental implant and tooth replacement industry headquartered in Switzerland;
- the founder of a Latin American agricultural biotechnology company;
- the owner of a family bakery in Serbia;
- the former managing director of a Hungarian brewery;
- the managing director of an Australian breakfast and health food manufacturer;
- the CEO of a cooperative owned by the credit unions in Saskatchewan, Canada; and
- the first African American Presiding Bishop of a church headquartered in New York City.

Aside from the first and last case studies—both focused on organizations in the United States—the other seven organizational examples appear in the book according to the length of time they've spent so far on their culture change journey. This arrangement helps to underscore a key point of this book, which is that creating an organization in which people can solve a broad swath of problems and adapt to changes is an *ongoing* journey—one that is often bumpy and is certainly not linear. It's a venture that members of all these organizations have found essential to positioning themselves for long-term sustainability as well as intermediate financial success, customer satisfaction, organizational adaptability and innovation, and employee engagement and loyalty. As you will discover, these facets of success are consistent across organizations ranging from an e-commerce company in Germany to a church in the United States.

Finally, by sharing with you the results of our culture research along with client experiences and insights, this book addresses a key question that is often lost in conversations about leadership and organizational culture:

> As a leader, how can you both directly and indirectly influence your organization to ensure that members can independently and interactively solve problems and achieve the organization's goals more readily and effectively?

As you will see, the biggest obstacle to changing an organization's culture is its culture! Consequently, to create change, leaders must approach culture and their leadership in a different way—one that consistently reflects and supports the cultural norms they want to strengthen rather than those they want to extinguish.

We begin our journey with an exploration of why Constructive cultures are optimal for most organizations and what leaders aim for when they want to change and improve their cultures.

Part I

Why and How Leaders Create Constructive Cultures

Chapter 1

Why Create a Constructive Culture?

> If you define strategy as what it is you want to do, the culture is how you get it done.
> Steven Baert, Head of Human Resources, Novartis[12]

In this chapter we'll cover seven sets of reasons why leaders should strengthen norms for Constructive thinking and behavioral styles:
- Attracting, engaging, and retaining talent
- Teamwork and problem solving
- Strategy implementation and change
- Innovation and adaptability
- Financial and other performance outcomes
- Consistency with organizational values
- Closing the gap between their organization's current and ideal cultures

As demonstrated by the research studies and case examples presented in this chapter and throughout this book, the types of behaviors supported by an organization's culture don't affect just one outcome. Rather, these cultural norms affect a wide variety of outcomes both directly and via their impact on problem solving.

The Effectiveness of the Most and the Least Constructive Organizations

To quickly illustrate the strong and pervasive relationship between Constructive cultures and effectiveness, we identified the top 10 percent and bottom 10 percent of Constructive organizations from a recent data set of more than nineteen thousand respondents from approximately two hundred different organizations. The composite culture profiles for these two sets of organizations, based on their members' aggregated responses to the *Organizational Culture Inventory*, are shown in Figure 1.1. The chart below the profiles shows the effectiveness results for the two sets of organizations. The latter results are from the *Organizational Effectiveness Inventory*™, a climate survey often administered along with or after the culture inventory to measure outcomes of cultures as well as possible levers for culture change.

Figure 1.1. Effectiveness of Most and Least Constructive Organizations

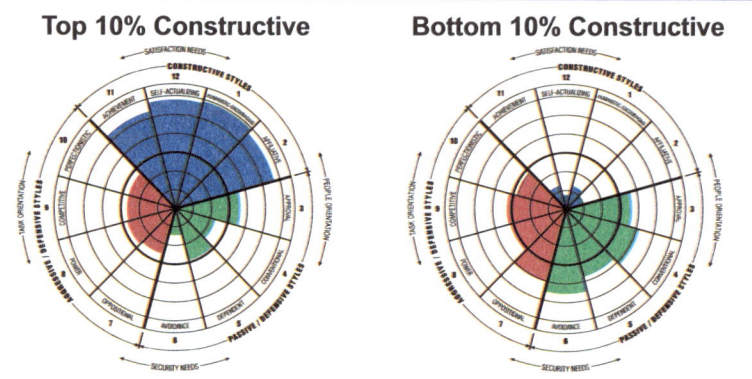

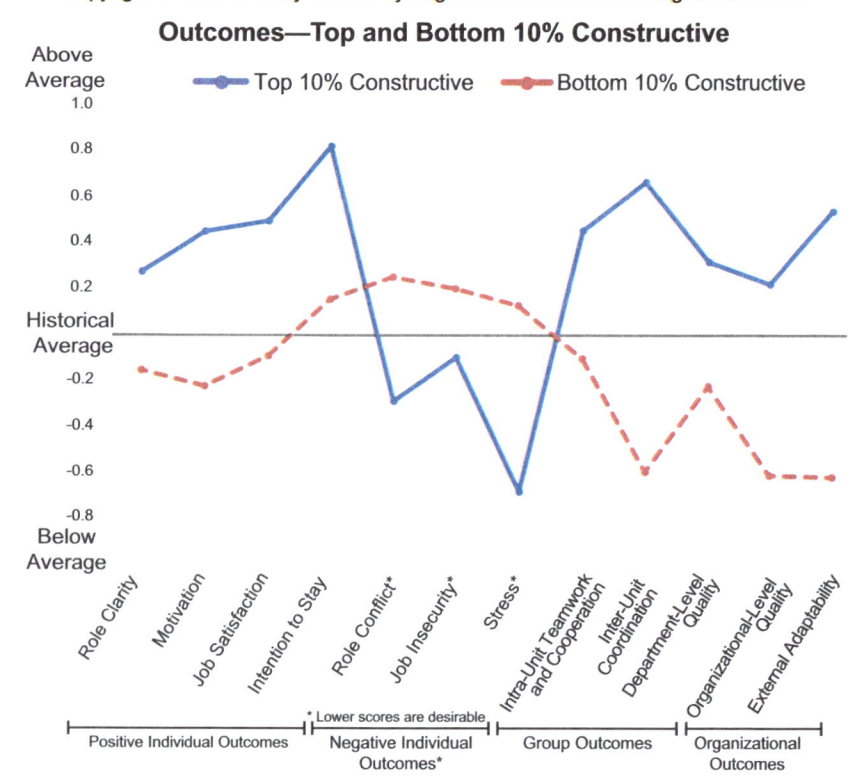

The visual shows that the organizations with the most Constructive cultures outperformed those with the least Constructive cultures along every individual-, group-, and organizational-level outcome. Additionally, the organizations with strong Constructive cultural norms demonstrated better-than-average performance along all measures. (The historical averages are based on a different data set of approximately one thousand organizations selected for research purposes.) In contrast, the organizations with weak Constructive norms scored below average along all but one measure—intention to stay. Nevertheless, even along this measure, they did not score as favorably as the organizations with strong Constructive cultures. More generally, these and the other examples in this book confirm why it's important for leaders to pay attention to culture and emphasize strengthening Constructive cultural norms.

Attracting and Retaining Talent (and Other Individual-Level Outcomes)

Given the importance of attracting and retaining talent, more and more organizations regularly use surveys to monitor the engagement or satisfaction of their employees. In turn, many of these organizations then use the *Organizational Culture Inventory* to identify cultural obstacles to improvement. Data from such organizations, as well as from organizations participating in research, have generated numerous opportunities to examine the relationship between culture and employee-level outcomes.

For instance, our previously published studies based on cross-organizational samples ranging from a few hundred to more than sixty thousand respondents show that the strength of Constructive norms is positively associated with employee intentions to stay and likelihood of recommending the organization as a good place to work.[13] In addition, these studies show that Constructive cultural norms are positively related to employee motivation, satisfaction, and role clarity and are negatively related to stress, role conflict, and job insecurity. In contrast, Passive/Defensive as well as Aggressive/Defensive norms are associated with more stressful, dissatisfying, and demotivating work situations that people want to leave and would not recommend.

Employer-of-choice designations and awards are another way that organizations gauge their attractiveness to potential applicants. Building on this approach, Canadian consultancy First Light identified more than forty of the best employers in Canada based on three lists: "Canada's

50 Best Managed Companies," "The Top 100 Companies to Work for in Canada," and Hewitt Associates' "Best Employers in Canada."[14] They then used survey measures of outcomes such as quality of service as well as conducted interviews with the CEOs and rank-and-file employees of the selected companies to identify the "best of the best" in terms of values and employee attitudes. We collaborated with them to measure the operating cultures of these top organizations using the *Organizational Culture Inventory*. As shown by the profile in Figure 1.2, the cultural styles of these highly rated organizations were more Constructive and less Passive/Defensive and Aggressive/Defensive than the average organization (which is indicated by the heavy concentric circle in the middle of the profile).[15]

Figure 1.2. Composite Operating Culture Profile of the "Best of the Best"

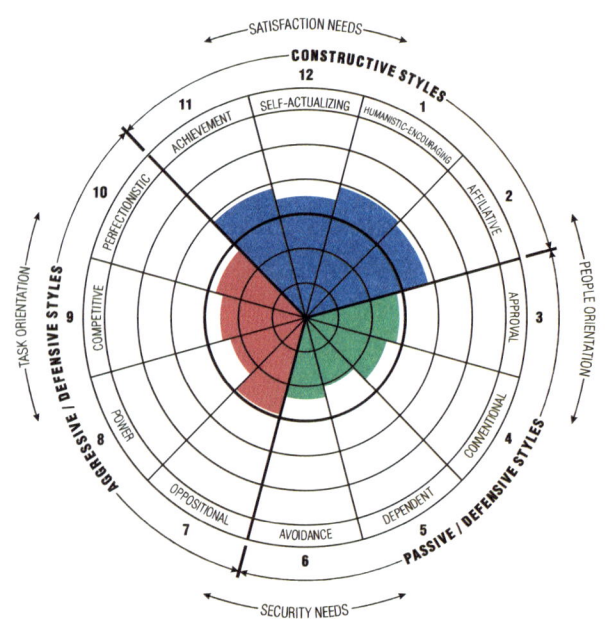

Research and development by Robert A. Cooke, Ph.D. and J. Clayton Lafferty, Ph.D.
Copyright © 1987-2019 by Human Synergistics International. All Rights Reserved.

Employee turnover rates are another important metric used by organizations to monitor their success in retaining talent. Predicting employee turnover was the focus of a study carried out by Charles Glisson and Lawrence R. James on child welfare and juvenile justice case management teams located in thirty different counties. High employee turnover plagued child welfare and juvenile justice systems nationwide at the time of the study—and discovering what could be done to reduce it was critical. The researchers administered the *Organizational Culture Inventory* to identify the cultural norms within welfare teams. They also administered a *team climate* survey that James had codeveloped to measure employees' emotional exhaustion, role conflict, and depersonalization. In addition, they measured characteristics of the teams' structure, members' work attitudes, and perceptions of service quality along items specifically developed for these organizations. Employee turnover in the teams was then measured one year later. The researchers concluded that "team constructive culture was the most important predictor of work attitudes, service quality, and turnover, and the only variable that predicted all three outcomes. Members of teams with more constructive cultures had more positive work attitudes, perceived the services they provided to be of higher quality, and were less likely to quit their jobs."[16]

Similarly, case studies on culture change show that strengthening Constructive cultural norms results in improvements in employee recruitment and retention, along with a variety of other outcomes. For example, a case study published in *Academic Medicine* describes how Dr. Fred Sanfilippo—Senior Vice President and Executive Dean for Health Sciences at the Ohio State University Medical Center and later its CEO—along with his team focused on leadership and culture to improve employee engagement, customer satisfaction, and performance. As part of their change process, they used the *Organizational Culture Inventory* to measure both the actual operating culture and the ideal culture toward which they wanted to move. (We'll revisit using the *Inventory* to measure ideal cultures later in this chapter.) Their results were impressive: after successfully moving the Center's culture in a more Constructive direction, they experienced a 38 percent increase in medical school student applicants. By way of comparison, the national average for medical school applicants during this period had increased by less than 10 percent. Based on confidential surveys of more than seven thousand of the Medical Center's faculty and staff, employee job satisfaction also rose to a level substantially above the benchmark for academic health centers. All of this was coupled with dramatic tangible improvements in the Center's academic, clinical, and financial performance, as well as in customer satisfaction.[17]

The changes documented at the Medical Center parallel those found in other studies on the effects of culture on staff turnover. One of the first, carried out in the early 1990s at Northwestern University, focused on intensive care units in a stratified random sample of twenty-six hospitals selected based on bed size, geographic region, and teaching status.[18] The researchers found that the quality of "caregiver interaction," a composite measure that included Constructive norms and factors such as communication, was negatively and significantly related to nurse turnover, while other important factors (such as technological availability and staffing ratio) were not. The caregiver measure was also negatively related to risk-adjusted length of patient stay and was positively related to evaluations of quality of care and ability to meet family members' needs. More recently, a presentation by Scott Goodspeed—formerly a director at Stroudwater Associates and now program director at Brown University—includes a case example of two front-line managers with highly Constructive impact profiles (based on our *Management/Impact* survey) who achieved a 2 percent turnover rate over a five-year period. The rate for the hospital, on the other hand, was 22 percent, compared to 17 percent statewide.[19]

We see similar patterns of employee turnover and retention in other industries. In the manufacturing arena, for example, GM Nameplate realized a dramatic decrease in turnover rates over their seven-year culture initiative. Paul Michaels, Aerospace Director, notes that when they embarked on the journey, "We were not really in bad shape. We just got our first Boeing Supplier of the Year reward."[20] However, after seeing their culture profile and discussing the results with their consultants from Excellent Cultures, the questions became *How are we going to sustain that culture?* and *How are we going to grow into something...truly excellent?* The development effort resulted in significant waste reduction, quality improvements, better earnings—and "less than 1 percent turnover since 2011."

The case studies featured in this book provide evidence that the impact of culture on attraction and retention is pervasive not only across industries but also across countries. For example, while focusing on developing a more Constructive culture, the Port of San Diego experienced a 67 percent drop in voluntary employee turnover, along with significant increases in revenues and both tenant and public satisfaction (see chapter 3 for more about the port). Similarly, the culture journey of Dreher Brewery in Hungary (chapter 8) shows how strengthening Constructive norms and expectations significantly affected and improved employee retention, which had been a major problem and became an impetus for their culture "reshaping." This outcome was coupled with other improvements, including in financial performance.

SaskCentral's journey (chapter 10) shows how creating a more Constructive culture and sticking with it under three different CEOs resulted in a designation for this medium-sized nonprofit organization in the financial services industry as one of the Best Places to Work® in Canada, a designation that has remained consistent for over a decade. As important, SaskCentral has been able to sustain improvements in customer service as well as successfully adapt to the various changes in its industry, which were the main reasons the organization and its leaders embarked on culture change in the first place.

Yet another example is Pons Bakery in Serbia (chapter 7). Motivated by a desire to grow their business, leaders at Pons initiated culture change and watched as these changes supported the growth and expansion of the business they had hoped for. In addition, the organization unexpectedly started attracting more talent, including hires from more "prestigious" kinds of businesses.

Teamwork and Problem Solving

Board rooms, team rooms, and other meeting areas are like theaters in which you can see the cultural norms play out. In organizations with strong and pervasive cultures, meetings across diverse functional areas and hierarchical levels seem to be guided by the same script—positive or negative. While the personal needs and objectives of team members have an impact on how things proceed, the interaction styles pervading meetings clearly are also influenced by the culture. In turn, these interaction styles represent one of the most important routes though which culture impacts effectiveness.

As discussed in the introduction, Constructive styles at the individual level are associated with better problem solving, whereas Aggressive/Defensive and Passive/Defensive styles detract from effective problem solving. Similarly, groups and teams with Constructive interaction styles develop more effective solutions to problems than those with Passive/Defensive or Aggressive/Defensive styles. While the effectiveness of solutions can be defined and assessed along multiple dimensions, we find most straightforward and valuable the criteria originally proposed by psychologist Norman R. F. Maier for evaluating decisions:

Solution Effectiveness = Solution Quality x Solution Acceptance[21]

Maier considered acceptance necessary, given that even a high-quality decision won't be fully implemented unless those responsible for doing so understand and accept it. Relatedly, our writing and research on the *Group Styles Inventory* have focused on the way Constructive versus Defensive styles affect the quality and acceptance of solutions.[22] Task-oriented Constructive styles, such as Achievement, promote high-quality solutions as group members set goals, analyze the situation, and consider multiple alternatives. People-oriented Constructive styles, such as Affiliative, promote solution acceptance, as members treat one another with respect and listen attentively to each other. Teams demonstrating such styles benefit from good group processes and synergy.

In contrast, Passive/Defensive interactions detract from solution effectiveness. Conventional and Approval styles, for example, interfere with quality by limiting the diversity of viewpoints and constructive criticism (which are withheld to minimize disagreement) that otherwise might improve solutions. Similarly, these styles fail to promote true acceptance. Instead, members tend to feign agreement to solutions to which they have little attachment. Management Professor Jerry B. Harvey called this situation—in which members agree to a solution that inwardly they don't endorse—the "Abilene Paradox."[23] He coined the term after an experience with a group of family members who, on a long, hot, and dusty summer afternoon in Texas, collectively decided to get in the car and travel fifty-three miles to the town of Abilene to have what turned out to be an awful dinner and an equally miserable drive. It was only later that they discovered (during the family's "debriefing" of the experience) that no one had really wanted to go to dinner in Abilene in the first place.

On the other hand, groups with strong Aggressive/Defensive styles are characterized by confrontation, conflict, power struggles, and time wasted by members trying to get their way. The quality of their solutions—although inconsistent and difficult to predict—typically ends up being only as good as the quality of the solution proposed by the member who won the argument or dominated the group. Similarly, acceptance tends to be mixed, with those who prevailed being much happier with the decision than those who lost the battle.

Similar effects are evident in virtual teams, in which members rely on electronic means to communicate. Constructive interaction styles and trust within such teams are positively related to cohesiveness and, in turn, higher levels of performance.[24] Interestingly, when driven by Constructive interaction styles, this kind of cohesiveness does *not* seem to result in groupthink—that is, dysfunctional processes that lead some tightly knit groups to ignore alternatives and discourage disconfirming opinions.[25] As a study of nurses' interactions with physicians confirmed, it is Passive/Defensive rather than Constructive norms that are associated with conflict avoidance.[26]

Constructive styles are as important to the problem-solving effectiveness of virtual teams as they are to groups whose members work face-to-face.[27] The early research on virtual problem-solving teams showed that they are more prone to interacting in Defensive ways than teams working face-to-face. This is illustrated by the composite profile in Figure 1.3, which shows the interaction styles of thirty-one virtual teams based on members' responses to the *Group Styles Inventory*. This tendency, which we refer to as *the electronic disintegration of interpersonal processes,* is partly due to the lack of nonverbal cues and the deindividualization promoted by the technology.

Figure 1.3. The Electronic Disintegration of Interpersonal Processes

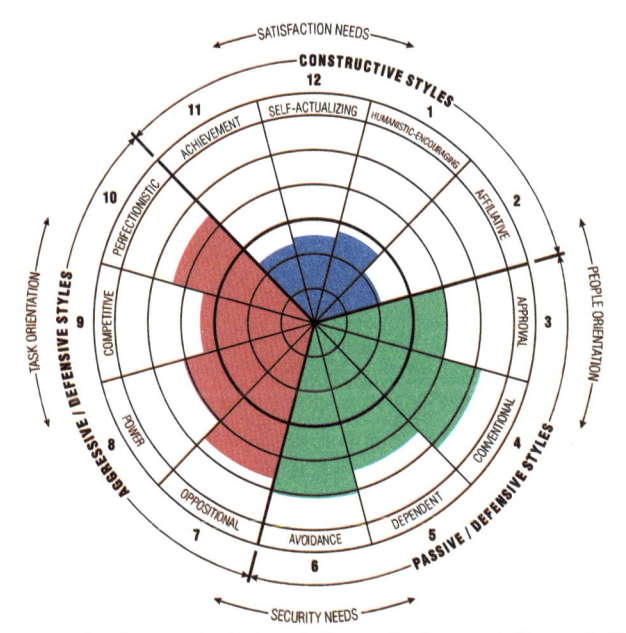

Research and development by Robert A. Cooke, Ph.D. and J. Clayton Lafferty, Ph.D.
Copyright © 1987-2019 by Human Synergistics International. All Rights Reserved.

The strong connection between the Constructive styles and effectiveness is evident beyond the problems teams solve during meetings. Most importantly, team members might face recurring problems of *coordination* on a day-to-day basis, due to the interdependence of the tasks being carried out by those performing the core activities of the organization. These problems become increasingly difficult to resolve as interdependencies become more challenging to manage—moving, for example, from sequential interdependence (as we see on a traditional assembly line) to reciprocal interdependence (as on a surgical team)—and higher levels of uncertainty and change exist. Teams facing the complex coordination challenges posed by reciprocal interdependence and high levels of uncertainty—such as those who work in hospital emergency departments and critical care units, nuclear power plants, and airline cockpits—must coordinate their activities through communication and mutual adjustment. Coordination by means of more basic devices, such as hierarchy and rules, simply is not sufficient.[28]

Research carried out on intensive care units in France shows that work teams with relatively strong Constructive cultures attain higher levels of cooperation, teamwork, and, therefore, performance than those with Defensive cultures.[29] Similar conclusions have been drawn by those who have used the *Organizational Culture Inventory* to improve safety in nuclear power plants. Plants that have experienced such improvement include PPL Susquehanna, a two-unit nuclear plant in the United States, and Asco Nuclear Power Plant in northeastern Spain. Working with the organizational development consultancy Tosan (now part of Ephektiv consultancy), both plants experienced dramatic improvements in safety and performance once their leaders focused on steering the culture in a less Defensive and more Constructive direction that better supported communication, collaboration, and problem solving across departments and organizational levels.[30] Cross-organizational research on nuclear power plants also substantiates the connection between Constructive norms and safety.[31] As further discussed in the next chapter, these studies show that Constructive norms are associated with better communication and trust—which are essential to the effective coordination and problem solving that prevent accidents and maintain safety.

More generally, the cases featured in this book confirm that solutions are more likely to be effective (equal to quality and acceptance, per Maier's formula) when people think and behave in a Constructive manner.

And this is true regardless of whether we are talking about identifying a solution to a problem or selecting and implementing a strategy.

Strategy Implementation and Change

Most leaders now recognize that culture is as critical to success as business models and strategies.[32] Thus, the question has changed from *whether* culture affects strategy to *what type* of culture facilitates strategy implementation and strategic change. Research carried out by Professor Andrew Klein on more than three hundred organizations shows that, regardless of the business strategy, Constructive cultural norms are more strongly related to desired outcomes than are Defensive norms. More fundamentally, as will be discussed in the next chapter, Constructive norms are as strongly related to, for example, the successful implementation of defender strategies as they are to prospector strategies. Klein concludes that Constructive norms give organizations an intangible competitive advantage in qualities such as trust, reputation, collaboration, and teamwork that are valuable, rare, and difficult to imitate and that lead to better strategy implementation and organizational performance.[33]

Consistent with this conclusion, our studies of several hundred organizational units across industries show that Constructive cultural norms are positively related not only to teamwork and coordination *within* work groups, but also to integration and coordination *between* groups.[34] Concurrently, research has demonstrated the positive relationship between Constructive cultures and trust within organizations.[35] High trust and coordination across units diminish silo effects and explain why some organizations outperform others with respect to strategy execution and, more generally, change implementation.

Despite such findings and other writings that highlight the importance of collaboration and agility to business strategy, implementation continues to be the phase at which strategy stumbles. Underlying reasons for this phenomenon are proposed by Donald Sull, Rebecca Homkes, and Charles Sull, based on their study of over eight thousand managers in more than 250 organizations.[36] They conclude that coordination and collaboration are rarely recognized or rewarded in organizations and are not typically emphasized in hiring and promotion decisions. This is consistent with our finding many years ago which (as summarized in the introduction) showed that many organizations fail to reward individuals with Constructive personal styles (which promote collaboration) and instead reward Aggressive/Defensive styles (which work against collaboration).[37] As a result, it is not unusual for managers to find themselves stymied by colleagues in other departments and unable to make the real-time adjustments necessary to be agile—as Sull, Homkes, and Sull's findings confirm. Furthermore, they note that these problems persist even when formal or structural remedial fixes such as cross-functional committees and centralized project-management offices are put into place. As we've learned from our research and our clients' experiences, the existing behavioral norms and expectations will simply be played out within any new strategy, formal system, or structure when other key forces—such as reward systems and the habits, skills, and personal qualities of leaders and managers—are not addressed.

We had an early opportunity to learn about the effects of cultural norms on strategy implementation in our work with the Defense Logistics Agency (DLA) back in the early 1990s. Specifically, the DLA's Medical Directorate wanted to better understand why certain units were more effective than others in getting medical supplies to deployed personnel during the Operation Desert Shield buildup. The DLA had already been using our Circumplex-based surveys with their leadership, and their internal consultant hypothesized it had something to do with leadership and subcultures—with different styles of certain leaders creating somewhat more positive unit-level cultures than that of the Directorate as a whole. Thus, she requested that we administer the *Organizational Culture Inventory* in the selected units.

As shown in the profiles in Figure 1.4, the behavioral norms of the top-performing units were characterized by significantly stronger Constructive styles—particularly Affiliative and Humanistic-Encouraging—and generally weaker Defensive styles, particularly in terms of Competitive and Avoidance, as compared to the average performers. At the same time, Oppositional and Perfectionistic norms were slightly stronger in the more effective units. These norms apparently were played out in less abrasive and impersonal ways in the more Constructive units, given that they were complemented by positive personal-centered norms as opposed to the more aggressive Power and Competitive norms. More generally, because Constructive cultures support better communication and coordination, these norms likely enabled members to more quickly and effectively carry out the assigned tasks, address problems, minimize errors, and get medical equipment and supplies where they were needed.

Figure 1.4. Subcultures of Average Performers versus Top Performers

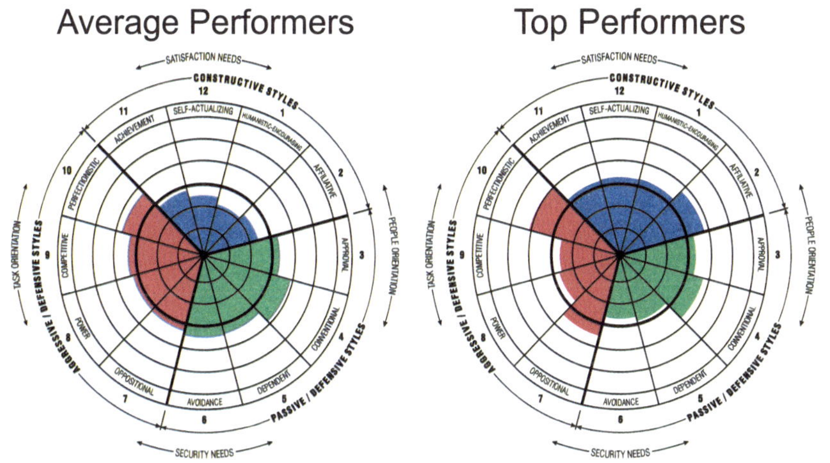

Research and development by Robert A. Cooke, Ph.D. and J. Clayton Lafferty, Ph.D.
Copyright © 1987-2019 by Human Synergistics International. All Rights Reserved.

Another more recent example of the way Constructive cultures can support strategic management and change is provided by a multiyear case study involving the Joint Mine Resistant Ambush Protected Vehicle (MRAP) Program Office within the US Department of Defense. A coalition of Navy, Army, Marine Corps, and Air Force offices, the Joint Program Office (JPO) initiated a culture change effort that was driven by its strategic planning process to a) catch up on human resources issues such as recognition, training, and mentoring, and b) move from "heroic expediting and implicit local processes" to more systemic, widely communicated, and connected processes. The organizational development initiative was guided in part by interview data and results from the *Organizational Culture Inventory* and *Organizational Effectiveness Inventory*. External consultants from the Strategic Management Support team of Transformation Systems, Inc., designed and implemented a series of interventions focused on leadership, organizational development, and processes (e.g., knowledge transfers between locations and a reorganization prioritizing service). Qualitative and quantitative data collected two years after the JPO began this initiative confirmed significant improvements in critical levers for culture change, such as upward and downward communication. The data also revealed a notably more Constructive culture and, as the authors put it, "mission success."[38] Consequently, many components of the enterprise integration strategy developed at this level were adopted by the larger Army Program Office and the Marine Corps Program Office.[39]

Similarly, all the cases featured in this book in some way show how movement toward a Constructive culture can facilitate strategic execution. Particularly relevant to this topic is chapter 6, "Deploying Levers for Cultural Change to Expedite Strategy Implementation," focusing on Agroenzymas in Mexico.

Finally, Constructive cultures not only support strategy implementation but also organizational learning. INSEAD Professor of Strategy and Organization Design Phanish Puranam points out that when implementation doesn't work, leaders can't assess whether the failure is due to a strategy that is poor to begin with.[40] In contrast, when implementation of a strategy is effective, leaders can learn about whether the strategy itself worked, which can help them to improve their decisions. Given that strategy failure rates are "considerably higher than would be desirable" (ranging anywhere from 7-10 percent to 80-90 percent, depending on the study),[41] organizational learning—which is facilitated by Constructive cultural norms—is particularly important.

Innovation and Adaptability

Innovation is now back at the top of corporate agendas, and for good reason. Despite the increased investment by organizations in research and development, measures of productivity growth in the United States and in countries in the European Union indicate that organizations are struggling to realize the benefits of these investments. According to the Bureau of Labor Statistics report from January 2017, annualized labor productivity growth since 2007 slowed to 1.1 percent—notably lower than the historic average.[42] Countries such as Belgium, France, and Spain, as well as Japan, are even lower than the United States in "total factor productivity," a proxy for innovation that measures growth due to more efficient use of labor and capital.[43] While differences across countries are attributed to many factors (including individualistic societal values), the important point for our purposes is that the global rates of innovation and productivity are generally low.

Analysts note that the increasingly wide disparity in productivity between the top 5 percent of companies and the rest indicates that the development and diffusion of innovations just aren't distributed among organizations as they should be. The advantages of certain very large organizations—such as their patents on technological innovations—make it difficult for the average organization to keep up.[44] Strategy Professor Anne Marie Knott points out that the problem isn't so much that R & D is getting harder as it is that companies are just getting worse at it.[45] Her research shows that managers as well as investors tend to have misconceptions about innovation (such as assuming it's small companies that are the most innovative) and that most don't know how to measure it. That said, "creating a culture for innovation" is currently seen by C-suite members as the most important strategy to improve innovation.[46]

Everett M. Rogers, author of the seminal book on innovation, defines it as "an idea, practice, or object that is perceived as new by an individual or other unit of adoption."[47] Accordingly, innovations can be big or small, come from any source (not just R & D), and be tangible (like a product) or intangible (like a process or technique). An organization can benefit not only from developing innovations but also from being an early adopter of innovations developed by others—which is one of the reasons we are focusing on external adaptability as we look at innovation.

So what does a culture that supports innovative behavior look like? Some important clues are provided by a recent study by Great Place to Work of approximately five hundred thousand employees of nearly eight hundred public and private organizations. The research and consultancy firm compared the top and bottom quartiles of companies in terms of the extent to which employees reported that their leaders and managers actively sought out and were interested in their ideas and encouraged them to try new approaches in their work. The high-scoring companies tended to establish special structures and practices that helped people generate and contribute ideas. Their employees were more motivated in those companies to put in extra effort than in the low-scoring companies. The payoff was significant, with the top-quartile companies achieving five times the revenue growth of the bottom-quartile companies. Marcus Erb, Vice President of Innovation & Development at Great Place to Work, said in a *Wall Street Journal* article about the findings: "Companies need to 'open up their mindset' about what employees can offer in the way of new ideas. Leaders that don't see that are going to miss out."[48]

Using the language of our Circumplex, then LinkedIn Vice President Fred Kofman (now Advisor, Leadership Development at Google) describes cultures that support innovation this way:

An innovative culture encourages learning behaviors such as asking questions, seeking feedback, experimenting, reflecting on results and openly discussing errors or unexpected outcomes. It creates a safe environment that promotes creativity.

An innovative culture discourages aggressive-defensive attitudes such as perfectionism, criticism and authoritarianism. For example, at LinkedIn we ask people to "criticize by proposing" an alternative solution, and to "make the other right" (e.g., recognize the kernel of truth in her argument) "before you make her wrong" (e.g., point out where you think she's mistaken).

An innovative culture also discourages passive-defensive attitudes such as conformism, conventionalism, and traditionalism. At LinkedIn, for example, we encourage each other to "take intelligent risks" and "celebrate (and learn) from intelligent failures."[49]

In this vein, early research by Deborah Weber and Peter Sorenson provided critical insights into *how* Constructive norms enable organizations to be more adaptive and innovative. They identified several activities that distinguished organizations that had successfully implemented and sustained changes and improvements from those that had not. The former

- set baselines for implementation of change initiatives from the start;
- adopted a common language around their goals;
- focused on both internal and external customers (in other words, they paid attention to both their external relationships with customers and internal relationships among units);
- relied on cross-functional teams to continue to identify and make improvements; and
- made good use of survey feedback (as opposed to shoving it in a drawer).

These activities reflect the Constructive (as opposed to Defensive) thinking and behavioral styles that were expected and rewarded in these organizations, as confirmed by the "expanded Constructive styles" in their *Organizational Culture Inventory* profiles.[50]

As we showed earlier with both problem solving and strategy, Constructive norms promote acceptance and therefore lead to more effective solutions that are more likely to be implemented. The same is true with respect to innovations. For instance, a study on two hospitals in Australia with very different cultures focused on clinicians' attitudes toward a specific innovation—computerized provider entry systems (CPOE). The researchers found that those who worked in the hospital with Constructive norms tended to hold positive attitudes toward CPOE, whereas those who worked in the hospital where the norms were more Aggressive/Defensive tended to express negative views of CPOE.[51] In the United States, a similar comparative study focused on the acceptance of evidence-based practice (EBP) by approximately three hundred public sector mental health service providers associated with forty-nine different programs providing mental health services for youths and families. Controlling for the effects of provider characteristics, the results showed that Constructive norms were associated with more positive attitudes toward EBP.[52]

Adaptability and innovation were the focus of two studies conducted by Northwestern University's Readership Institute, a joint venture of the Medill School of Journalism and the Kellogg School of Management. The studies focused on the newspaper industry in the United States and Canada, which had been experiencing declining readership and circulation figures for years. That said, some newspapers were faring better than others. The research team suspected that an internal organizational factor—organizational culture—was at play. Thus, in the first Readership Study project, they measured the culture and climate of approximately one hundred newspapers using the *Organizational Culture Inventory* and the *Organizational Effectiveness Inventory*. Beyond identifying factors causally related to their cultures, the effects of culture on adaptability and many other outcomes were statistically analyzed. Among the findings was that, overall, the industry was characterized by relatively strong Aggressive/Defensive as well as Passive/Defensive norms and relatively weak Constructive cultural norms. The bottom-line conclusion of the study was that newspapers would have to make a number of fundamental changes—including developing more Constructive cultures—in order to innovate, grow readership, and compete in an increasingly digital world.[53]

The findings of the Readership study are relevant not only to innovation and adaptation but also to the issues discussed earlier in this chapter, including recruitment, attraction, teamwork, and interunit coordination.[54] As reported by employees, the newspaper organizations with stronger Constructive cultures had significantly lower rates of employee turnover; lower rates of stress and higher rates of engagement; and better cooperation and teamwork within work groups and better coordination between groups. In addition, Constructive norms were positively related to the newspapers' profitability and to their *readership*, measured in terms of the amount of time customers spent reading a particular newspaper. More than thirty thousand customers were surveyed by the Readership Institute for this purpose. Simply put, customers spent more time reading the newspapers published by organizations with stronger Constructive cultural norms.

In contrast, newspapers with relatively strong Passive/Defensive and Aggressive/Defensive norms were plagued with lower levels of employee engagement, higher levels of stress, and poor teamwork, as well as less effective intergroup coordination. Those with particularly strong Aggressive/Defensive norms also experienced significantly higher rates of employee turnover and dissatisfied customers. Given the challenges that they were facing internally, it was not surprising that the research showed that the newspapers with less Constructive and more Defensive cultures were also struggling more than others to innovate, adapt to technological changes, and engage readers beyond the shrinking market of older loyal readers.

A second study carried out by the Readership Institute a few years later looked at newspapers' adaptability and readiness to innovate, specifically with respect to engaging a new young, diverse market. Their findings indicated that those newspapers that were focused on customers' needs and adapting to the changing market had

- more Constructive, less Defensive cultures;
- more readership in general and in the larger market;
- a clear readership strategy that was shared with employees at every level;
- employees who were more engaged, motivated, and innovative; and
- more women and minorities in positions of authority, which helped in connecting with underserved markets.

While it might seem that having the "right" people in place would be enough, the study showed that it wasn't. Innovative newspapers also had a clear strategy that informed everything they did and a culture that supported both the strategy and diversity in teams.[55]

In this book, the story about the culture change journey of Sanitarium Health and Wellbeing in Australia (chapter 9) demonstrates the causal relationship between culture and innovation and adaptability. Specifically, their story describes how strengthening Constructive thinking and behaviors at the leadership level helped to solidify Constructive behavioral norms across the company, which in turn rejuvenated the agility and innovativeness of this centenarian organization. As this investment of effort continues, Sanitarium is developing and introducing more new products more quickly and successfully than ever before. As well, its members are exploring new areas and trying new ways of doing things that collectively have elevated Sanitarium's brand and reputation both as an employer and a competitor, propelling the organization into the number two spot in the breakfast cereal market. This leads us to the next set of outcomes to be discussed.

Financial and Other Performance Outcomes

Given that the cultural norms on which we are focusing are related to so many critical attitudes and behaviors, it is no wonder that organizations and subunits with stronger Constructive cultures perform significantly better along "hard" criteria than those within which these norms are relatively weak. Constructive norms were related to the profitability of organizations in the newspaper industry. Similarly, in a study of sixty-nine organizations in different industries in the United States, Constructive cultural norms were positively associated with higher average earnings/sales ratios over a three-year period while Aggressive/Defensive norms were associated with greater volatility or variability in earning/sales ratios.[56] Likewise, a study focusing on nineteen organizations in Pakistan in different industries found that Constructive cultural norms had a significant positive impact on profitability over a five-year period.[57] Analyzing multiple units of a service organization, yet another study demonstrated how cultural norms are related to the financial performance of not-for-profits.[58] Though the focus on a single organization limited the extent to which the units varied in terms of cultural norms, the differences that did exist with respect to expectations for Passive/Defensive behaviors were negatively related to fund-raising success as well as to team attitudes.

Cultural norms have also been shown to be related to sales growth. The first study to suggest this was carried out by Martin (Merom) Klein, who administered the *Organizational Culture Inventory* in a chain of forty-four apparel stores in the Eastern United States.[59] He found that cultural norms within the stores that were *high-growth* in terms of both sales volume and sales increases were significantly more Constructive and less Defensive (particularly in terms of Avoidance and the Aggressive/Defensive behaviors) than the *no-growth* stores, which had the smallest sales volumes and growth (see Figure 1.5). In organizations with strong Aggressive/Defensive norms, members compete internally, fight with one another to "own" customers, and blame other employees for problems. These behaviors, in turn, result in frustrated customers and fewer sales. In contrast, in organizations with Constructive cultures, members take initiative and work together to quickly solve problems and delight customers, resulting in more sales, customer loyalty, and positive referrals. By collecting data on different *subgroups*—in this case, different stores that were part of the same organization—the leaders and managers of the retail chain were able to see quite clearly how culture was related to performance within their own organization. This subgroup approach is something that you will see again in chapter 5.

Figure 1.5. Cultural Norms and Sales Growth

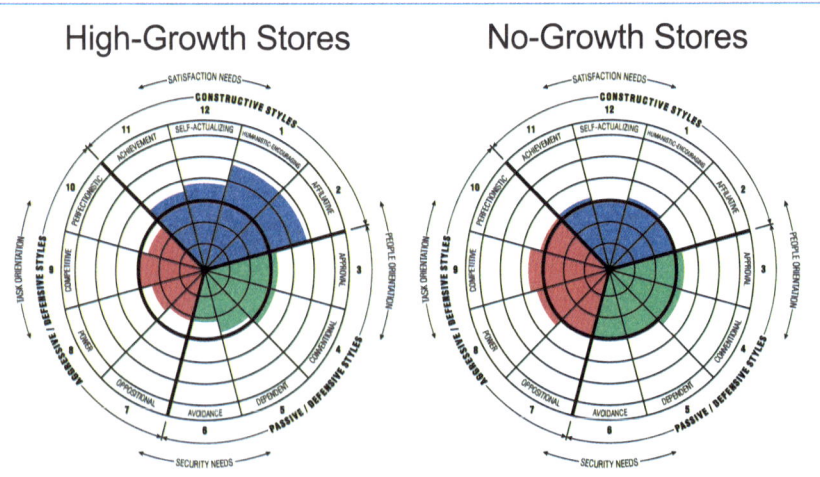

Research and development by Robert A. Cooke, Ph.D. and J. Clayton Lafferty, Ph.D.
Copyright © 1987-2019 by Human Synergistics International. All Rights Reserved.

Why Constructive Culture? 41

Various cultural change case studies provide evidence of the value of strengthening both Constructive thinking and behavior styles and, over time, Constructive cultural norms. The Ohio State Medical Center case study, introduced above, describes a dramatic turnaround in revenues, operating margin, and operating cash reserves, as well as research funding, academic performance, and clinical performance.

Australia/New Zealand beverage (and now also food) company, Lion (formerly Lion Nathan), also demonstrates the positive financial impact of working toward a more Constructive and less Defensive organizational culture. Like the other examples described in this book, their leadership and culture transformation has contributed to a variety of improvements that together enabled the company to perform much more effectively and profitably. A longitudinal case study by Human Synergistics Australia and New Zealand documented Lion's increases in return on capital over an eight-year period of progressively stronger Constructive norms.[60] Bob Murray, former CEO and now Non-Executive Director of Lion, shared parallel data showing the upward trend in Lion's share prices associated with their culture transformation (see Figure 1.6).[61]

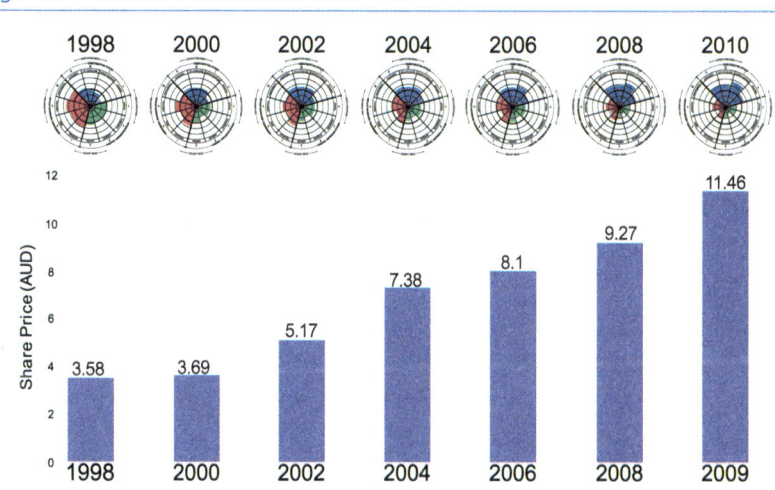

Figure 1.6. Cultural Norms and Share Price

Year	Share Price (AUD)
1998	3.58
2000	3.69
2002	5.17
2004	7.38
2006	8.1
2008	9.27
2009	11.46

From Rob Murray (2017, September). Presentation at Human Synergistics' 19th Annual Australian Culture & Leadership Conference, Sydney, Australia.
Circumplex: Research and development by Robert A. Cooke, Ph.D. and J. Clayton Lafferty, Ph.D. Copyright © 1987-2019 by Human Synergistics International. All Rights Reserved.

These cases, along with the cases featured in this book, illustrate that cultural norms affect how leaders approach *any* kind of change—whether that change concerns innovation, adapting to turbulence in the external environment, developing and implementing new business models and strategies, or changing the culture itself. As cultural norms become more Constructive, problems of change and adaptation are resolved more effectively, and, consequently, organizational performance along key financial outcomes steadily improves. More generally, Constructive norms enable organizations to more efficiently and effectively provide clients with valued products or services or fulfill needs important to the larger community. This, in turn, makes it possible for such organizations to garner more resources, grow, and generate a profit.

Consistency with Organizational Values

The four Constructive styles prescribe behaviors associated with the *core values* of many organizations across industries and around the globe—such as responsibility, integrity, innovation, respect for people, and teamwork. As a result, many leaders and managers find it useful to examine their organization's espoused values in the context of the Circumplex. This can be done by semantically linking stated organizational values to the Circumplex or by administering the *Ideal* form of the *Organizational Culture Inventory*. Analyzing espoused organizational values in either of these ways draws attention to the Constructive styles that should be exemplified in the day-to-day culture as well as to Defensive norms that are antithetical to those values and therefore should be minimized.

The styles identified either by semantically linking stated organizational values to the Circumplex or by administering the *Organizational Culture Inventory—Ideal* provide a benchmark for interpreting the results when measuring an organization's current operating culture, identifying culture gaps, and selecting levers for change. These approaches also *operationalize* the organization's values in the sense that they enable leaders and members to better express and practice specific behaviors associated with those values. The experiences of three global organizations, each deeply serious about culture change, provide examples of this focus on values.

AXA, one of the world's largest insurance and financial services companies, began using the *Organizational Culture Inventory* back in 2011 to measure progress in shifting their operational culture in the direction of the company's two main espoused values of "trust" and "achievement."[62] These values were viewed as essential for realizing AXA's ambition of becoming the preferred company in the industry. In a case study published about their culture journey, AXA's CEO and Chairman at the time, Henri De Castries, explained that the challenge resided in embedding these values in the organization's day-to-day norms and operations:

> In order to create a trust relationship with our customers, we need something similar among us. As of now we have a culture of success, but we still need a culture of trust and achievement. We have been working on developing such a culture for a while, but are not there yet in terms of a daily practice.[63]

These espoused values aligned with the Constructive styles on the Circumplex, particularly Humanistic-Encouraging, Affiliative, and Achievement. Thus, the *Inventory* and the results along these three styles provided an important way to monitor and guide progress in moving the existing culture in the desired direction with the involvement of, back in 2011, almost a hundred thousand employees around the world. The following year, George Stansfield, AXA General Counsel and Head of Group Human Resources, noted,

> The results clearly revealed the continuing impact of our "historical" culture, with all its strengths and limitations. This made it easier to identify drivers for change and enabled managers to draw up their own personal development plans. I am pleased to see that behaviors are beginning to adapt.[64]

Later in the process, comments by AXA Life Japan's Human Resource Director, Takashi Tanemura, illustrate how the Circumplex styles served as an indicator of movement toward the values:

> We concentrated on nurturing a culture of "Trust & Achievement" in all of our people processes. As a result, employees are now able to demonstrate a "constructive" culture in their everyday work and we believe that we are ready to leverage on this foundation to pave the way for the future—a future where all employees have a common goal to put our customers first at the heart of all our actions.[65]

Another important global example is Novartis, one of the world's largest pharmaceutical companies. Moving the culture of Novartis in a direction consistent with its values has been particularly important to its

Chairman, Jörg Reinhardt, who rejoined the company in 2013. Reinhardt explained in a 2015 interview, "We have introduced a new value system and it includes a few which are particularly close to my heart: teamwork, courage, and integrity."[66] These values are consistent with the Constructive styles—particularly, Affiliative, Achievement, and Self-Actualizing—and were in contrast with an operating culture that Reinhart described in the interview as "aggressive" and "top-down" in orientation.

Speaking at the 2016 WorldCity HR Connections roundtable, Novartis's Vice President and Head of Human Resources for Latin America and Canada, Marcelo Fumasoni, explained that the company used the *Organizational Culture Inventory* to review its current culture. He shared that they had made the new core values and behaviors part of each employee's annual review and had started to see some changes. "Putting courage as a value was a little uncomfortable for us, but we wanted to promote the 'ability to speak up' mentality," said Fumasoni, noting that employees would often play it safe and hesitate to offer ideas that could disrupt the status quo. "It's a journey," Fumasoni said. "We are becoming less red [Aggressive/Defensive]. We're becoming more blue [Constructive]. But we're not there yet."[67]

Values and culture continue to be of critical importance within Novartis. "The company has become known for having placed culture at the heart of the business," reports Gavin Hinks of *Board Agenda*, who had the opportunity to interview Novartis's Head of Human Resources, Steven Baert.[68] According to Baert, culture was a key consideration in the appointment of the company's new CEO, Vas Narasimhan, in 2018. Under his leadership, their culture journey has "accelerated." Consistent with the themes covered earlier in this chapter, Baert describes, in Hinks's article, how culture is seen as key to both strategy implementation and innovation:

> If you define strategy as what it is you want to do, the culture is how you get it done. ...If you really want to get great innovation, and great performance, you need to spend as much time and energy on how you get it done versus what it is you want to achieve.

Importantly, while Novartis continues to use the *Organizational Culture Inventory* and other measures to gauge the progress, Baert notes, "We want to avoid the culture becoming a workstream that is completely separate from the business reality, that it is an HR or corporate initiative.

It should be fully embedded in how you do the business."[69]

A third example is one of the cases featured in this book. Straumann is a leading global player in the dental implant industry with, as of 2018, approximately five thousand employees worldwide. Back in 2014, the company embarked on a journey to build a "high-performance culture," which they defined as one that fosters and promotes "delegation, empowerment, taking responsibility, risk taking, challenging, and creative thought."[70] Their ideal culture profile confirmed that they wanted to create a predominantly Constructive culture, particularly in terms of Achievement, Self-Actualizing, and Humanistic-Encouraging. The profile, along with the story of their culture change journey, is shared in chapter 5.

As these examples show, multinational firms tend to purposefully define a common set of values for the entire organization rather than designating different values for different geographical locations. The espoused values toward which they gravitate typically are consistent with the Constructive styles and, in turn, promote integration and performance when they are converted into day-to-day behavioral norms.

If your organization has a stated set of values or guiding principles, compare them to the descriptions of the twelve styles presented in the Introduction to this book to identify the behavioral norms that are consistent with these values and therefore should be encouraged and promoted. If your organization is developing or updating its value statement, the Constructive styles are among those that should be considered in delineating a meaningful and measurable set of values.

Ideal Cultures

When the *Organizational Culture Inventory* was initially released years ago, only one form of the survey was printed—that is, the version that measures current norms and expectations. However, respondents within many of our client organizations and research sites were interested in a benchmark, a description of a culture toward which they should aim. To generate target profiles, we wrote another set of instructions guiding respondents to answer the survey items in terms of the extent to which each of the behaviors listed *should be expected* to maximize effectiveness. That was when we discovered that the ideals generated by vastly different organizations were strikingly similar. This was despite the fact that members of these different organizations were completing the survey on the basis of seemingly distinct criteria of effectiveness (for example, some organizations would ask members to think about "service quality" and "customer satisfaction" when answering the survey, while others would specify "safety" or "reliability").

Because the ideal cultures described by most organizations were so similar, we combined data and provided clients with a "typical ideal" profile. Ironically, regardless of whether we were dealing with service- or reliability-oriented organizations, those in leadership (and other) positions would view the standardized ideal with a certain degree of skepticism. Members tended to assume that their organizations were "different"—carrying out specialized activities and operating in unique environments. Therefore, so that leaders and members of a given organization could generate their benchmark for themselves, we created the *Ideal* form of the *Organizational Culture Inventory* and made it available to our clients.

The *Ideal* form of the *Organizational Culture Inventory* specifically asks people to evaluate the extent to which each of the 120 behaviors listed *should be* expected to maximize their organization's performance and long-term effectiveness. Their aggregated descriptions of the ideal culture are profiled on the same normed Circumplex that is used to profile the current operating culture (which is based on actual rather than ideal responses and scores). This process allows meaningful comparisons to be made between the organization's current culture profile and its ideal.

> To experience a brief preview of the *Organizational Culture Inventory—Ideal*, see how it works, and obtain a general picture of your own ideal in terms of the three sets of styles, visit *www.humansynergistics.com/culturebook*.

A typical ideal profile is shown in Figure 1.7, which is based on the combined responses of ten people randomly selected from each of fifty-six different organizations in the United States who completed the *Ideal* form of the *Inventory*. Though the organizations spanned a variety of industries, we simply averaged their results into a single profile given that the differences across industries are minimal. Over the years, we've continued to observe that members of very different organizations—ranging from day care centers to nuclear power plants, service organizations to manufacturing firms, voluntary agencies to prisons—

consistently specify a strong Constructive culture as ideal. Similarly, other studies have found that the values of organizations in different industries generally are not significantly different from one another.[71]

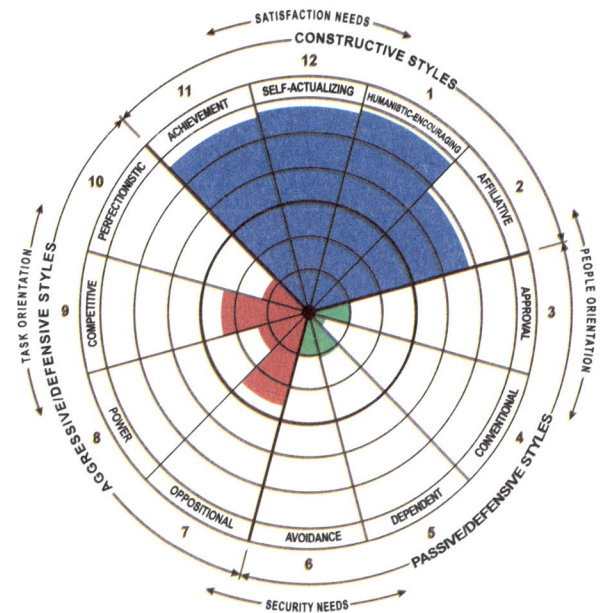

Figure 1.7. Typical Ideal Culture Profile

Research and development by Robert A. Cooke, Ph.D. and J. Clayton Lafferty, Ph.D.
Copyright © 1987-2019 by Human Synergistics International. All Rights Reserved.

The profile shows very strong extensions along the Constructive styles, weak extensions along the Passive/Defensive styles, and moderately weak though mixed extensions along the Aggressive/Defensive styles. As positive as this profile seems, we do occasionally see current culture profiles for organizations and subunits that are as strong as this one—as illustrated by the composite profile shown at the beginning of this chapter (see Figure 1.1). Thus, we are not asking people to describe a utopia, a culture that is unattainable.

The dividend of these ideal profiles is that they permit leaders and members to make quantitative comparisons to the current operating culture, thereby facilitating the identification of culture gaps—that is, disconnects between shared values (the ideal) and behavioral norms (current operating culture). This approach can validate the organization's stated values and help to bring them to life by a) confirming members' acceptance of the values delineated in statements and b) providing them with feedback on specific behavioral norms (at the level of the ten items associated with each style) that need to be strengthened or diluted to make the organization's ideal values a reality. This comparative technique confirms the direction of the cultural changes that, even when somewhat modest, can lead to better problem solving and task performance.

As noted earlier, ideal culture profiles across industries do not differ significantly. However, possible differences due to other factors need to be addressed. Thus, for the remainder of this section we'll share the results of ideal surveys completed by leaders located in different countries, by respondents in different age groups, and by women compared to men.

Ideal Cultures in Different Countries

One of the largest and most culturally diverse research projects using the *Organizational Culture Inventory* to describe ideal organizational cultures included approximately one thousand leaders from sixty countries who were associated with an international organization that helps young people develop their leadership potential. Specifically, the leaders were asked to complete an early version of the *Ideal* form of the *Organizational Culture Inventory* by describing the kind of organizational culture that would maximize goal attainment and the long-term effectiveness of their organizations. The ideal cultures described by leaders from different *societal clusters* (based on geography, language, and religion as described by the research of Simcha Ronen and Oded Shenkar[72]) are shown in Figure 1.8.

In general, Constructive styles are valued by leaders across the societal clusters, as shown by the blue extensions at the top of the profiles that extend well above the center (fiftieth percentile) ring of the Circumplex. Although there is some variance across countries in the extent to which the Constructive styles are viewed as ideal, there is visibly and statistically greater variance with respect to the Defensive styles. The exception is the Oppositional style, which is consistently viewed as relatively important to the leaders in the sample.

Why Constructive Culture? 49

Figure 1.8. Ideal Organizational Culture Profiles across the Globe

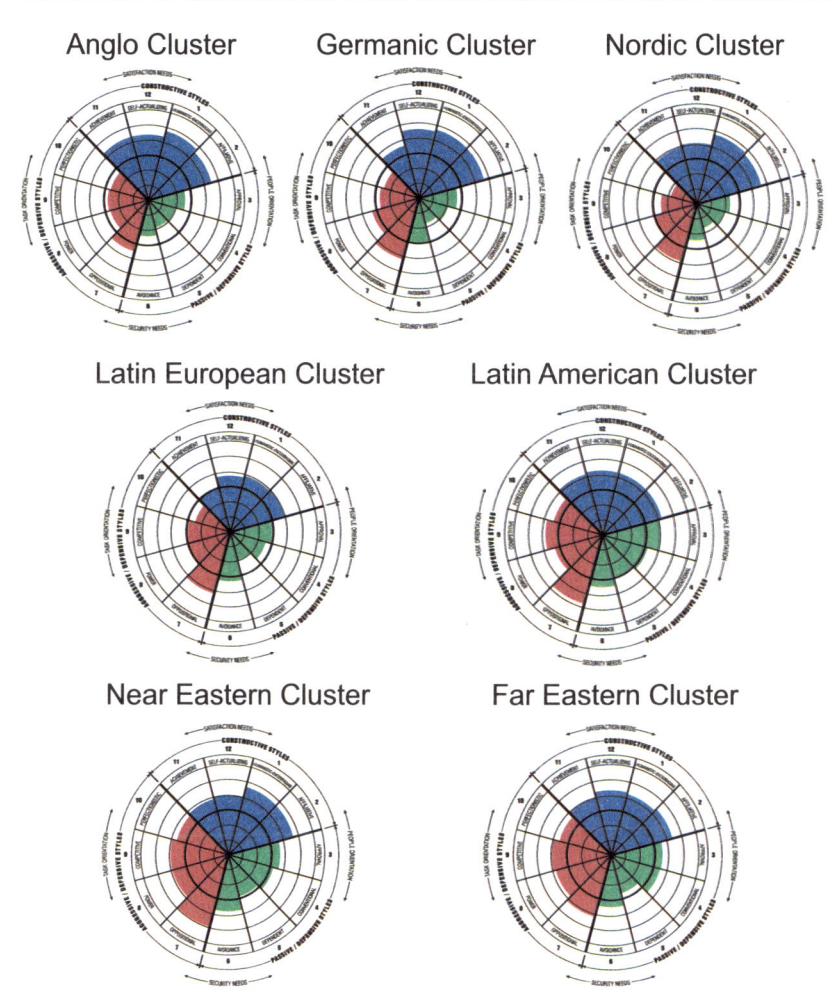

Anglo Cluster · Germanic Cluster · Nordic Cluster

Latin European Cluster · Latin American Cluster

Near Eastern Cluster · Far Eastern Cluster

Human Synergistics Circumplex: Research and development by Robert A. Cooke, Ph.D. and J. Clayton Lafferty, Ph.D. Copyright © 1987-2019 by Human Synergistics International. All Rights Reserved.

Ideal Culture Profiles: From Robert A. Cooke, *"Organizational Culture Inventory:* Ideal Culture Profiles (International Management Association)," presented at University of Illinois at Chicago, Chicago, IL, September 2001.

The differences in the ideal organizational cultures across these clusters most likely result from differences in societal values. As summarized in Table 1.1, the value placed on the Passive/Defensive and Aggressive/Defensive styles is related to the relative strength of three different societal values in the respondents' home countries—Individualism/Collectivism, Power Distance, and Uncertainty Avoidance.

Table 1.1. Ideal Organizational Cultures and Societal Values

	Individualism	Power Distance	Uncertainty Avoidance
Constructive	.07	-.13	-.29*
(11:00) Achievement	.16	-.15	-.39*
(12:00) Self-Actualizing	.21	-.21	-.24
(1:00) Humanistic-Encouraging	.33	-.30	-.36*
(2:00) Affiliative	.23	-.18	-.37*
Passive/Defensive	-.77***	.58**	.26
(3:00) Approval	-.51**	.48**	.37*
(4:00) Conventional	-.42*	.43*	.34*
(5:00) Dependent	-.54***	.59***	.33*
(6:00) Avoidance	-.45**	.45**	.56***
Aggressive/Defensive	-.72***	.55***	.37*
(7:00) Oppositional	-.40*	.15	.65***
(8:00) Power	-.42*	.23	.43**
(9:00) Competitive	-.42**	.38*	.44**
(10:00) Perfectionistic	-.46**	.39*	.39*

Note. Culture scores based on the *Organizational Culture Inventory®* from Human Synergistics. Societal values scores published in Geert Hofstede's *Culture's Consequences: International Differences in Work-Related Values* (Newbury Park, CA: Sage, 1980). N=40 countries for clusters, 29 countries for styles. Table from Robert A. Cooke, "Organizational Culture Inventory: Ideal Culture Profiles (International Management Association)," presented at University of Illinois at Chicago, Chicago, IL, September 2001. Copyright © by Human Synergistics International. All Rights Reserved.
*p<.05. **p<.01. ***p<.001.

As defined by Dutch social psychologist Geert Hofstede, the dimension listed in the first column of the table reflects the degree to which members of a society are loosely integrated and expected to look after themselves and their immediate family (Individualism) versus tightly integrated and expected to look after their extended families and any larger groups to which they belong and from which they cannot easily detach themselves (Collectivism).[73] The negative correlations indicate that Individualism at the societal level is negatively related to preferences for Defensive cultures at the organizational level. Combining Hofstede's research on the values of different countries relative to one another with the work of Ronen and Shenkar on societal clusters, countries in the Anglo, Germanic, Nordic, and Latin European clusters tend to be more Individualistic than countries in the Latin American, Far Eastern, and Near Eastern clusters, which are relatively more Collectivistic. Similarly, the profiles in Figure 1.8 show that the ideal organizational cultures described by leaders from the former countries are less Defensive than the ideal cultures described by those from the latter.

These trends are possibly due to the ability of people in Individualistic societies to move away from their extended families and to leave organizations that are not a good fit for them. Mobility and lack of attachment may lead them to view styles such as Approval and Conventional as somewhat unnecessary and even counterproductive in organizational settings. In contrast, members of organizations in Collectivistic societies may feel that expectations to fit in and gain approval (Passive/Defensive) are appropriate and necessary given the low likelihood of "escaping" from the organization. Moreover, they may view winning and being seen and noticed (Aggressive/Defensive) as appropriate ways to gain the approval and respect of others.

Hofstede defines Power Distance as the extent to which the less powerful members of a society accept and expect an unequal distribution of power. As shown in Table 1.1, societal values around Power Distance are positively and significantly related to the leaders' descriptions of ideal organizational cultures in all four of the Passive/Defensive styles and two of the Aggressive/Defensive styles (Competitive and Perfectionistic). Consistent with this finding, the profiles in Figure 1.8 show that respondents from Latin European, Near Eastern, Latin American, and Far Eastern countries (all relatively high in Power Distance) more strongly prefer Passive/Defensive and Perfectionistic and Competitive organizational cultures than do respondents from Anglo, Germanic, and Nordic countries (all relatively low in Power Distance).

Uncertainty Avoidance is described by Hofstede as the degree to which members of a society are intolerant of and uncomfortable with uncertainty, differences, and ambiguity. Per the correlations in Table 1.1, Uncertainty Avoidance is positively and significantly related to all the Defensive styles and is negatively and significantly related to all the Constructive styles except Self-Actualizing. As you can see from the profiles in Figure 1.8, the extent to which Self-Actualizing is valued varies the least across countries. Hofstede's research shows that countries in the Latin European, Latin American, and Near Eastern clusters are relatively high in Uncertainty Avoidance. These countries also have the strongest Defensive extensions in their ideal culture profiles. Countries in the Germanic cluster (particularly Austria and Germany) tend to be lower in Uncertainty Avoidance than those in the clusters just mentioned. However, they have higher Uncertainty Avoidance than countries in the Anglo and Nordic cluster and some of the countries in the Far Eastern cluster (such as Malaysia, Indonesia, and the Philippines). Uncertainty Avoidance helps us to better understand ideal organizational cultures in terms of the Defensive styles as well as the Constructive styles, particularly Achievement. Given that expectations for Achievement include taking reasonable risks, it makes sense that this style is not valued quite as strongly by leaders from societies that have a relatively low tolerance for ambiguity and uncertainty.

The leaders' descriptions of ideal organizational cultures are also related to their countries' World Competitiveness Rankings five and ten years after the ideal culture data were collected. To examine this, Rob aggregated leaders' ideal descriptions to the country level and then correlated these country-level averages with the countries' World Competitiveness Rankings five years and ten years after the ideal culture descriptions were collected. The rankings, which are published annually in IMD Switzerland's *World Competitiveness Yearbook*, are based on multiple indicators of economic performance, government efficiency, business efficiency, and infrastructure, and range from a numerical rank of 1 (indicating most competitive) to a rank of 63 (indicating least competitive).[74] As shown in Table 1.2, countries in which leaders place greater value on the Defensive styles (such as those in the Latin American, Near Eastern, and Far Eastern clusters) tended to rank more poorly in world competitiveness than countries where these styles were not valued as strongly by leaders (such as those in the Anglo, Germanic, and Nordic clusters). Interestingly, the relationship between the aggregated descriptions of ideal at the country level and the countries' World Competitiveness Rankings grew stronger over time (from five years later to ten years later in Table 1.2). The lack of significant correlations with the Constructive styles was not surprising, given that the scores for these styles did not vary as much as the Defensive styles from one country to the next.

The three most important takeaways from the research on ideal organizational cultures in different countries are:
- a) across countries, leaders generally agree that Constructive styles are important for maximizing the performance of their organizations;
- b) leaders differ on the extent to which they believe Defensive styles are ideal, and these differences are driven, at least in part, by societal values; and
- c) Defensive styles are negatively associated with the world competitiveness of countries.

These takeaways have clear implications for locally owned and operated companies in countries ranked low in international competitiveness, as well as for global corporations with facilities located in those countries. First, for leaders who want to initiate change, focusing on strengthening Constructive norms rather than suppressing Defensive norms is the most respectful and realistic way to start the journey. An initiative designed to accentuate Constructive styles is more likely to be accepted and supported by members, given the generally high value placed on those styles across the world (in contrast to the lack of agreement around the value of the Defensive styles). Second, to the extent that the initial changes lead to improvements in local effectiveness, members are more likely to become open to decreasing the strength of Defensive norms, particularly if they find that such norms interfere with the implementation and/or impact of the other changes being made. For example, existing norms for Power and Dependent styles can limit the progress of otherwise successful employee involvement and empowerment initiatives. Moderating these norms to achieve greater participation could lead to many valued outcomes, ranging from higher engagement and teamwork to greater innovativeness and quality to better financial performance. Such successes could pave the way for addressing other Defensive norms.

Table 1.2. Ideal Cultures and World Competitiveness Rankings Five and Ten Years Later

Countries' World Competitiveness

	Five Years Later	Ten Years Later
Constructive		
(11:00) Achievement	-.30*	-.19
(12:00) Self-Actualizing	-.29	-.25
(1:00) Humanistic-Encouraging	-.21	-.16
(2:00) Affiliative	-.17	-.08
Passive/Defensive		
(3:00) Approval	.36*	.51**
(4:00) Conventional	.41*	.48**
(5:00) Dependent	.44**	.55***
(6:00) Avoidance	.44**	.57***
Aggressive/Defensive		
(7:00) Oppositional	.17	.28
(8:00) Power	.22	.21
(9:00) Competitive	.32*	.43**
(10:00) Perfectionistic	.31*	.49**

Note. Culture scores based on *Organizational Culture Inventory*® data from Human Synergistics. World Competitiveness rankings published by IMD, Switzerland. Lower rankings indicate better management of competencies to achieve increased prosperity. N=31 to 34 countries. Table from Robert A. Cooke, *"Organizational Culture Inventory: Ideal Culture Profiles (International Management Association),"* presented at University of Illinois at Chicago, Chicago, IL, September 2001. Copyright © by Human Synergistics International. All Rights Reserved.
*$p<.05$. **$p<.01$. ***$p<.001$.

Interestingly, over time, information about developing a Constructive culture can spill over the boundaries of an organization—whether it is locally owned or part of a multinational company—and gradually lead to changes in values and norms within other local organizations, the community, and even the country. These secondary effects occur as members share what they've experienced and learned with others outside of their organization (a phenomenon we've observed with several of our clients). Such an influence in the broader community may lead to a decrease in the relative strength of Power Distance, Uncertainty Avoidance, and Collectivism. These are the societal values related to Defensive organizational cultures (as shown here) and to lower global or national competitiveness (as shown by other research[75]). In turn, our observations suggest that as more organizations continue to strengthen their Constructive styles and improve their performance, their communities may begin to support innovation, encourage better communication, and, as a result, attract more investment and talent. These trends, particularly when accompanied by enlightened leadership at the national level, have the potential to increase the country's world competitiveness and to improve its citizens' quality of life.

The survey-based approach to setting goals and providing a benchmark for culture therefore can be particularly helpful in global organizations. If you use this approach and collect cross-national data, you may notice that the differences in ideal profiles across cultures may not be as pronounced today as they were when we collected the data described above—particularly at the higher levels of your organization. As leaders travel more frequently, take on assignments in different countries, and further their education overseas, it is likely that their values and preferred norms shift away from the Defensive styles. Nevertheless, data collected via the *Ideal* form of the *Organizational Culture Inventory* may reveal differences in values (especially at lower levels of the organization) that should be considered in launching a culture initiative.

Ideal Cultures and Age

Millennials (born 1981–1997) have now surpassed Baby Boomers (born 1946–1964) as the nation's largest living generation.[76] Thus, from a sustainability perspective, it would make sense for leaders to be thinking about how their organizations' cultures align with the values of those who compose, or likely will compose, much of their employee pool. This issue raises the question *Are the cultural values of younger generations really that different from those of the older generations?*

According to Kevin Moidzik and Kenneth De Mueuse of talent management firm Korn/Ferry International, the claims made by the media—and particularly the popular press—about generational differences in organizational loyalty, employee motivation, and work-related values and attitudes are "greatly exaggerated." Their review of twenty-six different peer-reviewed studies on generational differences in the workplace reveals many more similarities than differences.[77]

Google's People Operations also concluded, based on their own research, that every generation of workers basically wants the same things. "If you look at what their underlying needs and aspirations are, there's no difference at all between this new generation of workers and my generation and my father's generation," stated former Head of People Operations Laszlo Bock in a *New York Times* article. "Every single human being wants the same thing in the workplace—we want to be treated with respect, we want to have a sense of meaning and agency and impact, and we want our boss to just leave us alone so we can get our work done." As columnist Farhad Manjoo points out, shared desires don't imply that the different generations are identical but rather that generational stereotyping can lead people to overlook *even more important similarities* across generations that influence workplace behavior and decisions.[78]

Similarly, the *Organizational Culture Inventory—Ideal* profiles based on a recent sample drawn from a variety of organizations and industries show that, overall, people of different ages strongly endorse the Constructive styles. However, in developing these profiles, we found that it was important to take societal culture into consideration to better understand values associated with the Defensive styles. Thus, we created separate age-group profiles for respondents in Anglo counties versus those in other country clusters (see Figure 1.9).

Why Constructive Culture? 57

Figure 1.9. Ideal Cultures Described by Different Age Groups

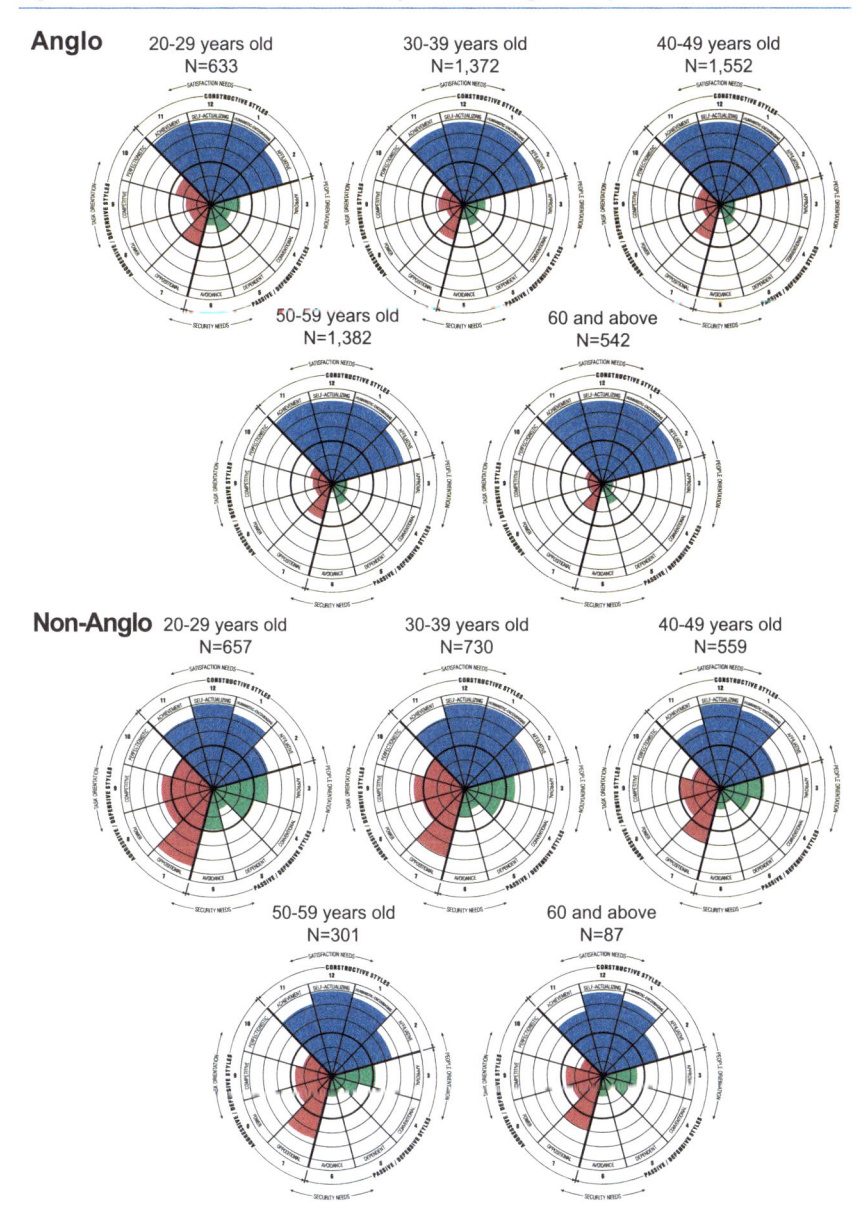

Anglo

20-29 years old
N=633

30-39 years old
N=1,372

40-49 years old
N=1,552

50-59 years old
N=1,382

60 and above
N=542

Non-Anglo

20-29 years old
N=657

30-39 years old
N=730

40-49 years old
N=559

50-59 years old
N=301

60 and above
N=87

Research and development by Robert A. Cooke, Ph.D. and J. Clayton Lafferty, Ph.D.
Copyright © 1987-2019 by Human Synergistics International. All Rights Reserved.

The results for respondents in the Anglo cluster of countries show strong consistency across age groups, not only with respect to the Constructive styles but also the Defensive styles. The extensions for the youngest group are slightly longer along the Oppositional and Competitive styles (Aggressive/Defensive) and Approval and Dependent styles (Passive/Defensive). We have noticed these relatively minor differences, particularly along the Aggressive/Defensive styles, in our Circumplex data sets over the decades. Thus, these trends are more likely due to age (and associated factors such as education, experience, and organizational level) than generation. Certainly, there are observable and distinctive differences in the ways that people of different generations behave given, for example, advances in technology and city versus suburban or rural living. However, in North America, these differences do not necessarily reflect or imply changes between generations in the types of values measured by the *Organizational Culture Inventory—Ideal.*

On the other hand, in the data we collected in non-Anglo countries, the differences across age groups are more pronounced. This is most noticeable, again, for styles such as Oppositional, Competitive, and Approval—though the profiles look somewhat more expanded in general for the younger respondents. Further research is needed to determine whether these differences are generational or due to, for example, the organizational levels and education of respondents. As noted previously, the values and ideal profiles reported by leaders at the top of organizations in certain countries may be changing due to travel, education overseas, and opportunities associated with certain assignments. This movement away from Defensive styles might be weaker or slower at lower organizational levels. Nevertheless, it is important to consider the possibility that, in non-Anglo countries, the norms viewed by younger people as ideal are somewhat more Defensive. Younger members who value Defensive styles may resist culture change programs, a reaction that can be dealt with, as noted earlier, by focusing on strengthening the Constructive styles when initiating change. As Constructive styles gain a foothold and their positive impact becomes visible, leaders can direct attention toward reducing Defensive behaviors.

Ideal Cultures and Gender

Women now make up nearly half of the workforce in the United States. Yet, among the companies in the S&P 500, they represent only one-third of managers, just over a quarter of senior managers and executives, 11 percent of board members, and 5 percent of CEOs.[79] Just 3 percent of leaders in the world's top five hundred companies are women.[80] According to Pew Research, only fifteen world leaders are women (less than 10 percent of UN member states), eight of whom are their countries' first.[81] Gender discrimination and harassment are key issues in many organizations, as well as in many countries and societies. Although societal values and norms contribute to the breadth and depth of the problem, organizational culture provides the fuel that either escalates or reverses discrimination and harassment in the workplace.

Discrimination and harassment persist despite the fact that both men and women place a much greater value on Constructive than on Defensive norms and, in doing so, describe ideal cultures that are far more similar than different. Ideal profiles based on recently collected data from over eight thousand leaders, managers, and other members of a wide array of organizations show this to be the case in Anglo and in non-Anglo countries (see Figure 1.10). If these commonly held values were consistently translated into Constructive operating cultures, the concomitant high levels of fairness and respect for all members would counteract these troubling and persistent trends.

Yes, the ideal organizational culture profiles do in fact show that, in Anglo countries, men place somewhat greater value on Aggressive/Defensive norms than do women. In addition, and possibly contrary to popular belief, men also place slightly more value than women on Passive/Defensive norms. However, the message regarding gender that is most clearly conveyed by the Anglo profiles in Figure 1.10 is the mutual desire for and strong belief in the value of a Constructive culture.

For people in non-Anglo countries, the ideal descriptions of men and women are even more similar to one another. As in the Anglo countries, both men and women in these countries show a strong preference for the Constructive styles over the other two sets of styles.

Focusing strictly on gender, parallel findings were reported by Andrea Simon based on a completely different tool (the *Organizational Culture Assessment Instrument* by Professors Robert Quinn and Kim Cameron of the University of Michigan) and a sample of over three thousand men and over three thousand women in the United States. According to Simon, "**both preferred** a strong Clan culture that emphasizes collaboration, teamwork and focus on people."[82] These three attributes correspond to the Affiliative and Humanistic-Encouraging styles on the Circumplex.

Figure 1.10. Ideal Cultures Described by Females versus Males

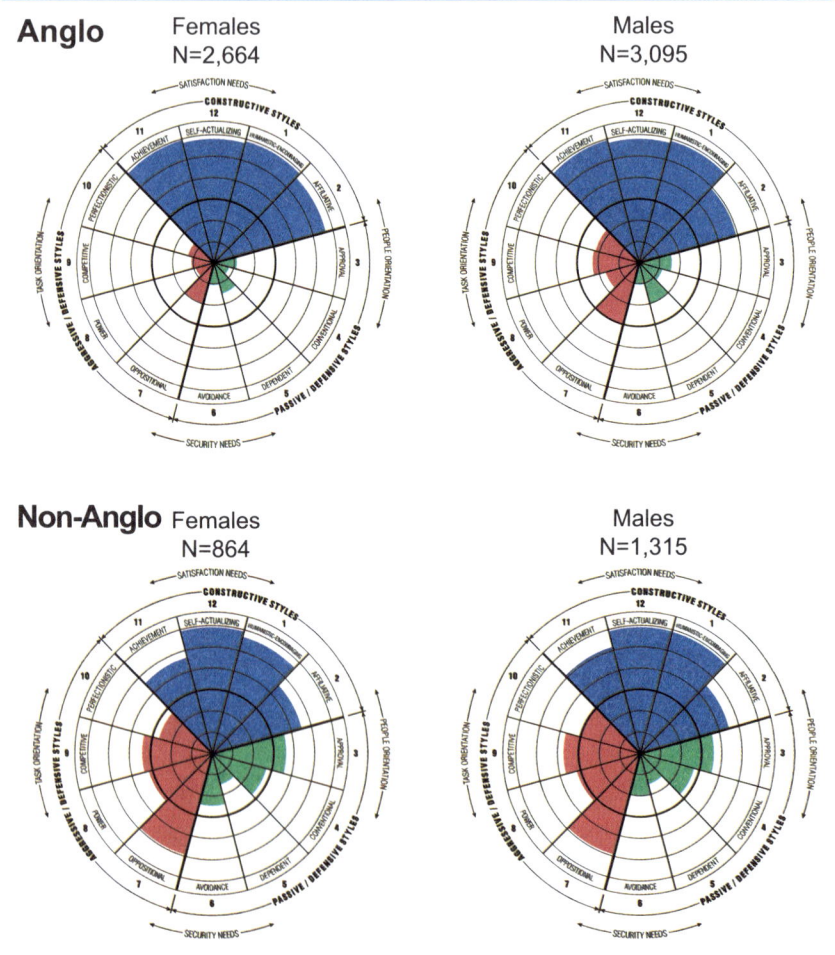

Research and development by Robert A. Cooke, Ph.D. and J. Clayton Lafferty, Ph.D. Copyright © 1987-2019 by Human Synergistics International. All Rights Reserved.

Using the *Organizational Culture Inventory*, Drs. Cynthia Emrich and Aarti Shyamsunder of Catalyst also found that the ideal cultures described by nearly five hundred high-potential men and women who were working in one of forty-three countries at the time of the survey were very similar and strongly Constructive. In addition, the researchers compared the ideal culture profiles to the behaviors that the respondents described as currently expected in their organizations. They then examined the style-by-style gaps between the ideal culture and the current operating culture and the impact of those gaps on satisfaction and retention. According to their findings, both men and women agreed that the largest gaps in their workplace cultures were in the Constructive styles. Those who experienced a wide gap between their ideal and current cultures frequently signaled their intentions to leave their organizations, while of those who experienced a narrow gap, 50 percent fewer men and 90 percent fewer women reported that they were planning to leave. In addition, when the gap between ideal and current culture was narrow as opposed to wide, both men and women reported higher levels of satisfaction with work and advancement, pay, supervisors, and their organizations' commitment to work-life quality and diversity.[83]

Even though men and women agree that Constructive behaviors are important in organizations, disconnects between espoused values and the day-to-day operating cultures of organizations continue to exist. As we'll talk about more in the next chapter, the disconnect between values and current operating cultures is in large part due to structures and systems that are expedient, short-term, easy to understand, or driven by leaders' personal needs rather than by shared organizational values. Thus, ironically, the programs that are put into place to address organizational issues and problems often reflect and reinforce Defensive norms and end up exacerbating rather than improving the situation. For example, in a relevant and insightful article, "Why Diversity Programs Fail," Frank Dobbin and Alexandra Kalev emphasize that so many diversity programs fall short of producing any of their target changes because of the way in which most organizations approach the problem. Specifically, they note:

> Executives favor a classic command-and-control approach to diversity because it boils expected behaviors down to dos and don'ts that are easy to understand and defend. ...You won't get managers on board by blaming and shaming them with rules and regulations.[84]

A command-and-control approach is consistent on the Circumplex with Power and Dependent norms and expectations; the emphasis on rules and regulations reflects a Conventional mindset; and blaming and shaming are part of an Oppositional approach and potentially lead to Avoidance norms. These norms influence not only the solutions that organizations adopt but also the way in which such solutions are implemented—ironically, reinforcing the existing culture rather than changing it.

For instance, according to Dobbin and Kalev's research, three-quarters of diversity programs rely on negative messaging and offer avoidance of adverse consequences as the reason why the people in the training programs should change (which is consistent with an Oppositional approach). Forty percent of organizations use hiring tests—yet Dobbin and Kalev note that many use them inconsistently, with some applicants but not others, and downplay or ignore the results when making actual decisions around who to hire. This trend is consistent with Conventional norms—where members simply do what others are doing—and does not address the issue in an Achievement-oriented way. And what about performance appraisals, which 90 percent of midsize to large organizations use? According to Dobbin and Kalev, managers will often "lowball" women and minorities or rate everyone highly to avert conflicts—which reflects behavioral norms that are at the heart of what we refer to as Avoidance cultures. Finally, the authors point out that half of midsize to large organizations have grievance procedures, yet many people are afraid to use them for fear of retaliation. This is consistent with cultures where expectations for Power, Dependent, and Avoidance behaviors prevail.

So what kinds of organizational cultures are effective in promoting both diversity and equality? Cross-cultural research by Linda Bajdo and Marcus Dickson shows that values and practices emphasizing both gender equality and a *humane orientation* are key. When these values and practices are combined, they contribute significantly to the percentage of women in management.[85] Likewise, Catherine Kwantes and Arief Kartolo at the University of Windsor's Centre for Cultural and Organizational Research found that Constructive norms lead to the lowest levels of perceived discrimination, while Aggressive/Defensive norms lead to the highest. They point out that Constructive norms promote inclusion based on organizational membership rather than demographic characteristics such as gender and race.[86] Along similar lines, research on gender diversity in management teams in relation to firm performance shows that a supportive organizational culture is necessary before the beneficial aspects of gender diversity can be realized.[87] This finding echoes those of the Northwestern University readership studies discussed earlier.

In conclusion, given that Constructive behaviors are more consistently and positively related to effectiveness and organizational performance *and* to the stated values of organizations, it makes sense that ideal culture profiles are consistently and strongly Constructive. We are not implying that Defensive behaviors are not valued—they simply are not valued as strongly or as consistently. These results also make sense given that, on the one hand, Defensive behaviors are negatively or inconsistently related to effectiveness and performance and, on the other hand, they are in some cases (particularly with respect to Aggressive/Defensive behaviors) associated with higher salaries, higher-level positions, and/or broader society values.

Although a strong Constructive culture is achievable, for many organizations there is a fairly large gap between what their leaders and other members say is ideal and the behaviors that are actually required to fit in and meet expectations on a day-to-day basis. Fortunately, we've found that leaders have the influence and power to both directly and indirectly steer the cultures of their organizations in a more Constructive direction. How they achieve this—and, in the process, attain higher levels of effectiveness and performance for their organizations—is the topic of the next chapter and those that follow.

Chapter 2

How Leaders Directly and Indirectly Influence and Change Culture

> There is a pervasive belief that if you lose the red, you'll lose your drive and capacity to lead. You'll become "fluffy" or a "tree hugger," and then you can't lead because leaders are red. However, there is a way that leaders can be even more assertive, better express their core truth, and be honest and respectful without being brutal and hurting other people. But this isn't something that's easy to see when you're in a culture that is strongly Defensive.
>
> Ricardo Gil, Founding Partner, Axialent[88]

Do your managers and employees act in ways that are consistent with and reflect the stated values, mission, and philosophy of your organization? Or do their decisions and behaviors communicate that something different is more important and expected? If your organization is not living up to its values, then it is experiencing what we call a *culture disconnect*, a situation in which the day-to-day norms (the organization's operating culture represented by the current culture profile) differ from or are out of alignment with its values (as represented by the ideal culture profile). Consider the following example:

> A recent public investigation revealed that call center employees had been incentivized to "sell, sell, sell" with a single goal in mind: to win the trips, cruises, and cash offered as prizes. The problem wasn't the prizes. Rather, it was the understanding that the employees could win the prizes regardless of how they achieved their sales targets. A combination of drivers—including goal-setting systems; compensation systems that required the sales agents to pay for potential client lists or caller leads; and direct communications by managers and leaders, including emails)—together reinforced what was described as an "old-school boiler room culture" where salespeople "cut corners" and sold products regardless of whether they were suitable for the customer or met the customers' wants or needs.[89]

Is Your Organization Experiencing a Culture Disconnect?

Culture disconnects arise when the organization's structures, systems, and technologies—as well as the skills and qualities of its leaders and managers—are not driven by, are inconsistent with, and/or run counter to its stated values. Under these circumstances, the *climate* of the organization—that is, members' shared perceptions of their work environment—fails to communicate the importance, appropriateness, and efficacy of those values. Instead, members infer from the prevailing climate that they are expected or implicitly required to think and behave in ways that are markedly different than those described in the value statement on the corporate website, in the employee handbook, or in annual reports. Shared inferences and beliefs about expected behaviors are the *norms* that define an organization's day-to-day operating culture. In practice, the breakdowns between values and norms lead members to behave in less Constructive and more Passive/Defensive or Aggressive/Defensive ways than desired. While these informal, unintended norms might seem to temporarily address an immediate problem or accomplish a specific goal, they more generally and over the longer term intensify, lead to counterproductive consequences, and pull the organization and its members further away from the mission and vision. Consequently, culture disconnects put organizations and their leaders, employees, members, clients, customers, suppliers, and shareholders in greater jeopardy the longer they persist.

The data we've collected over the years consistently indicate a strong tendency for leaders to describe their operating cultures as more Constructive and less Defensive than do others within their organizations. This is illustrated by the culture profiles shown in Figure 2.1, based on recently collected data using the *Organizational Culture Inventory*. Beyond the likelihood that things are objectively more Constructive at the top of the hierarchy, these relatively optimistic descriptions may be due to leaders' failure to recognize that any Defensive norms driving their own behavior are amplified as one moves down the hierarchy. In addition, their more positive descriptions could also be the result of misreading the impact of the systems they have put into place and assuming that the organization's espoused values will automatically drive behavioral norms at lower levels. As a corollary, many leaders do not realize the extent to which culture disconnects pervade their organizations—which is one of the reasons why feedback on their operating cultures is so important. Just as critical, however, is that leaders understand how culture works so that they can address gaps and keep the organization connected to its purpose and values.

Figure 2.1. Operating Culture at Different Organizational Levels

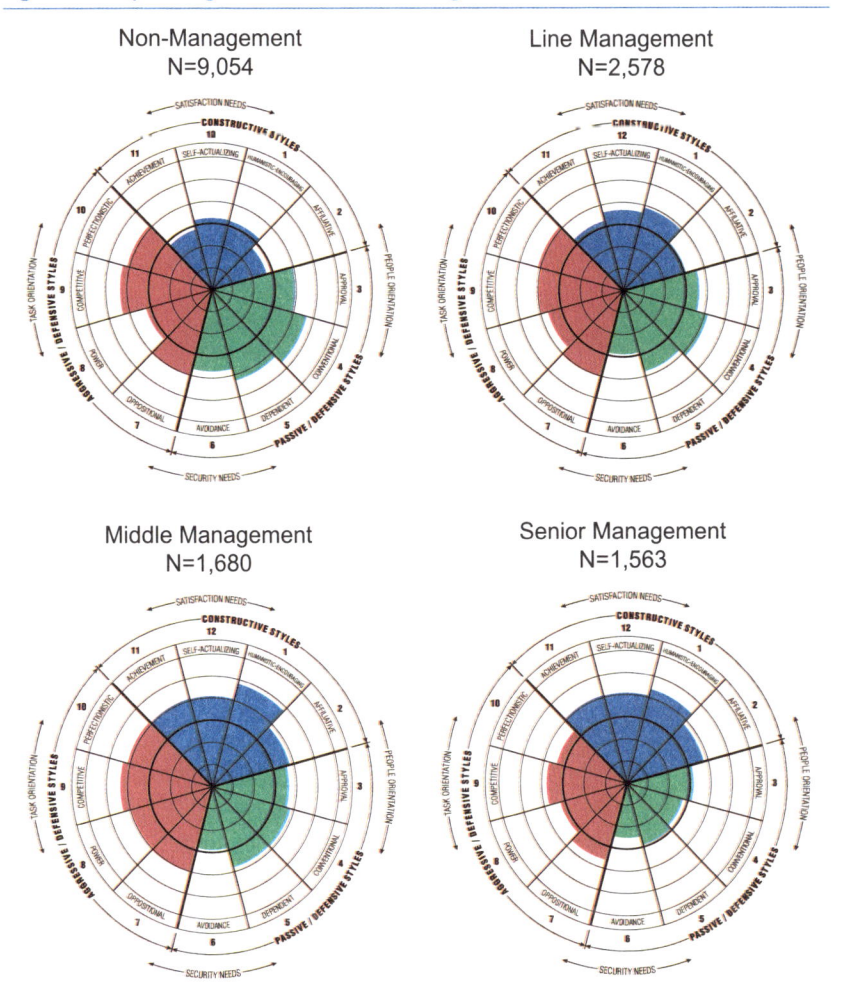

Non-Management
N=9,054

Line Management
N=2,578

Middle Management
N=1,680

Senior Management
N=1,563

Research and development by Robert A. Cooke, Ph.D. and J. Clayton Lafferty, Ph.D. Copyright © 1987-2019 by Human Synergistics International. All Rights Reserved.

How Culture Works

Though the shared values and ideal cultures described by leaders influence their organizations' operating cultures, our research confirms that other internal forces are more strongly related to the norms and expectations that emerge in day-to-day operations. That's because the behavioral norms that evolve in organizations are predominately the product of members' collective learning regarding what it takes to succeed—or to stay out of trouble and survive—in the system. In deciding what behaviors are required, members may react cautiously or even skeptically to mission and value statements, change initiatives, and what leaders say they want. Instead, they infer what's really expected based on the conditions and realities that they face daily, as shown in our "How Culture Works" model (Figure 2.2). These internal *causal factors* are the primary determinants of the operating culture of the organization regardless of whether they are consistent with the organization's values and what leaders say is expected. Therefore they potentially are also the most powerful *levers* available to leaders interested in redirecting cultural norms. Leaders at the top of the organization can make changes to causal factors so that they are consistent with the ideal culture and, by doing so, make them levers for Constructive culture change.

Figure 2.2. How Culture Works

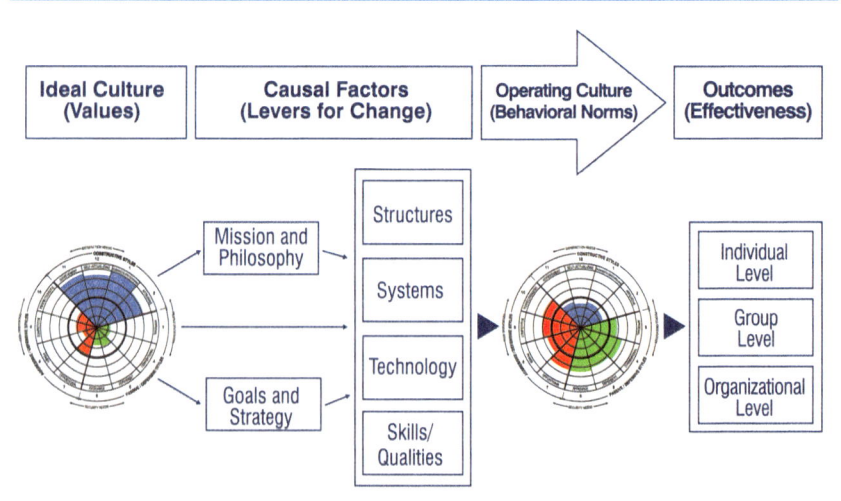

From *Organizational Culture Inventory/Organizational Effectiveness Inventory Feedback Report* by Robert A. Cooke, Ph.D. and Janet L. Szumal, Ph.D.
Copyright © 2003 by Human Synergistics International. All Rights Reserved.

In the model, the factors listed between the ideal culture Circumplex and the operating culture profile depict some of the important means through which leaders can have a *direct impact* on culture (which involves their presence and interactions with others) as well as an *indirect impact* (which doesn't require their presence).

Leaders indirectly influence culture through their decisions about the organization's mission, philosophy, values, goals, and strategies, as well as through the structures, systems, and technologies they put into place. This indirect influence is further magnified by the skills and qualities of the people that leaders choose to hire, fire, reward, and punish.

Leaders directly influence culture through their interactions with others and through their own skills and qualities, including their personal styles, leadership strategies, and management approaches. Given leaders' position and status, their behaviors set a standard and are often emulated by those with whom they interact, regardless of whether their behaviors exemplify or run counter to the stated values or philosophy of the organization. Their styles also can provoke unforeseen or dysfunctional reactions or counteractions in others. Moreover, their behaviors directly influence the operating culture by constraining or facilitating other members' work activities and interactions.

What we've found is that leaders who use both direct and indirect levers have the greatest impact on culture. As illustrated by the scenario at the beginning of this chapter, it's rarely just one force that promotes and reinforces cultural norms. Indeed, one of the biggest problems we face in organizational life is the tendency to unintentionally support and even reward, in multiple ways, Passive/Defensive and Aggressive/Defensive thinking and behavioral styles rather than those that are Constructive. Consequently, if you keep in mind how culture really works and remain sensitive to the subtle effects of how you lead and the decisions you make, you can create a culture that supports rather than inadvertently detracts from your organization's mission and vision.

Table 2.1 summarizes the various indirect and direct causal factors that promote Constructive, Passive/Defensive, and Aggressive/Defensive cultural norms, based on our cross-sectional research and client case studies. Although we describe the causal factors one at a time, their interrelated nature will become evident as you read about the experiences of clients who used the *Organizational Culture Inventory* as early as the 1980s. These clients include General Motors (GM), International Business Machines (IBM), General Electric (GE), and Cincinnati Gas & Electric (CG&E). These or similar forces might be at work in your organization—and may or may not be sending the messages you desire.

Table 2.1. Causal Factors Related to Constructive and Defensive Behavioral Norms (Summary of Findings)

Behavioral Norms

Causal Factors	Constructive	Passive/Defensive	Aggressive/Defensive
Mission and Philosophy			
Articulation of Mission	Clear, understood	Unclear	Unclear
Customer Orientation	Strong	Weak	Moderate or variable
Structures			
Authority	Decentralized	Centralized	Unrelated
Influence	Decentralized	Centralized	Centralized
Employee Involvement	High	Low	Low
Empowerment	Sufficient	Insufficient	Insufficient
Systems			
Performance Appraisal	Fair, unbiased	Unfair, biased	Unfair, biased
Rewards: Praise	Very likely	Unlikely	Unlikely
Rewards: Raise or Bonus	Very likely	Unlikely	Likely
Use of Punishment	Unlikely	Very likely	Very likely
Punishment: Criticism	Unlikely	Likely	Very likely
Selection/Placement	Good employee-job fit	Poor employee-job fit	Poor employee-job fit
Training and Development	Sufficient	Insufficient	Insufficient
Goal Clarity	Clear	Unclear	Variable clarity
Goal Challenge	Reasonably challenging	Too easy	Too difficult
Goal Participation	Set jointly or by employees	Set by superiors	Set by superiors
Goal Acceptance	High acceptance	Low acceptance	Low acceptance
Technology (Job Design)			
Autonomy	High	Low	Low
Skill Variety	High	Low	Low
Task Identity	High	Moderate or variable	Moderate or variable
Job Significance	High	Low	Low
Feedback from Job	High	Low	Low
Interdependence	High	Low	Low
Leadership Skills/Qualities			
Thinking and Behavioral Styles	Constructive	Passive/Defensive Aggressive/Defensive	Aggressive/Defensive
Interaction Facilitation	Strong	Weak	Weak
Task Facilitation	Strong	Weak	Moderate or variable
Goal Emphasis	Strong	Weak	Weak
Consideration	Strong	Weak	Weak
Reliance on Positional Power	Moderate or variable	Strong	Strong
Reliance on Personal Power	Strong	Weak	Weak
Communication	Clear, open, multi-directional	Unclear, restricted	Unclear, restricted
Leadership Strategies	Prescriptive	Restrictive	Restrictive
Management Approaches	Facilitating	Inhibiting	Inhibiting

Mission and Philosophy and Cultural Norms

According to management guru Peter F. Drucker, every organization—business or not—has a "theory of the business" that consists of assumptions about, among other things, the organization's mission or purpose. However, while missions are fundamental and critical, they are often forgotten, overlooked, or misunderstood. Drucker points out that as this happens, the organization becomes "sloppy," "cuts corners," "begins to pursue what is expedient rather than what is right," and stops thinking and asking questions.[90] Consistent with this point, our research on causal factors indicates that strong philosophies and missions that are clearly articulated, defined, and understood by members are associated with Constructive behavioral norms (see Table 2.1). In contrast, philosophies and missions that are poorly defined, communicated, and understood tend to be associated with Passive/Defensive and Aggressive/Defensive cultures.

Similarly, with respect to philosophies, we have found that strong customer service orientation is positively related to strong Constructive norms and is negatively related to Defensive norms, particularly Passive/Defensive. That said, mission statements and company philosophies alone do not determine the direction of operating cultures. Though philosophies or methods such as customer experience, Agile, Lean Six Sigma, total quality management, quality of work life, and human-centered design theoretically *should* drive operating cultures to be more Constructive, this does not necessarily happen. Specifically, when other causal factors are promoting strong Defensive behavioral norms, these norms interfere with and limit the successful implementation of philosophies and overpower the more positive norms they would otherwise engender.

One of the first clients to give us deep insights into how a new philosophy can be undermined by the existing culture—or instead can inspire and enable leaders to make changes that will foster new norms and expectations—was the GM Powertrain plant in Toledo, Ohio. The story of how this transmission plant began working on culture change dates to 1983, when its managers and the United Auto Workers' (UAW) Local 14 union leaders agreed to initiate a philosophy around employee involvement and quality of work life based on union-management cooperation. Although the plant was operating at full capacity, it had lost some major contracts due to quality issues and had accumulated more than two thousand outstanding employee grievances while the local union and the plant's management were gridlocked (for over twelve months) on a new labor contract. Oscar Bunch, the UAW Local 14 president who signed the joint statement of commitment (along with the union chairman, the plant manager, and the personnel director), recalled,

> At the time, we only had about 40 percent buy-in from the people on the floor, and several people told me that signing that statement would be political suicide. However, I realized that we couldn't survive with the union and management at war with each other. We had to change for the company to be able to continue to compete and stay in business.[91]

In 1991, we met with the plant's most senior leaders from both union and management, along with UAW members Gary Thompson and Wes Bunch (who then were two of the plant's internal facilitators and had previously worked on its factory floor), to hear their observations of the change process so that we could document them.[92] They explained that during the first few years, as they attempted to implement the new agreed-upon philosophy, the plant struggled with "trying to create a participative culture in a dictatorial manner." Managers continued to give orders and demand loyalty, and union reps continued to deal with problems by filing grievances—because that was how they had always done business. Even the hourly workers didn't recognize how their own behavior continued to reinforce a culture that insiders described as "hierarchical" and "contentious." Wes recalled,

> Everyone was looking at things from their own perspective. We would create these teams, and it would just turn into a "bitch fest" because there wasn't a Constructive place toward which people could direct their energy.[93]

During the initial meeting of the first employee involvement group, the hourly workers basically "ate the supervisor alive" by telling him every thought they had about how he ran the department. They then informed the union committeeman that they weren't particularly pleased with him either. By the third meeting, the group consisted of only hourly workers.

Bit by bit, the facilitators, along with the plant's managers, union leaders, and employees, identified and addressed obstacles to implementing the philosophy—including the organization's structure, certain terms of the union-management contract, job design, the skills and qualities of leaders and managers, and, more generally, the plant's culture. However, it wasn't until individual members from both union and management realized how their own behavior affected the culture that things really started to change. Gary observed,

> We had groups of managers and union officials identify the ideal culture using the *Organizational Culture Inventory* and then had a couple hundred of them do the *Life Styles Inventory Self Description* and *Description by Others* to show them the difference between what they said they wanted, what they thought they were acting like, and how others actually saw them. That's when we started using the notion of culture intelligently. ...Once we started internalizing and aligning our personal goals with organizational goals that we could work on together, the transformation we were seeking got easier.[94]

The plant's first success with this approach was in the assembly area, historically considered one of the worst areas in the plant in terms of quality of work life. Employees worked on a traditional assembly line attaching 2,800 parts per day with no opportunity for movement, interaction, or involvement in decision making. Acting on the feedback about their own behavior in comparison to the ideal culture that they wanted to create, the union and management leaders in the assembly area, along with a group of hourly employees, worked together in a more Constructive way to design and implement a plan for improvement. They decided to reorganize the assembly workers into six-member autonomous work groups in which members would rotate tasks and have the authority to make decisions that impacted their jobs. It was also decided that the newly designed jobs would be implemented by hourly workers on a voluntary basis, contingent on a majority vote of support from the area's employees and continued support three months after the plan was implemented. Because the new design required employees to learn five additional jobs, volunteers received a nominal increase in pay. Those who chose not to participate were also placed into the groups, but only those members who had volunteered to participate rotated their jobs.

The plan was initially endorsed by 60 percent of the hourly employees, which was enough to move forward. Three months after it was implemented, 85 percent of hourly employees endorsed the plan. Absenteeism, grievances, and the number of visits to the medical department by assembly area workers all significantly declined. Costs decreased while quality and demand for the plant's product increased. Employees in other areas began taking notice of what the assembly area had achieved and wanted to go through a similar process to identify and implement improvements.

By 1990, people in several areas of the plant as well as the plant's leadership had gone through the process of connecting their own behavior to culture. Customer surveys indicated significant improvements in product satisfaction. The plant achieved a 55 percent reduction in warranty expenses. Assembly plant returns of items shipped directly to customers decreased by 28 percent from 1987 to 1990. Costs decreased by $100 million from 1986 to 1990.[95] Scrap costs alone were reduced by almost 50 percent (from $30 per unit to approximately $15.50). All of these changes positively affected the bottom line. To this day, the plant continues to successfully operate under a joint-partnership process with UAW Local 14.[96]

Another more recent example of the connection between culture and organizational philosophy is provided by IBM. Their 2008 Global CEO study on readiness for change revealed that the two greatest challenges to change were a) mindsets and attitudes and b) corporate culture.[97] Realizing that both could be impediments to improving adaptability and efficiency, the leadership team at IBM's Integrated Supply Chain Operation in Poughkeepsie, New York, embarked on a transformation that tied Lean Manufacturing Principles to the Circumplex styles. They used the Principles together with the styles and their results from the *Organizational Culture Inventory—Ideal* to define their vision for change. Their change process integrated Lean tools, techniques, and assessments with leadership development (which included *Leadership/Impact* for executives and the *Life Styles Inventory* for managers), team building (which included the *Group Styles Inventory*), and culture change (which they evaluated and monitored using the *Organizational Culture Inventory*). By recognizing and addressing the role of individual mindsets and organizational culture in the implementation of their new philosophy, the team was able to better enact the espoused philosophy and values. In turn, the changes enabled IBM to realize benefits along multiple criteria, including exceeding financial goals, inventory management targets, and quality goals, as well as improving employee satisfaction.[98] As summarized by Chanchal Saha, Sarah S. Lam, Sreekanth Ramakrishnan, and Warren Boldrin:

While the common understanding of LT [Lean Transformation] only considers the tools and techniques it uses to effectively minimize waste and standardize processes, overall LT is most successful through the creation of a LC [Lean Culture] with the development of leadership behaviors, styles, and strategies. It is observed that nearly 80% of Lean's success relies on changing the mindset of organizational leaders. IBM mostly uses the organizational culture inventory tool to diagnose an organization's behavior or culture.[99]

These cases, along with the more recent client examples featured in the chapters that follow, illustrate that realizing a mission, vision, or philosophy requires more than just words. Successful implementation also depends on the skills and qualities of leaders and managers (reflected in their thinking and behavior) as well as the structures, systems, and technologies they put in place to support the philosophy itself and the Constructive norms that make it real.

Goals and Strategies and Cultural Norms

Constructive ideal cultures should translate into goals and strategies that are positive and beneficial in terms of both their content and their properties (e.g., their clarity, degree of difficulty, and comprehensiveness). Such goals and strategies should lead to effective structures and systems and, both directly and indirectly, to a Constructive operating culture. However, our research and observations indicate that this is not always the case. Constructive ideals and value statements do not necessarily ensure that exemplary goals and strategies are a) developed at the enterprise level, b) translated into meaningful objectives and plans for subunits, and c) converted into structures, systems, and behavioral norms that would support their implementation and attainment.

Our survey-based research indicates that managers who clearly translate organizational goals and strategies into meaningful objectives and goals for their units tend to have a relatively Constructive impact on the behavior of those around them. In contrast, managers who fail to translate goals and strategies appropriately or who instead base their unit's goals and objectives on personal agendas or self-interest do not have this positive impact.[100] Thus, leaders and managers have the potential to promote Constructive expectations by clearly articulating meaningful goals and, in turn, moving their organization toward the desired state of future affairs. Nevertheless, many leaders fail to do so even though they personally express an interest in having such an impact.

As mentioned in the previous chapter, research by Andrew Klein on organizations in a wide spectrum of industries shows that Constructive cultures facilitate strategy implementation and lead to quality and effectiveness regardless of the type of strategy being pursued.[101] Indeed, Constructive norms are just as relevant in organizations pursuing differentiation or *first in* strategies as they are to organizations pursuing cost leadership or *second in* strategies. Interestingly, further analyses of Klein's data show no significant relationships between type of strategy and type of culture. Constructive norms are just as likely to emerge in organizations competing on the basis of cost and efficiency (i.e., *defender/low-cost*) as in those competing on differentiation (i.e., *prospector/differentiation*).

Given the advantages of Constructive over Defensive cultures for implementing any strategy, consultant Cathy Perme has asked, "Does culture *have* to eat strategy for lunch?" Based on her experiences, she points out that it's possible to start improving cultural norms *during* the strategic planning process:

> Oftentimes, the way we do strategic planning simply reinforces the current culture. And if that culture is already defensive, we are probably fortifying those defenses instead of breaking them down. Today, as an integral part of my strategic planning with a client, I start with [the] *Organizational Culture Inventory*. I need to determine the current culture, establish why it is that way, and identify levers for changing it. From there I can design a strategic planning process that actually begins to change a client's workplace culture while helping them plan their strategy.[102]

Thus, consultants and leaders can start with setting goals and developing strategies in more Constructive ways to promote cultural change and break Defensive syndromes. For example, different *silos*, or subcultures that tend to form around the functional units of organizations, are often fueled by their own very different goals.[103] Establishing cross-functional goals is one of the levers that we've seen organizations use to help break down silos and foster expectations for greater collaboration between units. However, the success of this approach usually requires changes in other forces or causal factors. This challenge is illustrated by the story of Dreher Brewery in chapter 8.

Other ways in which goals and strategies have been used by organizations as a lever for change include

a) making culture and culture change part of the company's strategy (see chapter 5 about Straumann and chapter 9 about Sanitarium),
b) incorporating culture in the organization's balanced scorecard (see chapter 10 about SaskCentral), and
c) setting individual goals and aligning them with organizational goals (see chapter 7 about Pons Bakery).

Like philosophy and mission, changes to goals and strategies alone—no matter how well articulated—do not create culture change (as exemplified by the story about Agroenzymas in chapter 6). Rather, to be effective, the various forces that are part of the day-to-day work environment—particularly the skills and qualities of leaders—also must change to be better aligned with and supportive of a Constructive culture.

Structures and Cultural Norms

In their classic book *The Management of Innovation*, sociologist Tom Burns and psychologist George Stalker show how organizations that are innovative and responsive to changing market situations rely on structures that differ from those designed for organizations operating in stable environments. The findings of their landmark study conducted in the early 1960s are just as relevant today as they were back then. Specifically, they identify and describe two "polar extremities" of organizational design: mechanistic and organic.

Mechanistic organizational designs, like bureaucracies, are intended to maximize efficiency in highly stable external environments. They do so by relying heavily on

- hierarchical structures of control, authority, and communication that emphasize vertical linkages and relationships;
- highly specialized knowledge, tasks, roles, and functions that emphasize local competency over general competency; and
- strict definitions of roles, responsibilities, rights, and methods that emphasize obedience and loyalty.

Organic organizational designs feature characteristics that are better suited for innovation and adaptability in complex and changing

environments. These characteristics include
- network structures of control, authority, and communication that emphasize lateral linkages and relationships;
- continual redefinition of tasks, roles, and functions through lateral (as well as vertical) interactions and communications that emphasize knowledge sharing, collaboration, and consultation; and
- the "shedding" of narrowly defined and limiting responsibilities, rights, and methods so that problem solving and contribution to the broader common task of concern are emphasized.[104]

Building on this and more recent research,[105] we propose that the characteristics of mechanistic organizational designs interfere with innovation and adaptation, at least in part because of the Defensive norms these designs promote and reinforce. Specifically, as suggested by Table 2.1, expectations for both Passive/Defensive and Aggressive/Defensive behaviors are stronger in organizations in which decision-making authority and influence are centralized, the involvement of employees in organizational improvements is low, and employee empowerment is not sufficient. In addition, our interviews with managers confirm that Defensive cultures are maintained through micromanagement, extensive rules and procedures, and narrowly defined jobs and functions—all attributes of mechanistic systems.

In contrast, Table 2 shows that Constructive cultural norms are communicated and reinforced in organizations that decentralize authority and influence, sufficiently empower people at all levels to solve problems and make decisions, and involve employees in improving the organization. These norms support personal styles—such as thinking ahead and planning, approaching things in creative ways, and sharing ideas—that are critical in carrying out the various activities required for effective change and adaptation. Thus, organic structures lead to these outcomes at least in part as a function of the Constructive norms they promote.

Some organizations seek to combine the best of both worlds by creating ambidextrous structures, with some departments or divisions designed for exploration and innovation and others for exploitation and efficiency.[106] However, for this differentiation to work, the subunits must be effectively integrated.[107] Other organizations may seek to achieve ambidexterity within departments, with subunit members switching between organic and mechanistic structures as dictated by the demands of the situation. This within-unit approach requires, among other things, that members are prepared not only to carry out the decisions of superiors but also to take on responsibility and implement decisions that they make on their own. While more research is needed, it appears that both the cross-unit and within-unit approaches to ambidexterity are facilitated by Constructive norms. This is expected, given that such norms have been shown to lead to interunit coordination (which would enable the first type of ambidexterity) and to motivation and adaptability (which would enable the second type). The challenge inherent in ambidextrous structures is accentuating and capitalizing on organic culture-shaping forces rather than mechanistic design characteristics. We'll return to the issues of ambidexterity and culture in chapter 5.

The impact of structure on culture also comes into play with respect to how leaders approach change. One of the first times we noticed this critical detail was during the late 1980s, when the Cincinnati Gas & Electric Company was using our surveys to guide their culture change process. The change initiative was intended to support innovation and improvements in service quality (and, ultimately, to enable CG&E to expand by acquiring a utility across state lines—which at that time required special approvals). Rather than structuring a change team made up only of top leaders, which would have been the norm, the company formed a diverse group that represented a diagonal slice of the organization, including, for example, a woman who worked on the power lines. The approach was consistent with the kind of inclusive, open-minded, and Constructive norms that the leaders wanted to strengthen in the organization. In turn, the group was able to effectively identify changes that were accepted and supported throughout the organization and, importantly, that positioned the company to expand. Thirty years later, we see many other organizations structuring their change process in an inclusive way that is consistent with their Constructive ideal culture profiles (for instance, Straumann's teams of "culture change champions" in chapter 5 and Dreher Brewery's "Visegrad Group" in chapter 8).

Culture change initiatives that are driven by mechanistic structures and Defensive norms send the wrong message, are viewed as disingenuous, and end up reinforcing those norms rather than moving the culture in a more effective direction. Again, the existing culture is often the greatest obstacle to culture change! In contrast, the ways in which structural variables shape cultural norms—and can be changed so that they modify those norms—are illustrated by the cases featured in this book. These cases show that a multifaceted approach to change, guided by and reflecting the culture toward which the organization aspires, is most likely to succeed.

Systems and Cultural Norms

The systems that an organization uses to set goals, select new talent, and appraise performance optimally should be designed and driven by its mission and ideal culture. However, in practice, the systems that are put into place are often determined by other factors, such as cost, administrative expediency, or industry trends. Organizational systems, like structures, create the climate within which members work. Shared perceptions of the work climate lead members to develop beliefs, Defensive and/or Constructive, regarding how they are *really* expected to think and behave—regardless of the culture deemed ideal in the organization's mission and value statements. The systems we focus on in this section are related to reinforcement; performance appraisal; goal setting; selection and placement; and training and development.

Reinforcement Systems

At the outset, it is important to note that all systems having to do with performance management shape cultural norms in two important but different ways. This relationship is most clearly exemplified by reinforcement systems. First, since as early as 1985, Edgar Schein and other culture scholars have highlighted the allocation of rewards as a mechanism for reinforcing desired behaviors and shaping culture.[108] Making rewards contingent on the demonstration of desired behaviors (e.g., setting and achieving goals or helping colleagues) can directly promote the specific behaviors being sanctioned. Similarly, making punishments contingent on specific behaviors (e.g., not showing up for work or working while intoxicated) can discourage those behaviors from occurring.

However, what is less widely recognized is the impact of the use of rewards and punishments beyond the specific behaviors they're contingent upon. What we've found is that the extent to which rewards and punishments are used more generally can create a culture that is safe and supportive, or indifferent and lackadaisical, or punitive and combative. In other words, the system of reward and punishment in an organization contributes to and reinforces norms for behaviors above and beyond those which such a reinforcement system is intended to promote or discourage.

The use of rewards has the potential to strengthen Constructive norms. While leaders in some organizations might contend that they do not have the resources to positively reinforce desired behaviors, our research shows that recognition and praise (which don't cost any money) are as strongly and positively related to Constructive norms and expectations as are monetary rewards. Furthermore, intangible rewards, such as praise, are less frequently used in organizations with strong Defensive cultures (Passive, Aggressive, or both), likely reflecting as well as solidifying the prevailing norms.

Equally important is the type of feedback provided when things go wrong, when people make mistakes, or when employee performance falls short of expectations. In some organizations, the prototypical reaction or procedure is to problem solve and provide people with support and, within reasonable parameters, the opportunity to learn and improve. This developmental response not only reflects but also strengthens Constructive behavioral norms—particularly Achievement, Self-Actualizing, and Humanistic-Encouraging. In contrast, when the modus operandi is to criticize and punish people for mistakes, norms for Defensive behaviors prevail. Members develop a fear of failure and come to believe they must hide their shortcomings and errors, shift blame to others, and avoid getting involved in anything that seems risky.

More specifically, Passive/Defensive norms emerge when feedback and reinforcement systems primarily or exclusively focus on punishments *and* don't provide much in the way of recognition or rewards for effort, improvement, good performance, or going the extra mile. In contrast, when reinforcement reflects more of a "carrots and sticks approach"—where high performance is monetarily rewarded (with raises or bonuses) *and* low performance is met by criticism along with other forms of punishment—norms for Aggressive/Defensive behaviors tend to emerge.

Norms and expectations for Aggressive/Defensive behaviors can become even stronger when raises and bonuses are designed specifically to reinforce the Oppositional, Competitive, Power, and Perfectionistic styles. The most frequently heard example of such reinforcement is from organizations that espouse internal teamwork yet reward sales or other "wins" by members who compete with and outperform rather than cooperate with and work collaboratively with peers. Other examples come from organizations that disproportionately reward members who skillfully promote or "advertise" their accomplishments and make sure they're noticed. Yet more serious issues arise when members receive rewards for performing well along certain dimensions even though they treat others in disrespectful or arrogant ways. There is no doubt that the use of rewards, tangible and intangible, can lead to a negative, potentially toxic culture when they (even inadvertently) sanction Defensive styles.

Given these dangers, you might conclude that it is best not to use monetary rewards at all. However, as mentioned above, the use of rewards (tangible as well as intangible) is also positively associated with Constructive norms, while a lack of rewards is associated with Passive/Defensive cultures. That's why understanding the impact of your organization's reinforcement systems and what you are actually reinforcing in terms of behavior is essential to effectively managing culture.

Performance Appraisal Systems

Performance appraisal systems similarly influence norms and expectations in ways that go beyond the specific behaviors and/or outcomes they were designed to promote and reinforce in the first place. Referring again to Table 2.1, our research on culture consistently shows that performance appraisal practices that are perceived to be fair promote Constructive norms. Appraisals viewed as unfair lead to Defensive, particularly Passive/Defensive, norms.

Our work with clients also suggests that when members view appraisals as subjective, they tend to report that they are implicitly required to stay on people's good side and please those in positions of authority (Approval and Dependence norms). Other important features to consider include team-based systems, which tend to promote Humanistic-Encouraging and Affiliative norms (Constructive). In contrast, appraisal systems that focus exclusively on individual performance can inadvertently promote Competitive norms (Aggressive/Defensive). The Aggressive impact can be even greater when appraisal systems require managers to evaluate employee performance along a normal distribution, so that the number of employees ranked as poor is equal to the number ranked as excellent.

Goal Setting Systems

Constructive ideal cultures should translate into goals for the organization and its members that are clear and comprehensive, challenging yet realistic, and developed with the participation of those responsible for their attainment. Goals and goal setting systems of this type would also be consistent with

- the writings of Edwin Locke and Gary Latham, which prescribe goals that are clear and challenging and not unnecessarily complex[109];
- the extension of their work by George Doran delineating SMART goals;[110] and
- Andrew Grove's prescriptions for establishing objectives and key results (OKRs) in high-technology organizations.[111]

However, our research suggests that, despite organizations' Constructive ideals and values, the goals toward which individual members work may not be particularly well designed. When this is a reality, it negatively impacts motivation and performance directly as well as indirectly via the Defensive norms that emerge. Per Table 2.1, leaders who make sure that members participate in goal setting promote Constructive norms and attenuate Defensive norms. In addition, goals that are clear, appropriately challenging, and accepted by those responsible for achieving them send signals for Achievement-oriented behaviors and further boost motivation. Goals that are too difficult and unrealistic lead to Aggressive/Defensive cultural norms and, more specifically, promote Perfectionistic and Oppositional behaviors. In contrast, setting goals that are too easy or not setting them at all tends to be associated with Passive/Defensive cultures.

Selection and Placement Systems

The quality of selection and placement systems (in terms of effectively matching people to roles) tends to be better in organizations with strong Constructive cultures than in those with relatively weak Constructive cultures. In contrast, Defensive norms emerge when members, on a regular basis, find themselves and/or others placed in positions or roles for which they are not suited.

In addition to considering experience, skills, and performance, several of the leaders we interviewed emphasized that hiring, promoting, and retaining people with skills and qualities that exemplify the organization's ideal culture and values are important for creating more Constructive norms. As we'll discuss in chapter 6, this is different than hiring people who fit in with the current operating culture—particularly when the current culture is more Defensive than Constructive. As with the other systems and levers for change, Defensive cultures tend to emerge when the organization's ideal culture and values are overlooked in the design and implementation of selection and placement systems.

Training and Development Systems

Opportunities for training and development also tend to be better in organizations with strong Constructive cultures. In contrast, Passive/Defensive and Aggressive/Defensive norms are stronger in organizations in which training and development opportunities are minimal or unfairly distributed.

More generally, training and development programs have been critiqued for failing to have a significant business impact.[112] Reviewers note that such programs are often designed without the involvement (and the follow-up support) of participants' superiors; that they lack any connection to the work that people are doing; that they have little or no continuity; that they lack accountability; and that they are not tied to any kind of meaningful results (beyond employee evaluations of the program). These shortcomings make it unlikely that such programs will contribute to members' growth and development. Similarly, they are unlikely to communicate that members are expected to invest in self-development or the development of the people around them (Self-Actualizing and Humanistic-Encouraging norms, respectively). As mentioned earlier, culture and changes in culture are rarely the product of a single force; rather, a combination of forces (e.g., not only the availability of employee development but also its quality, impact, and fairness) together leads to Constructive norms.

One of the earliest and most noteworthy examples of successful training and development programs is the one spearheaded by Dr. Linda Sharkey, who at the time was manager of global executive development at GE Capital. Offered during CEO Jack Welch's tenure, the program was globally recognized and detailed in various books, articles, and webinars, including *Best Practices in Leadership Development and Organizational Change* by Louis Carter, David Ulrich, and Marshall Goldsmith.[113] Specifically, when GE was experiencing rapid global expansion during the 1990s, maintaining its values and culture—which were viewed as a competitive advantage—became increasingly important, particularly with the influx of emerging leaders. Early on, Linda and her team engaged the business's leaders in both the design *and* delivery of the training and development program. The program emphasized the connections between individual, team, and organization; focused on the future; and addressed the challenges likely to be faced moving forward.

Participants learned about the behaviors associated with their peak performance (using an appreciative inquiry approach) and about their psychological preferences and personality type based on the Meyer-Briggs Type Indicator® (MBTI®). In addition, they received feedback on their leadership strategies and their ideal and current impact on others based on *Leadership/Impact* and the Circumplex. Regardless of whether the emerging leaders were in the US, Europe, or Asia, the impact they described as ideal tended to be strongly Constructive.

Coaching, case studies, and "fireside chats" with the business's leaders (who shared their personal defining moments and lessons learned) were also built into the initial sessions. Internal coaches used an adaptation of Marshall Goldsmith's behavioral coaching model, which they also taught to program participants. After the initial training sessions, there was considerable follow-up, which included progress check-ins, coaching, special forums on leadership issues, and remeasurement. Participants' *Leadership/Impact* results were analyzed along with measures of both personal success (in terms of raises and promotions) and leadership effectiveness (in terms of performance). The results demonstrated that the most successful and effective leaders in their organization had a strong Constructive impact on others. In contrast, those who were least successful and effective had a strongly Defensive impact on the behavior of those around them. Follow-up measures showed that 95 percent of participants improved in their jobs—and sustained their improvement over time.

Turning to more recent cases, we see various aspects of human resource systems being used as levers for change. For instance, the leaders at Port of San Diego incorporated culture into their training and development programs as well as their performance appraisal systems (see chapter 3). At Agroenzymas (chapter 6), leaders changed the criteria for selection and placement as well as promotion decisions, which traditionally had been based on past performance and tenure, with little regard for behavior and attitude. At Dreher Brewery (chapter 8), a comprehensive and ongoing training and development program for middle managers was created. This was complemented by executive development, changes to the criteria for promotions and rewards, and changes to goals—all of which were modified to be supportive of the Constructive norms they wanted to strengthen. At Pons Bakery (chapter 7), the use of criticism and punishment for mistakes and errors was scaled back to provide a more supportive environment for people to learn to take on new responsibilities. Pons also implemented an individual-level goal setting system that was tied to the goals of the organization. SaskCentral (chapter 10) adjusted selection and promotion criteria, performance evaluations, reward systems, and training and development programs to emphasize culture and reinforce the Constructive behaviors the organization espoused. And, at the Chicago Diocese (chapter 11), a human resource management system (which previously did not exist) was put in place to strengthen Achievement-oriented norms. As these cases show, such changes would have had little influence had they not been supported by other forces, including improvements in the skills and qualities of leaders and managers.

Technology and Cultural Norms

The methods by which organizational inputs are transformed into outputs also shape behavioral norms and expectations. The impact of technology on behavioral norms was first demonstrated by Eric Trist and Kenneth Bamforth's classic study of coal miners.[114] Their research showed that the consequences of a change in technology (in this case from the hand-got method of mining coal to the long-wall method) on performance were due to the effects of the new technology on the behavior of those who had to use it. With the hand-got method, the coal miners had worked in autonomous groups that were each responsible for an identifiable piece of work. However, the more sophisticated tools required by the long-wall method simplified the jobs of the workers and, in doing so, made working in groups and making decisions less necessary. The coal miners experienced a reduction in their autonomy, in the variety of skills they used, and in their interdependence. The perceived meaningfulness of their jobs decreased, as they were neither producing an identifiable product nor having a significant impact on the work or lives of others. Under the old method, employees communicated and coordinated with one another and readily took the initiative to collaborate and solve problems. Under the new method, they stopped communicating and coordinating with each other and felt less responsibility for their work and the achievement of goals. In the language of the Circumplex, the culture went from Achievement and Affiliative to Oppositional and Avoidance. Absenteeism increased, and productivity plummeted.

Some of the key lessons from this and related studies on the social and psychological implications of technology provided the foundation for Professors Richard Hackman and Gregg Oldham's "Job Enrichment" approach to job design.[115] Their research and writings identified five "core job characteristics" that lead to three critical psychological states: meaningfulness of work, responsibility for outcomes, and knowledge of results. In turn, relatively high levels of these states lead to higher performance, motivation, and satisfaction (which, today, some people refer to as *employee engagement*). The five core job characteristics identified by Hackman and Oldham are

- *autonomy*, the extent to which members have the discretion to make decisions about how they carry out their work;
- *skill variety*, the extent to which members' jobs require that they use a number of different skills and competencies;
- *task identity*, the extent to which members carry out, from beginning to end, a complete and identifiable service or "product";
- *job significance*, the extent to which members view their work as having a significant impact on other people; and
- *feedback from job*, the extent to which members can discern for themselves how well they are carrying out their work.

In several early consulting projects using the *Organizational Culture Inventory*, we noticed the influence of job design on behavioral norms. For example, we unexpectedly observed a Constructive culture profile for the custodians who worked in a children's hospital that more generally was characterized by relatively weak Constructive norms. Upon further investigation, we learned that the manager of the custodians had created a more Constructive culture within his area, not only by his supervisory style but also by enriching the jobs of the custodians. Rather than continuing to assign them to different areas of the hospital each day (which was the way it had traditionally been done), the manager redesigned their jobs so that there was continuity in terms of the rooms and patients for which they were responsible. This allowed the custodians to regularly interact with beneficiaries of their work and see for themselves the impact of the quality of the work on others. Their perceptions about the significance of their jobs increased, which led to greater perceived meaningfulness of their roles. In addition, their beliefs about the extent to which they should do even simple things well (Self-Actualizing), emphasize quality (Achievement), communicate openly with others (Affiliative), and demonstrate concern for others' needs (Humanistic-Encouraging) also were positively affected.

Our subsequent quantitative research confirmed that the five core job characteristics, in addition to leading to the psychological states proposed by Hackman and Oldham, shape the shared behavioral norms and expectations that develop, particularly when members of a unit are carrying out the same or similar jobs. Specifically, our studies have consistently shown that high levels of autonomy, skill variety, task identity, task significance, and feedback are all positively associated with Constructive cultural norms (see Table 2.1). In contrast, jobs that lack autonomy, skill variety, job significance, and feedback are associated with stronger norms and expectations for both Passive/Defensive and Aggressive/Defensive behaviors. In addition, our research indicates that the degree of interdependence among members is also important. Jobs with high interdependence among members tend to be associated with stronger norms for Constructive behaviors, whereas jobs with low interdependence tend to be associated with more Passive/Defensive and Aggressive/Defensive norms.

Job design was one of the keys levers for change used in the GM Powertrain case, with redesign efforts focusing on job rotation, increased interdependence, and greater autonomy. In terms of the cases featured in this book, job significance was among the forces addressed by Sanitarium leaders to move culture in a more Constructive direction (see chapter 9). Similarly, job significance as well as interdependence were among the factors addressed by the leaders at the Chicago Diocese to reduce norms for Avoidance and encourage a greater Achievement and Affiliative orientation (chapter 11). And, at Dreher Brewery, job rotation among managers was one of the levers used to help break down silos and move norms in a more collaborative direction (chapter 8).

Leadership Skills/Qualities and Cultural Norms

The skills and qualities of members at all levels influence culture. However, for the purposes of this book, we highlight the skills and qualities of leaders. Up to now we have been focusing on how leaders *indirectly* affect culture via their decisions regarding mission and philosophy, strategies and goals, structures, human resource management systems, and technology in terms of job design. In this section we'll focus on some of the most important ways in which leaders *directly* influence people and culture, including

- personal thinking and behavioral styles,
- leadership styles,
- bases or sources of power and influence,
- communication skills and qualities, and
- leadership strategies and management approaches.

We will also discuss some of the ways that skilled consultants help leaders develop their personal thinking and behavioral styles.

Personal Thinking and Behavioral Styles

The connection between culture and personal thinking and behavioral styles measured by the *Life Styles Inventory* (LSI) was first demonstrated by a 1986 study sponsored by the Coca-Cola Retailing Research Council on approximately five hundred store- and department-level managers from fifteen different chains in the grocery and supermarket industry.[116] Data on the managers' personal styles and the cultural norms within their departments or stores were collected using the *Life Styles Inventory* and the *Organizational Culture Inventory*, respectively. Employee and manager interviews about personal styles and culture were also conducted. Additionally, corporate leaders provided evaluations of managers' performance.

The store managers who were evaluated as highly effective had significantly stronger Constructive personal styles than their less effective counterparts, especially in terms of Humanistic-Encouraging and Affiliative styles. They tended to be good listeners, to keep people informed, to include others in planning and problem solving, and to give their employees leeway to try out better ways of doing things. They also maintained high standards for themselves, their staff, and their stores, and they treated failures and mistakes as opportunities for learning rather than excuses for punishment. In turn, the cultures they created in their departments or stores were also Constructive, as confirmed by the *Organizational Culture Inventory*. Employees indicated that they were expected to think for themselves, to research and experiment with new ideas, to be helpful and friendly with coworkers as well as customers, and to accomplish their goals. They also reported a lack of tolerance for slacking off or shirking responsibilities.

In contrast, the least effective managers were more Aggressive/Defensive (particularly in terms of Competitive, Power, and Oppositional personal styles) than their more effective counterparts and, on the Passive/Defensive side, were also more Avoidance-oriented. They focused on trying to control the people around them. They dominated conversations. They excluded others when solving problems and making decisions. They opposed suggestions and new ideas. And they tended to avoid situations that involved any risk of failure. The cultures that they created in their departments and stores were particularly strong with respect to Oppositional and Avoidance norms.

The causal relationship between the styles of leaders and the cultures of their organizations has since been observed in many case studies and via subsequent data-based analyses.[117] Across organizations, the typical patterns observed are:

- Constructive leadership styles promote Constructive cultural norms;
- Passive/Defensive leadership styles promote Passive/Defensive cultural norms; and
- Aggressive/Defensive leadership styles promote Aggressive/Defensive and Passive/Defensive cultural norms.

Moreover, the results of our early research and the ongoing observations of numerous researchers and consultants, including Ricardo (Richi) Gil of Axialent, confirm that the relationship is reciprocal. Thus, when the culture is Defensive, it reinforces Defensive thinking and behavioral styles on the part of leaders. Defensive norms and ingrained but untested beliefs—such as "if you lose your red (Aggressive/Defensive styles) you're going to lose your drive"—can make it difficult to get leaders to buy into individual development initiatives.

Similarly, Francisco (Fran) Cherny, Managing Director of Axialent, notes that in many organizations people view the Aggressive styles as "getting things done," the Passive styles as "procrastinating and delaying things," and the Constructive styles as "an uncertain combination of softness and being kind."[118] He points out that without feedback and coaching, it can take a long time for leaders who work in organizations with Defensive cultures "to understand that curiosity, openness, and learning—which are characteristic of the blue styles—are what really make things happen." Richi adds,

This is a story that we help leaders deconstruct. One way we do this is by role playing and demonstrating how one can be even more assertive and express more of their core truth with a blue style. When I act out the blue style with them in a role play, they say, "Oh my God!" I ask them whether they felt I was being disrespectful to them and they say, "Well no, you weren't." And then I ask whether they thought I was being honest, and the response is, "Oh, you were being incredibly honest."

The *Ideal* version of the *Organizational Culture Inventory* can be used along with role playing to legitimize and gain acceptance for the Constructive styles. Richi notes that after administering the *Ideal* inventory and presenting the results to an executive team, you "can hear a pin drop." Relative to their own *Life Styles Inventory* results, the significantly longer Constructive extensions (and shorter Defensive extensions) on the ideal culture profile are difficult to ignore. "This does not by itself create the change in habits prescribed," Richi says, "but it does give us the permission, the humility, the ritual space for us to teach them something—about the way they interact, the way they think, the way they feel, and then how they take action."

Based on Axialent's use of our Circumplex-based inventories with thousands of people throughout the world, Fran and Richi shared with us numerous other ideas for promoting understanding and acceptance of the styles and initiating individual and organizational change from Defensive to Constructive. For instance, to create interest in the styles, Axialent consultants focus on the outcomes important to the client and the culture styles that most likely support or detract from the attainment of those outcomes. So, for example, Fran notes that, "Today, innovation and agility are among the main things that everyone wants. Most people can very easily connect with how styles such as Perfectionistic or Dependent can interfere with agility and entrepreneurship given what is currently happening in their organization." In addition to identifying styles that get in the way of the client's objectives, they also accentuate one or two of the Constructive styles that most plausibly support what the client wants to achieve.

They also relate the blue, green, and red styles to activities or processes that currently are viewed as suboptimal or problematic. For example, Fran described an organization in which communication became critical largely because no one was sharing what they really believed.

He explains, "Initially we assess whether the issue is being too brutal or too respectful. If the issue is more on the side of brutal, usually the red styles are expanded on the Circumplex. If the issue is being too respectful, the underlying problem is on the green side." When consultants use the Circumplex to illustrate why specific factors—such as communication—are an issue, it's easier for leaders to see how the styles can be used as a model for change.

Axialent consultants also place importance on the leader's mindset and how it affects the way in which the styles are interpreted. Richi explains,

> For example, when an individual is looking at the Circumplex from a self-altering mindset, the Achievement style could mean delivering on one's work, getting things done, and the like. When you're with someone who is looking at this through a self-transcendent kind of mindset, which recognizes interdependencies within and between systems, the Achievement style can mean developing the capacity to execute, building the capabilities of self and others, and focusing on system responses and implications.

The *Life Styles Inventory* profile can also provide hints as to leaders' mindsets. For instance, those with strongly Constructive profiles may tend toward self-transcendence while those with primarily Aggressive/Defensive profiles may tend toward self-altering. More generally, as Fran points out, it's important for consultants to consider the shape of the leader's profile when debriefing his or her *Life Styles Inventory* results.

In addition to connecting the styles to priorities, issues, and mindsets, Fran suggests accentuating the connections between the personal styles of leaders, the cultural norms of their immediate group, and the norms of the larger organization:

> Ideally, if we're working with a leadership team at a global level (or a regional or even country level), we usually do the culture inventory at the organizational level and at the leadership group level, and then the *Life Styles Inventory* with all of the leaders. That's the ideal situation to create engagement in this process. By doing it this way, leaders can see the connection between the three layers—how they are influencing the group and how the group and they individually are influencing the culture.

This multilevel measurement approach reduces the likelihood that leaders will either acknowledge or claim that they don't like the culture—and then attribute its negative characteristics to others.

Finally, regarding the pace of change, Fran notes,

> We are coming from a world in which we used to tell clients that this will take three to five years—and today clients are saying, "Thank you very much, but we need to do this in three months." Thus, we discuss how our offerings can connect with that, for instance, by doing one-hundred-day sprints where we really go deep into their processes and the way they work and provide more consulting than training.[119]

Given the various ways in which leaders impact culture, it makes sense to start working on change with the leadership team before working with the rest of the organization. That said, change can also be initiated by starting with a specific functional area, intervening with a specific process, or beginning with a training program to introduce members to the concepts and create a common language. Regardless of where change begins, the pace of implementation is quicker when leaders are committed to supporting it both indirectly through their decisions and directly through their thoughts, behaviors, and actions.

Leadership Styles

We've also looked at the relationship between the cultural norms measured by the *Organizational Culture Inventory* and David Bowers and Stanley Seashore's Four-Factor Theory of Leadership.[120] In a groundbreaking study of forty agencies in the insurance industry, Bowers and Seashore identified four leadership styles and then demonstrated the relationship between these styles and employee satisfaction and performance. Our cross-sectional research and case studies suggest that at least part of the reason leadership styles have an impact on effectiveness is that they directly affect the behavioral norms and expectations of an organization.

As indicated near the bottom of Table 2.1, our research shows that leadership styles that emphasize interaction and open communication among employees (labeled *interaction facilitation* by Bowers and Seashore) and the achievement of goals (*goal emphasis*) are positively associated with Constructive norms and negatively associated with

Passive/Defensive norms. In addition, leaders who demonstrate a concern for employees (*supportiveness*) and help them to identify ways to solve problems and complete their assignments (*task facilitation*) are also more likely to promote expectations for Constructive behaviors than are leaders who do not demonstrate these styles. Leaders who exhibit all four of these styles demonstrate a positive concern for both people and tasks. This trait is apparently not lost on the people around them, who gain an appreciation for the importance and appropriateness of maintaining this balance—an inherent feature of a Constructive orientation.

A cross-sectional study carried out by Rob with Andrew Klein and Joseph Wallis confirms, as noted at the beginning of this subsection, that these leadership styles promote organizational effectiveness via their effect on culture.[121] Similarly, in this book, there are various examples that illustrate these relationships. For instance, to reduce Competitive, Power, and Dependent norms as well as foster expectations for more collaborative behavior, the founder of Agroenzymas (chapter 6) began delegating decisions to teams made up of people who held diverse views instead of taking over the problem and resolving it for them—an example of interaction facilitation. At Dreher (chapter 8), middle managers started meeting with employees one-on-one to talk about the issues that the employees wanted to discuss and to support them in identifying solutions—an example of supportiveness and task facilitation. This facilitation was in turn one of the levers used to create a more collaborative and Achievement-oriented environment. And at Sanitarium (chapter 9), quarterly lunch clubs that focused on both accomplishing goals and setting new quarterly goals—an example of goal emphasis— helped leaders strengthen expectations for Achievement behaviors and reduce the pervasiveness of Passive/Defensive norms.

Bases of Power and Influence

The bases or sources of power used by leaders to influence people (as identified by John French and Bertram Raven[122]) represent another dimension of leadership that is directly related to culture. For instance, reliance on *organizational* bases or sources of power and influence—such as the power inherent in one's position, control of rewards, and ability to punish or coerce others—tends to promote Passive/Defensive and Aggressive/Defensive norms and expectations. Conversely, reliance on *personal* bases of power—such as expertise and the respect or admiration of others (referent power)—tends to be positively associated with Constructive norms and negatively associated with Passive/Defensive and Aggressive/Defensive norms.

Strong reliance on organizational bases of power was one of the factors that sustained Defensive thinking styles and norms at the GM plant before their culture change journey began. One of the levers for change was division offsites, meetings at which attendees were not allowed to wear their usual attire or company uniforms (which signified positions) and were asked not to reveal their positions to other attendees. With over four thousand people working at the Toledo plant and many more working in the overall division, attendees found themselves in a situation in which they didn't know who was a manager, a supervisor, an hourly worker, or a union representative. One of the things they discovered was that they had a lot more in common than they had assumed, which was a step in helping everyone who attended to develop and rely on more personal sources of power and influence.

As you'll see in chapter 6, bases of power and influence were also a key part of Agroenzymas' culture change journey. Their story shows that as leaders build and use personal bases of power, share and exchange influence, and decrease their reliance on organizational sources, their influence as well as the influence of others (including that of their employees and colleagues) also increases.[123]

Communication Skills and Qualities

Although communication channels and networks are structural, we are talking about communication specifically in relation to leadership because the skills and qualities of members—particularly leaders—determine how well such channels and networks are used. As indicated in Table 2.1, the quality of upward and downward communication, as well as communication for learning,[124] is positively related to Constructive cultures and negatively related to Defensive cultures. Specifically, Constructive norms and expectations are supported by communication that is multidirectional, clear, open, timely, forthcoming, credible, focused on the "big picture," understood, accepted, and acted upon. In contrast, expectations for both Passive/Defensive and Aggressive/Defensive behaviors are reinforced by communication that is unclear, restricted, delayed, censored, distorted, focused on minutia and blame, misunderstood, questioned, and ignored. Thus, the nature of both sending and receiving is important when assessing communication and using it as a lever for change.

Early studies examining the relationship between the cultural norms discussed here and communication include those that focus on nuclear power plants and hospitals, where effective communication is critical to safety and reliability. For instance, a study of nuclear facilities by researchers at Brookhaven National Laboratory demonstrated a positive relationship between Constructive norms and communication in terms of trust, accuracy, interaction, and overall satisfaction with the communication process. Although Perfectionistic norms were also characteristic of the nuclear facilities studied, Constructive norms were critical. As the researchers point out, "It appears that a safety culture is one in which management expectations promote behaviors which strive for perfection, with an orientation of attention to safety, *but not at the expense of the satisfaction of members of the organization*" [emphasis added].[125] Similarly, a study by Beverly Haley showed that nurses in medical-surgical units with relatively strong Constructive cultural norms more readily reported errors than those in other units. In units with Defensive cultures, mistakes were more likely to be covered up and therefore went unreported—making it appear that such units were more effective than they actually were.[126] Comparable findings were reported by Amy Edmondson, who, in her qualitative study of psychological safety in hospital patient-care units (intensive care units and general care units), noted that in some units, reporting drug errors was seen as necessary, whereas in other units avoiding blame was viewed as more important.[127]

Communication seems to work both ways in that cultural norms can support or inhibit effective communication, and communication can support or inhibit Constructive cultural norms. For example, a recent study of five different nuclear power plants showed that Constructive norms are positively related to communication satisfaction and, in turn a "safety conscious work environment" that includes, for example, the freedom to raise concerns without fear of retribution and with the likelihood of being heard. The authors conclude that Constructive cultures should be supported and encouraged by communication channels that keep employees informed of the "big picture," practices that maintain effective two-way communication, and reward systems that reinforce the actions of employees who raise concerns.[128] Similarly, another recent study on nuclear power plants concluded that, of the twelve styles measured by the *Organizational Culture Inventory*, "the constructive styles are those that have the greatest influence on the safety culture results." The authors also recommended that steps be taken to improve and strengthen these behaviors, including those around communication.[129]

Several of the organizations featured in this book used communication as a lever for change. For instance, at Spreadshirt (chapter 4), having a shared language (provided by the Circumplex) to redirect conversations and behavior was invaluable in improving the quality of interactions, as well as in reducing the frequency of Power and Perfectionistic behaviors. Similarly, Sanitarium's leaders described how having a shared language allowed people to be more transparent and communicate about what they were doing and why, which also helped to generate greater support from others. This shift occurred in situations in which critical business problems were being discussed, decisions had to be made, and people were trying to approach the issues in a more Constructive way than they had in the past (see chapter 9). Communication was also a critical part of the Episcopal Church's culture change process at both the diocese level and at the national level (see chapter 11). As illustrated by these and the other cases in this book, when leaders leverage vertical and lateral communication channels and networks, their effort has a significant impact on behavioral norms.

Leadership Strategies and Management Approaches

The *strategies* used to carry out leadership responsibilities are also directly and causally related to culture. Two general types of leadership strategies identified by our research are:
- *Prescriptive strategies*, which "guide or direct the activities and behaviors of others toward opportunities, goals, and methods," and
- *Restrictive strategies*, which "constrain or prohibit activities and behaviors with respect to goals, opportunities, or methods."[130]

Almost any leadership role or responsibility can be carried out in either Prescriptive or Restrictive ways that, in turn, affect other people's behavior and the organization's culture very differently. To illustrate, Table 2.2 describes what it looks like to carry out various important leadership responsibilities in a Prescriptive versus Restrictive manner.

Table 2.2. Examples of Prescriptive and Restrictive Leadership Strategies

	Prescriptive leadership provides people with:	**Restrictive leadership** provides people with:
	Directions for channeling their efforts	Directions that should not be pursued
	Models regarding how things should be done	Models regarding behaviors they should avoid
	Positive reinforcement to encourage the repetition of desired behaviors	Negative feedback to discourage the repetition of undesired behaviors
	A set of parameters specifying their sphere of influence	A set of parameters limiting their sphere of influence
	Prescriptive Strategies *facilitate* activities and *promote* behaviors by:	**Restrictive Strategies** *constrain* activities and *prohibit* behaviors by:
Envisioning	Communicating goals and directions to be pursued	Communicating goals and directions to be avoided
Role Modeling	Personally exemplifying preferred behaviors	Actively avoiding objectionable behaviors
Mentoring	Helping others to learn by sharing personal experiences and knowledge	Expecting others to learn from their own experiences and mistakes
Stimulating Thinking	Challenging others to break through boundaries, question assumptions, and identify new approaches	Confining others to work within boundaries, accept assumptions, and look for "proven" approaches
Referring	Talking about the successes and competencies of other people	Talking about the mistakes and failures of other people
Monitoring	Actively looking for things that people are doing well	Actively looking for things that people are doing poorly or incorrectly
Providing Feedback	Letting people know when they are doing things well	Letting people know when they are performing below standards
Reinforcing	Rewarding accomplishments and excellent performance	Punishing mistakes and poor performance
Influencing	Using reciprocal and participative tactics that increase the influence of others	Using unilateral and controlling tactics that reduce the influence of others
Creating a Setting	Structuring the work environment to promote people's growth, development, and experiences	Structuring the work environment to limit people's growth, development, and experiences

Adapted from *Leadership/Impact Confidential Feedback Report*.
Copyright © by Human Synergistics International. All Rights Reserved.

Restrictive strategies, which emphasize minimizing undesired behaviors and avoiding unwanted outcomes, may be easier and are faster to use. However, leaders who rely on these strategies cause the people around them to behave in more Passive/Defensive and Aggressive/Defensive ways. On the other hand, Prescriptive strategies—such as specifying the desired outcomes to be achieved, noticing and acknowledging what people are doing well, and considering their ideas and suggestions—generally are more functional and lead to a Constructive impact.[131]

Table 2.3 highlights the most important leadership strategies to consider to increase your Constructive impact or decrease your Defensive impact along each of the styles, based on our research on thousands of leaders who have completed our *Leadership/Impact*. This 360-degree assessment provides leaders with feedback on their relative use of Prescriptive and Restrictive strategies and their personal impact on the behavior of other people in terms of the twelve Circumplex styles. The data suggest that if, for example, you want to increase Achievement-oriented behaviors within your organization or unit, you should begin by considering the extent to which you currently carry out Envisioning and Creating a Setting in Prescriptive versus Restrictive ways. If you are already performing these activities in Prescriptive ways, then focus instead on a leadership responsibility in which you are not as strong or one that you tend to carry out Restrictively.

The efficacy of developing more Prescriptive strategies with respect to improving one's impact, performance, and success has been demonstrated by a series of in-depth case studies of CEOs coached by Dr. Peter Fuda.[132] Feedback and coaching at the executive level were a vital part of the change process for many of the organizations featured in the upcoming chapters of this book, including Spreadshirt (chapter 4), Straumann (chapter 5), Dreher Brewery (chapter 8), Sanitarium (chapter 9), SaskCentral (chapter 10), and the Episcopal Church (chapter 11). For instance, the leaders at Spreadshirt focused on Prescriptively defining their vision of what the company could achieve as well as understanding the ideas of other people (exemplifying Prescriptive Envisioning and Influencing). They found, as a result, their impact on each other and their employees became more Constructive and less Passive/Defensive and Aggressive/Defensive.

Table 2.3. Leadership Activities to Target for Change

Increasing Your Constructive Impact

ACHIEVEMENT
Envisioning: Move toward Defining
Creating a Setting: Move away from Constraining and toward Facilitating

SELF-ACTUALIZING
Stimulating Thinking: Move away from Vertical and toward Lateral
Creating a Setting: Move away from Constraining and toward Facilitating

HUMANISTIC-ENCOURAGING
Influencing: Move away from Unilateral and toward Reciprocal
Mentoring: Move away from Passive and toward Active

AFFILIATIVE
Influencing: Move away from Unilateral and toward Reciprocal
Creating a Setting: Move away from Constraining and toward Facilitating

Decreasing Your Passive/Defensive Impact

APPROVAL
Stimulating Thinking: Move away from Vertical and toward Lateral
Role Modeling: Move away from Circumscribing and toward Exemplifying

CONVENTIONAL
Creating a Setting: Move away from Constraining and toward Facilitating
Stimulating Thinking: Move away from Vertical and toward Lateral

DEPENDENT
Influencing: Move away from Unilateral and toward Reciprocal
Monitoring: Move away from Managing by Exception and toward Excellence

AVOIDANCE
Monitoring: Move away from Managing by Exception and toward Excellence
Role Modeling: Move toward Exemplifying

Decreasing Your Aggressive/Defensive Impact

OPPOSITIONAL
Influencing: Move away from Unilateral and toward Reciprocal
Providing Feedback: Move away from Negative and toward Positive

POWER
Influencing: Move away from Unilateral and toward Reciprocal
Referring: Move away from Negative and toward Positive Referents

COMPETITIVE
Monitoring: Move away from Managing by Exception and toward Excellence
Mentoring: Move away from Passive and toward Active

PERFECTIONISTIC
Influencing: Move away from Unilateral and toward Reciprocal
Reinforcing: Move away from Punishing and toward Reward

From *Leadership/Impact Confidential Feedback Report.*
Copyright © by Human Synergistics International. All Rights Reserved.

Similarly, the leaders at Sanitarium started focusing more on how goals could be achieved and considering how ideas could work instead of readily dismissing potential solutions because of possible flaws. This reflects a combination of Stimulating Thinking and Influencing in more Prescriptive and less Restrictive ways. In turn, the changes they made increased their Constructive impact on culture—particularly with respect to the Achievement style—as well as decreased their Passive/Defensive and Aggressive/Defensive impact—including with respect to Conventional, Oppositional, and Perfectionistic styles.

At Dreher Brewery, *Leadership/Impact* was used with both top and middle managers. The changes they made to the ways in which they approached their responsibilities again helped to shift the culture in a more Constructive direction. In addition, this case demonstrates that efforts by middle managers to carry out their responsibilities in a more Prescriptive way can be a powerful force when complemented and supported by similar efforts by senior leaders.

The ways in which leaders and managers approach management activities and responsibilities can also move culture in a productive or counterproductive direction. Leadership activities involve setting an overall agenda for the organization in terms of the vision and strategies and inspiring others to achieve them. In contrast, management activities are more operational and include implementing strategies and turning visions into accomplishments by organizing, motivating, and guiding the efforts of others.[133] Through our research, we've identified two general approaches to management activities that evoke very different reactions and behaviors on the part of those working for or with a particular manager. This research is based on data collected through the use of *Management/Impact*, an assessment that provides managers with feedback on the approaches they use to carry out management responsibilities as well as feedback on their impact on the behavior of others in terms of the Circumplex. Specifically, managers who rely on *Facilitating approaches* carry out their responsibilities in ways that maximize the development of the people around them, expand their autonomy, and help to coordinate their work with that of others. This mode, in turn, is associated with a Constructive impact. In contrast, *Inhibiting approaches* are in play when managers carry out their responsibilities in ways that maximize their control over others and their work. Our research shows that a heavy reliance on Inhibiting approaches has a strong Defensive impact on the behavior of members and the culture of an organization.[134]

Table 2.4 offers examples of how fifteen different management responsibilities can be approached in Facilitating versus Inhibiting ways. Table 2.5 identifies the most important management approaches to consider to strengthen a Constrictive impact or to decrease a Defensive impact, based on data from thousands of managers who have experienced *Management/Impact*. The table also identifies the managerial responsibilities most strongly related to each of the twelve specific styles. For example, if you are most interested in increasing your Constructive impact with a specific focus on Achievement, you might start by examining the ways in which you manage rewards and learning, since these are the managerial domains most strongly related to a Constructive impact. In addition, you might consider how you manage goals and change, since these are also very strongly and specifically related to an Achievement impact.

On Human Synergistics' *Constructive Culture* blog, co-owner and vice-president of Ephektiv consultancy, Kevin Smith, provides a case example on how coaching and feedback based on *Management/Impact* can help managers implement strategies and achieve better results. He explains how one group of supervisors within a client organization significantly strengthened their Constructive impact on crew members. Simultaneously, they also reduced the tendency to promote Defensive reactions such as Dependent and Avoidance by changing the ways in which they managed goals, learning, and communication, all based on their *Management/Impact* feedback. The result was considerable improvements along a variety of outcomes, including role and goal clarity; time management; the quality of relationships and the level of trust between supervisors and front-line workers; and safety performance (a key strategic objective).[135]

The story of Pons Bakery in chapter 7 also illustrates how feedback and coaching on management approaches enabled the general manager to change the way he approached managing goals, rewards, and learning in less Inhibiting and more Facilitating ways. These changes resulted in a significant shift in his impact on people and culture and, in turn, on the growth and expansion of the business.

Table 2.4. Examples of Facilitating and Inhibiting Management Approaches

	Facilitating Approaches	Inhibiting Approaches
	Driven by *mutual* interests	Driven by *self-interests*
	Process *and* outcome focused	Process *or* outcome focused
	Oriented toward *long-term* effectiveness	Oriented toward *short-term* success
	Constructive in nature and impact	*Defensive* in nature and impact
	Empowering and supportive	*Hindering* and restrictive
	Yield *consistently* good results	Yield *inconsistent* or *poor* results
	Facilitating Approaches maximize the *autonomy of other people* and the *coordination of their efforts* by:	**Inhibiting Approaches** maximize the *manager's own control* over other people and their activities by:
Goals	Setting goals viewed by others as meaningful, relevant, and realistic	Setting goals that are meaningful, relevant, and realistic only to him/her
Change	Acting on new ideas and opportunities for changes and improvements	Resisting new ideas and opportunities for changes and improvements
Problem Solving	Focusing on causes of problems	Focusing on symptoms of problems
Results	Monitoring the quality and effectiveness of both processes and performance	Monitoring the quantity of what is accomplished
Resources	Effectively acquiring and allocating resources	Ineffectively acquiring and allocating resources
Work Activities	Delegating assignments that fully utilize people's talents, skills, and decision-making capabilities	Dictating assignments and how they should be carried out without regard to people's current interests or workload
Inter-unit Relations	Coordinating and cooperating with other units and their managers	Ignoring, criticizing, and competing with other managers and their units
Teams	Providing opportunities for people to meet and work together as a team	Focusing on individuals without regard for the team as a whole
Communication	Listening to what others have to say	Listening to only what he/she wants to hear
Rewards	Readily recognizing people's efforts and good performance	Overlooking effort or withholding recognition for good performance
Learning	Providing suggestions and guidance to help people learn	Presuming people will learn on their own
Personal Relations	Treating people with sensitivity and respect	Treating people with indifference and lack of regard
Integrity	Maintaining consistency in what he/she does and says	Being inconsistent in what he/she does and says
Self-Development	Taking advantage of opportunities to learn and improve	Reacting defensively to opportunities to learn and improve
Emotions	Thinking before reacting	Reacting before thinking

Adapted from *Management/Impact Confidential Feedback Report*.
Copyright © by Human Synergistics International. All Rights Reserved.

Table 2.5. Management Activities to Target for Change

Increasing Your Constructive Impact

ALL CONSTRUCTIVE STYLES	Manage **Rewards** in a more Facilitating and less Inhibiting manner Manage **Learning** in a more Facilitating and less Inhibiting way
HUMANISTIC-ENCOURAGING	Manage **Inter-Unit Relations** in a more Facilitating manner Manage **Personal Relations** in a less Inhibiting way
AFFILIATIVE	Manage **Communications** in a more Facilitating manner Manage **Personal Relations** in a less Inhibiting way
ACHIEVEMENT	Manage **Goals** in a more Facilitating manner Manage **Change** in a less Inhibiting way
SELF-ACTUALIZING	Manage **Change** in a more Facilitating and less Inhibiting manner Manage **Goals** in a more Facilitating way

Decreasing Your Passive/Defensive Impact

ALL PASSIVE/DEFENSIVE STYLES	Manage **Integrity** in a more Facilitating and less Inhibiting manner Manage **Communications** in a more Facilitating and less Inhibiting way
APPROVAL	Manage **Teams** in a less Inhibiting way Manage **Emotions** in a more Facilitating manner
CONVENTIONAL	Manage **Change** in a less Inhibiting way Manage **Work Activities** in a more Facilitating manner
DEPENDENT	Manage **Work Activities** in a less Inhibiting way Manage **Personal Relations** in a more Facilitating and less Inhibiting way
AVOIDANCE	Manage **Change** in a less Inhibiting way Manage **Emotions** in a more Facilitating manner

Decreasing Your Aggressive/Defensive Impact

ALL AGGRESSIVE/DEFENSIVE STYLES	Manage **Personal Relations** in a more Facilitating and less Inhibiting way Manage **Communications** in a more Facilitating and less Inhibiting manner
OPPOSITIONAL	Manage **Inter-Unit Relations** in a less Inhibiting way Manage **Emotions** in a more Facilitating and less Inhibiting manner
POWER	Manage **Self-Development** in a less Inhibiting way Manage **Emotions** in a more Facilitating manner
COMPETITIVE	Manage **Results** in a less Inhibiting way Manage **Integrity** in a more Facilitating and less Inhibiting way
PERFECTIONISTIC	Manage **Results** in a less Inhibiting way Manage **Integrity** in a more Facilitating manner

Adapted from *Management/Impact Confidential Feedback Report*.
Copyright © Human Synergistics International. All Rights Reserved.

Ultimately, understanding how culture works and applying this understanding to how you lead and manage can profoundly reduce culture disconnects and move behavioral norms and outcomes in the desired direction. Indirect levers such as performance management systems, restructuring, and job redesign are certainly important; however, their impact is strongly reinforced by the extent to which leaders and managers carry out their roles in more Prescriptive, Facilitating, and Constructive ways. To further illustrate this dynamic, we'll turn now to the culture change experiences and insights shared by the leaders of nine different organizations around the world, starting in the United States with the Port of San Diego.

Part II

Examples from Different
Countries and Key Learnings

Chapter 3

Launching— and Relaunching— Constructive Cultural Change (USA)

> At the time, we didn't realize that the culture initiatives had been set up as separate from the day-to-day activities of the business.
>
> Randa Coniglio, CEO, San Diego Unified Port District

Organization	San Diego Unified Port District
Location	San Diego, California, United States
Industry	Public Sector
Founded	1962
Market Position	Fourth-largest port in the State of California
Number of Employees	500+
Started Culture Journey	Initiated in 2004; reignited in 2016
Interviewees	Randa Coniglio, CEO
	Tim DeNike, Director of People Strategies
	Scott Laing, People Strategies Business Partner

PORT of SAN DIEGO
Waterfront of Opportunity

Embarcadero, located on the east side of San Diego Bay

If you have ever had the pleasure of walking along the wetlands and tidelands of San Diego Bay, as we have, you will have likely glimpsed just a fraction of the enormous responsibilities shouldered by the Unified Port of San Diego. You may, for example, have attended some of the many arts and culture programs that take place or wandered through several of the Port's twenty-two lavish waterfront parks. You'll no doubt have noticed the cruise ships whose incoming and outgoing schedules the Port prepares, along with the vast amount of cargo—much of it for the world's leading motor companies, including Volkswagen, Audi, Mazda, Hyundai, Toyota, Jeep, Porsche, Bentley, Lamborghini, Isuzu, and Mitsubishi—headed into the Marine Terminal. Perhaps you witnessed the Harbor Police in action, a force that is cross-trained in marine firefighting, or met the patrol officers who enforce laws and ordinances from state to district levels.

What you were less likely to appreciate is the extent of the stewardship undertaken by the Port's five hundred–plus dedicated employees and leaders in innovatively and courageously supporting San Diego Bay's commerce, community, and environment. Nor did we, until we spoke with Randa Coniglio, the first female CEO in the Port's fifty-five-year history, who, along with the director and business partner of the Port's People Strategies team, Tim DeNike and Scott Laing, shared the organization's vision of a Twenty-First Century Port. It's a vision that is predicated on "doing the greatest good, by doing remarkably well."

The Port was one of the vanguards in recognizing the connection between leadership and culture back in the early 2000s. Currently at the helm of the organization and rekindling its attention to culture is Randa, the only woman CEO featured in this book. As in all the other stories that follow, the Port's journey illustrates the ups and downs of culture change. It also illustrates key learnings they've offered about what does and does not work with respect to changing and managing culture—the most important of which is that *indirect* levers for changing and managing culture (such as the design of systems and processes) are more effective when supported by *direct* levers (such as changes in leaders' strategies, approaches, and behavioral styles).

"The Good Old Days"

But first, let's go back to 2004, when organizational culture initially became a priority for the Port. This is when culture was the mission of Bruce Hollingsworth (who had just been promoted to CEO) and Randa Coniglio worked in the Real Estate Operations department. During Bruce's tenure, he realized there were opportunities for improvement throughout the organization that needed to be underpinned by real culture change. According to the *San Diego Union-Tribune*, Bruce "wanted to bring a change in culture, to usher in a spirit of cooperation, collaboration, openness and something he calls 'a servant's heart.'"[136]

As a special district of the State of California, the Port receives no tax dollars from city, state, or federal governments. Instead, its revenues must be earned. Consequently, the Port has always supported itself through the revenues generated from its real estate and maritime operations. However, when Bruce took over as CEO, there was very little in the way of innovation going on or sense of urgency around important projects. In short, the organization had become very bureaucratic, top-down, and low-risk.

Among the actions taken to achieve the organization's vision of "a world-class port through excellence in public service" were the adoption of the Malcolm Baldridge Performance Framework and the use of a balanced scorecard to assess the Port's performance from a customer and stakeholder perspective. Under Bruce's leadership, the Port began assessing its culture, along with various outcomes and causal factors related to it, using the *Organizational Culture Inventory* and *Organizational Effectiveness Inventory*.

The assessment of the organization's operating culture in 2004 showed that the norms and expectations at the time primarily were oriented toward passivity, particularly Avoidance, with moderate expectations for Aggressive/Defensive behaviors and very weak expectations for Constructive behaviors (see Figure 3.1). Randa, who had joined the Port in 2000, explains,

> There were a lot of people who just wanted to keep their heads down, do really routine things, and avoid taking on anything that was controversial or had political complications associated with it. I came from the private sector, naïve to all of that, and my reaction was "bring it on."
>
> Not long after I arrived, a fellow employee told me to "slow down" and that, instead of committing to people, I should say, "We'll consider it" or "We'll run it up the flagpole." He pointed out that "If you tell them you're going to do it, then they're going to actually expect you to do it."

It was those kinds of norms that Bruce and the other leaders were intent on changing. They used the feedback about the various causal factors related to culture to identify and implement several changes, starting with themselves and their own understanding of Constructive behaviors.

Specifically, the Port's senior leaders participated in two personal development programs—the Pacific Institute's *Investment in Excellence®* and FranklinCovey's *7 Habits of Highly Effective People*—both of which they mapped to the various Constructive behaviors on the Circumplex. The senior leaders also learned to facilitate these programs, in which everyone in the organization eventually participated.

To reinforce the behaviors and concepts taught in the programs, the organization's members would review them at the beginning of each meeting (using the *7 Habits*). They were also incorporated into their human resource management systems. This included performance evaluations, reward and recognition programs, and the leadership selection process (not including the CEO, Port Attorney, and Port Auditor, who are appointed by the Board of Port Commissioners).

A reassessment of the organization's operating culture in 2007 showed evidence of a small positive shift (see Figure 3.1), indicating that some people were starting to believe that being more Constructive and less passive was expected and rewarded. Randa remembers that period well:

> At all different levels of the organization, we started to see people bringing forward new ideas, new ways of doing things,

rather than just coming to work, putting their heads down, and doing what they're told. The culture was more encouraging and accepting that process improvement was part of everyone's job. This meant that an administrative assistant or a gardener could go to their supervisors and say, "I don't think this is the most effective way to do that. Why don't we try doing it this way?"

Figure 3.1. Shift in Port of San Diego's Operating Culture

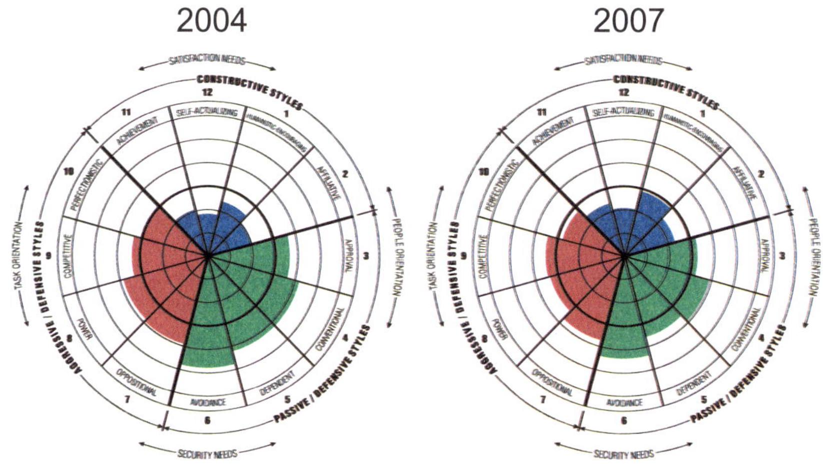

Research and development by Robert A. Cooke, Ph.D. and J. Clayton Lafferty, Ph.D. Copyright © 1987-2019 by Human Synergistics International. All Rights Reserved.

By the time Bruce retired in 2009, his focus on developing a more Constructive culture within the Port had resulted in many significant wins, from a 38 percent increase in revenue to high employee morale and low turnover.[137] The *Organizational Effectiveness Inventory*, two years into the culture change effort, showed statistically significant improvements in employee reports of interunit coordination, organizational-level quality, and external adaptability. Separately, customer surveys indicated a 5 percent increase in both tenant and public satisfaction during that same period. Voluntary turnover dropped from 6 percent in 2004 to 2 percent in 2009. The organization successfully implemented fifteen strategic projects between 2002 and 2006.[138] Certainly, it seemed as if this initial push to improve the culture had been effective and had made at least some people realize how important culture is to the performance of the organization.

Regression in Culture

The period leading up to Randa's promotion to CEO needs to be put in context at this point. As is the case with many organizations (including those showcased in this book), there followed one unexpected challenge after another. First came various changes in leadership following Bruce's departure. Other senior leaders at that time also left, including the executive vice president. Then the effects of the 2008 recession began to hit hard. Steps were taken to significantly reduce the employee count, for example, by flattening the organizational structure and implementing an early retirement program. Yet the amount of work to be done by the Port did not change. During this time, the organization also experienced its first deficit in five years, and, as many organizations do, the Port cut the training budget, along with any spending associated with the culture efforts. The financial difficulties and tough decisions that had to be made during the recession completely absorbed the attention of executives in most organizations, including at the Port. The second CEO after Bruce was succeeded by an interim CEO, who was brought in for a year before Randa Coniglio was appointed to the position.

Through this turbulence, the strides that the organization had made toward moving the culture in a more Constructive and less Defensive direction eroded. The changes in shared beliefs and behavioral norms had not yet been ingrained in the critical mass to the necessary extent. With the number of changes in key positions, along with the tough problems

Aerial view of Embarcadero

leaders were facing, culture became less a priority and instead was viewed as the responsibility of human resources personnel. By the time Randa took over as CEO, the norms around Avoidance and complacency were as strong as they had been in 2004. "Working on several different initiatives at once, it was often the case that we push each of them forward an inch or two rather than focus on just one and drive it all the way home," says People Strategies business partner Scott Laing.

Having been a part of the Port's initial culture change process, Randa was keen to reignite the leadership's attention to culture with the goal of increasing innovation and efficiency. Specifically, she wanted to create a culture that fostered disciplined practices as well as an environment in which employees would want to work and could feel a sense of accomplishment.

Lessons in How to Undo Culture Change

One of the biggest learnings for Randa, after seeing how the positive changes in culture had unraveled during the previous challenging six years, was the need to embed the transformation efforts in the day-to-day managing of the business—rather than relying so heavily on training and human resources to instill the organization's values into its operating culture. Because, while training and human resources had helped to push the needle during Bruce Hollingsworth's tenure, when times got tough and the senior leaders who were championing culture change were no longer there, it was too easy for the remaining leaders and employees to regress into Avoidance and other Defensive behaviors. Randa explains,

> When we undertook the cultural initiative back in 2004 to 2008, it was a standalone project. It was one of several different initiatives that we were doing at that time. When the executive team evaluated my performance, I reported on my behaviors and then, separately, on the status of my revenue goals, the progress on each of my projects, and my other business activities. At the time, we didn't realize that the culture initiatives had been set up as separate from the day-to-day activities of the business. When the CEO changed, and we didn't have leaders who had that same focus on culture, there was no longer any understanding that the Constructive behaviors should be a part of everything we do.

We see this often as organizations move forward with what they expect to be a major culture change. When responsibility for culture is largely considered the domain of the human resources or organizational development departments rather than that of leadership, culture change efforts become a source of conflict and frustration for employees. Given that most, if not all, of the causal factors that influence culture are controlled by senior leaders or delegated to people whom they select (see the "How Culture Works" model in chapter 2, Figure 2.2), changing culture can be like trying to swim against the tide for human resource directors or anyone else who has been tasked with sole responsibility for it. In the end, employees will become increasingly cynical, uninvolved, and focused on playing it safe. Says Scott Laing,

> The culture change effort was initially spearheaded by an organizational development function with upwards of seven people. But then after the transfer in leadership, the number of individuals involved in organizational development and training was reduced. What is interesting is that if you fast-forward to today, there's still a lot of that early culture work left in the system, but the people running the programs have no context around why or how they were designed that way.

This is an important point to consider: Structures, systems, and technology—not to mention people—are going to change within your organization over time. The people who are responsible for these functions today need to know historically why things are designed the way they are and have a good understanding of how culture works. If they don't, there's a risk as to whether any changes or decisions they make will reinforce Constructive behaviors or inadvertently encourage Defensive ones. Adds Scott,

> The human resources model that we used became very transactional and didn't necessarily have the strategic side that we needed. In the past, the organizational development people had led the cultural transformation efforts, and over time that all got watered down. We wanted to look at a more modern focus and approach, so we created two groups—Human Resources and People Strategies—that work closely together in carrying out the activities vital to the sustainability of our organization and the achievement of its strategic objectives. Human Resources is responsible for the regulatory, benefits,

A park on the waterfront of San Diego Bay

and transactional work necessary to support the organization's day-to-day operations. People Strategies is responsible for strategic activities like systems evaluation and design to ensure that the systems we use facilitate the accomplishment of the organization's strategic objectives.

What the CEO has been clear to avert this time around is making a single department become—as the director of People Strategies, Tim DeNike, described it—"the pill that would be responsible for all aspects of a cultural change." That's a message that is often missed in discussions of this kind.

Applying the Lessons Learned

Randa decided to relaunch the organization's culture change efforts with the key focus on making it part of everyone's job—including leadership's. She personally went to every department to ask people to complete the *Organizational Culture Inventory* and the *Organizational Effectiveness Inventory*. While this may not sound significant, it had been years since anyone from senior leadership had asked people for their opinions.

Among the most important issues highlighted by the survey results, which Randa wanted to address first, was moving the culture in a less Avoidance- and more Achievement-oriented direction. She recruited several new leaders from the private sector, including Tim, to serve as change agents and to contribute fresh ideas and perspectives. The leaders were selected not only for their experience but also in consideration of their personal styles and attitudes—which Randa felt reflected the Constructive characteristics she sought to strengthen in the Port's culture.

Tim and his staff in People Strategies started working with the senior leaders to support them in incorporating and reinforcing the desired behaviors in the ways they personally work, lead, and interact with one another. For instance, they sat in on meetings and provided feedback to help the leaders be more deliberate about establishing priorities to be discussed during the meeting and then accomplishing them. As Tim points out, although it may seem small, recognizing these kinds of "wins" in addition to those that are more salient is an important step toward developing more Achievement-oriented behaviors.

Of course, not everything they tried went smoothly or as expected. For example, the leaders on the operations side wanted to begin institutionalizing a new human-centered design process. The process involves gaining a deep understanding of the customer's experience and perspective, and incorporates techniques such as brainstorming, modeling, personas, and prototyping to come up with creative ideas.

A cross-departmental group of people (the Blue Team) was selected, the members of which the leadership team believed had the capacity to learn new Constructive behaviors by using the new process. The team was to work through a pilot project that focused on a new attraction intended to provide public good as well as additional revenue to invest in other strategies and plans. The hope was that the new process would promote the desired behaviors and, in doing so, illustrate how a Constructive approach accelerates progress on work directly relevant to the organization's mission and goals. At the same time, top leadership would define the structure to expand the work and engage other departments and teams in similar improvement efforts, not least by showing how Constructive behaviors are beneficial to achieving work-related goals.

However, one of the important things that the Port's leaders learned from the experience—which is often overlooked—is that Constructive behaviors do not necessarily automatically arise from the implementation of a new process. The Blue Team was given the new process to use, and the idea was to let them learn from their mistakes, make their own adjustments, and not have leaders intervene as they worked on the project. Consequently, the top leaders ended up relying on the Blue Team to carry the change flag. While the new process enabled the team to approach the project in different way, it was largely because of the enthusiasm of the team's members about having been chosen to participate. On its own, however, the process didn't help people *learn* new Constructive behaviors. Instead, the norms and expectations that were part of the organization's day-to-day culture guided how people used the new technique, particularly when they ran into problems.

"The focus of the experience was on the process and not necessarily the behaviors," Scott explains. "So what happened was that we replicated the organization's existing culture within this new process." The key lessons learned were 1) even with a new process, people still need some feedback and coaching to better understand and develop more Constructive behaviors; 2) senior leadership needs to be more engaged in this initial work by actively working on their own personal development; and 3) leaders also need to expand the learnings about culture beyond the pilot group.

Acting on these learnings, the Port has reestablished and redefined its vision with the involvement of cross-functional teams. They've established a framework of six Port-wide Competencies (humility, authenticity, trustworthiness, listening, growth, and collaboration), which were developed through the lens of servant leadership and are aligned with the organization's values. The Port's executives are participating in a six-month leadership development program, to be followed by simulations, assessments, and coaching based on the competency framework. As Randa points out, "I think it's going to take years, but we're trying some different things and not setting up a single team responsible for transforming the culture of the organization. Everybody has to take responsibility."

Key Learnings

The story of the Port of San Diego illustrates that culture isn't a destination or a "quick fix" where the work is done once you have achieved movement in the desired direction. It's an ongoing journey that has ups and downs and is defined by the assumptions and beliefs that people in the organization share about what's *really* important and *actually* expected. These assumptions and beliefs are shaped and reinforced by the actions and decisions of the organization's leaders and managers.

To keep the journey headed in a Constructive direction, both current and incoming leaders need to understand and be committed to their role in championing the culture, recognizing that it is continually affected by how they carry out their work and by the decisions they make. As the Port experienced, when leaders are personally engaged in creating more

Constructive cultures through how they carry out their work, people throughout the organization take more initiative, problems are more readily addressed, and performance improves. However, to sustain these improvements, leaders must continue to pay attention to their personal impact on the prevailing culture and its influence on effectiveness. While human resources and organizational development directors and departments can be invaluable sources of support (as you will read more about in subsequent chapters), leaders' personal transformation and attention to culture play a central role in embedding Constructive cultures in the everyday work of the organization. Says Scott Laing,

> I think our story is a good example of showing that it's not an easy road. You have to be committed to culture change, because some days it can be very difficult. But we have a lot going for us, including a CEO who wants and is driving this and an incredibly inspiring purpose and vision for the organization.

This observation allows us to segue nicely to the next chapter, which focuses on a problem we see time and again within organizations: chronic fear of failure and firefighting in the C-suite make trust and internal collaboration impossible—and the effects can take the business to the brink of disaster. To read how one organization addressed this set of challenges, we leave the west coast of the United States and shift our attention to the eastern part of Germany to examine the leadership and culture journey of a leading e-commerce company for on-demand printing of apparel and accessories.

Key Learnings

Constructive culture change is more feasible to achieve and sustain when:

- *indirect* levers—such as human resource management, training, and the implementation of new processes—are complemented by the *direct* impact of leaders (including their behaviors, strategies, and approaches) on people and culture;

- leaders purposefully embed transformation in the day-to-day work of the organization rather than approach it as a separate activity; and

- leaders make their own personal development part of the culture change process to establish transformation in how they carry out their leadership activities and responsibilities.

Chapter 4

Using a Shared Language to Increase Self-Awareness and Reduce Conflict (Germany)

> When problems with behavior and people not being able to work together really show is when times are tough.
>
> Philip Rooke, CEO, Spreadshirt

Organization	Spreadshirt
Headquarters	Leipzig, Germany
Industries	E-commerce and print-on-demand apparel and accessories
Founded	2002
Market Position	Market leader in Europe and fourth in the United States
Number of Employees	750
Started Culture Journey	2015
Interviewees	Philip Rooke, CEO
	Theresa Kretzschmar, Global HR Director
	Jochen Grotenhöfer, Transition Consult (Supporting Consultant)

Left to right: Theresa Kretzschmar, Jochen Grotenhöfer, and Philip Rooke

It all started at 6:00 a.m. Monday on a cold winter morning in Germany, when Spreadshirt's CEO, Philip Rooke, woke up thinking, "I don't want to go to work." Not a big deal—after all, who hasn't occasionally woken up feeling like that? But the CEO? Something was very wrong. Because it wasn't just this day that had started off with this feeling—for Philip, lately it was every day. It was especially odd given his passion for the company, which provides an e-commerce platform on which customers can buy, create, and sell their ideas and designs for print-on-demand apparel and accessories. Originally founded in 2002 by student Lukasz Gadowski and engineer Matthias Spieß, working from a university basement in Leipzig, Germany, Spreadshirt and its online shop system quickly expanded. They won numerous awards for their innovative business concept and extraordinary growth, and they had no problem recruiting talent to work for the growing company, which projected a fun, energetic, and youthful vibe.

The issue was largely that more than 80 percent of Philip's time was spent sorting out internal arguments about how things should be done, leaving little time for him to spend on strategic issues—the work he really enjoyed and what the company needed him to be doing. Customers, along with employees and projects, were left hanging while leaders tried to work out their differences, often with Philip as the reluctant referee. Decisions were delayed, resulting in some customers migrating to Spreadshirt's competitors, while employees would shift their efforts to working on less controversial and in some cases less important or less urgent assignments and problems. Projects were running over time and over budget. Company revenues, which had been growing steadily since 2010, had essentially gone flat.[139] Philip realized that if he didn't do something to change the situation, they would be heading back to where they had been six years ago, when the company was teetering on the brink of bankruptcy.

Back then, in 2009, sales on Spreadshirt's e-commerce platform had been plummeting to an extent that the company was likely to go out of business within eighteen months. Unlike some of the other organizations described in this book, in which leaders began addressing cultural issues before they experienced a serious crisis, Spreadshirt's combative culture had already taken the company to the brink of financial failure. That was until Philip, then Global VP and Managing Director, recognized that the challenges they faced were as much internal as external. Certainly, the market was changing. The increasing number of broadband connections, changes in the way people accessed and interfaced with the internet,

Spreadshirt head office, Leipzig (Source: Spreadshirt)

and the rising power of social media had all expanded the potential pool of clients, as well as brought new market players to the online original-design T-shirt sales industry.[140] However, the more formidable enemy that the company faced lay within Spreadshirt itself, in the form of constant disagreements between warring factions and unnecessary micromanaging, which meant that the company's leadership was continually taking its eyes off the prize: being the "go-to place" for anyone looking to realize their creative ideas on quality fabrics.

Finding the company so close to the edge of a cliff, Philip had had to rally everyone around a strategy and go into firefighting survival mode to keep the company solvent. They were fortunate to have succeeded and, in 2011, Philip became Spreadshirt's CEO. By the end of 2013, the company's sales performance had more than doubled to €72 million (euros). Sales also increased throughout the next year, when the company expanded into South America and launched a new brand. A happy ending, right? Except we now know that there never is an end to the challenges of keeping up with an ever-changing world—just brief respites. And for Spreadshirt, this breathing space didn't last long, because the leadership team hadn't yet recognized that the deeper issue they faced was cultural.

Firefighting and Fear of Failure

By 2014, Spreadshirt had operations in nineteen countries, offered more products and product lines than in previous years, and had recruited even more employees representing different generations of technical knowledge and experience. Because technology and the ways in which people interfaced with Spreadshirt continued to change, interaction between the business and its target audiences had also shifted. No longer was the company just one business selling customized apparel; it was now three businesses, each of which used customization as part of what the customer was buying:

- a *Spreadshop*, which provides a shop system that enables anyone to connect to an audience and earn money by selling merchandise online;
- a *Marketplace*, where partners can upload and sell their designs while customers can browse for clothing and accessories to express themselves; and
- a *Design Tool*, that people can use to create their own design ideas on any product.

At the same time, the popularity and number of "e-tailers" had skyrocketed,[141] and new competitors were continually cropping up, ready to take Spreadshirt's business away.

Nevertheless, Philip's perspective was "I've always found competitors much friendlier problems to have," referring to the increasing number of internal conflicts that the leaders seemed unable or unwilling to resolve. The firefighting survival mode that had helped to bring together the company and its leaders during the 2009 crisis had lost its unifying potency during these more profitable times. There were plenty of signs that indicated to Philip that the organization was starting to veer off course: loss of customers, flat revenues, too many projects over schedule and over budget, and the growing number of internal conflicts that were affecting Philip's motivation to go to the office. Says Philip,

> Our earlier firefighting approach had helped us address the simple problems we faced, but it wasn't working to solve the complex technological problems that we were now up against. We recruited some product and design experts into the business, but that just resulted in lots of infighting between old-school and new-school ways of approaching problems.

Indeed, one of the hallmarks of the warring factions within Spreadshirt was the tension between even slightly outdated approaches and cutting-edge technology in their ever-changing industry. The experience and expertise that had helped the company grow had also created a shared fear of failure with respect to implementing innovations—and a resistance to trying new approaches. "Rigidity is the mark of a failed expert," note knowledge-building pioneers and educational researchers Carl Bereiter and Marlene Scardamalia. "People get into ruts when they reduce problems to levels that can be handled by learned procedures and patterns."[142]

Issues between these warring factions weren't only happening in executive meetings. They were playing out throughout the organization, eventually landing in Philip's lap for resolution. It wasn't unusual for leaders to walk into design meetings or approach a team that was trying to rebuild a piece of technology and say, "Your current plans are all wrong." According to Philip, they would often rely on their own experience and positional power to change the plans and have the product built the way *they* wanted it. In some cases, people would come into his office in tears because of the problems caused by all the mixed messages and changes.

In other cases, people would avoid certain executives or simply do what they were told until the next person came along to change it.

Impact on Decision-Making Effectiveness

Perhaps the bickering and disagreement would have been worth it if they had led to better decisions, but they didn't. By an effective decision, we are specifically talking about what group process pioneer Norman R. F. Maier expresses very simply in the following formula, which we discussed in chapter 1:

Solution Effectiveness = Solution Quality x Solution Acceptance

At this point, it should already be clear that solution acceptance was an issue for Spreadshirt, which, in and of itself, means less-than-effective decisions were being made. However, let's also consider the effects of the then current culture on solution quality.

Fear of failure erodes confidence, discourages smart risk taking, and is an impediment to learning and innovation. It narrows people's focus to finding solutions that minimize failure and mistakes. Although senior executives generally recognize that risk-averse cultures are a key obstacle to innovation,[143] many of them struggle with how to shift that kind of fearful shared mindset in a more Constructive direction. As leadership guru Warren Bennis emphasized, effective leaders embrace positive goals and put their energies into what they want to achieve rather than dwelling on failure and what they want to avoid. Bennis called this critical leadership tendency "The Wallenda Factor," after the famous tightrope aerialist Karl Wallenda. He pointed out that Wallenda had always put his energy toward successfully walking the tightrope. However, while preparing for his 1978 walk in San Juan, Puerto Rico, Wallenda poured all of his energy into *not* falling, which made him "virtually destined to fall." Bennis wrote that the same is true of leaders—those who focus on succeeding and accomplishment, as opposed to avoiding failure, tend to be the ones who accomplish extraordinary things.[144] As described in chapter 2, the overreliance on Restrictive leadership strategies leads other people to respond in self-protective ways and promotes unwanted Defensive cultural norms and expectations. This was precisely what Spreadshirt was experiencing.

In Spreadshirt's case, the answer lay in letting go of their old firefighting mentality and shared fear of failure, which certainly were no longer helping the organization. How did the leaders achieve this? Broadly speaking, it was by

- adopting a shared language to talk about the impact they wanted to have on each other and the organization;
- clarifying the context of actions, proposals, and changes;
- developing self-awareness about their own behaviors and their impact on each other and the culture; and
- accepting responsibility to take action to improve their leadership, team, and organization's effectiveness.

This seemed to be exactly what was needed to get the leadership team (and the people reporting to them) to unify around a strategy, to collaborate, and to move forward in such a way that they could continue to evolve the company's offerings and grow the business. Just over eighteen months later, with revenues reaching €92.5 million, Spreadshirt achieved its most profitable year ever. In the course of doing so, a major product release was implemented during which problems were solved more quickly and effectively. Let's explore in greater detail how they achieved these results.

The Currency of Shared Language

"The most powerful change interventions occur at the level of everyday conversation," point out Karl Weick and Robert Quinn, professors at the University of Michigan Business School.[145] Indeed, the way people talked to each other seemed to lie at the center of the shared fears and counterproductive behaviors that had become part of Spreadshirt's culture. As Philip explains, communication becomes more difficult and debilitating as companies grow larger and put in place more complex processes:

> Often when internet businesses start, everyone is working in a one-room company made up of four or five people. Communication is not a problem. Everything is oriented around the launch, and it's very simple to run a company in firefighting mode during that time. However, when the company starts growing and expanding into multiple rooms, floors, and locations, the tendency is to introduce rules and processes to keep things flowing smoothly. That's when I've often seen teams struggle and fail, because managers are shouting and arguing with each other in an effort to maintain control.

Philip recognized that the communication and behavioral patterns that had become the norm at Spreadshirt were putting the company's future at risk. However, as he points out, "We didn't have the right words to describe it," nor the words to steer the conversation in a more effective direction. He decided to bring in a management consultant, Jochen Grotenhöfer of Transition Consult, and to use *Leadership/Impact*®. Jochen recalls some of his early observations and impressions:

> The C-level leaders' meeting room was in a very transparent part of the building. During their routine meetings, which seemed to take a lot of their working hours, they weren't aligned with one another, and other people could see them fighting. The company needed a new strategy, but there was no agreement on the direction to take. Half of the leaders would react in an oppositional, cynical way, and the other half would be avoidant and leave the room. Discussions about new products were taking place, but not necessarily at the C-level. While it created the opportunity for other people in the company to take the initiative in coming up with creative ideas for new products—which they did—it also created frustration, because people didn't have any idea if they were heading in the right direction.

Using *Leadership/Impact*, Philip and the other senior leaders defined their "ideal impact" by delineating the behaviors they needed

Digital Direct Printing, Spreadshirt (Source: Spreadshirt)

to encourage and develop—in each other and in the rest of the organization—to maximize performance and long-term effectiveness. Creating a composite profile of their ideal impact descriptions provided Spreadshirt's leaders with a clear picture of the behaviors they collectively wanted to motivate and drive throughout the organization (see Figure 4.1). It also provided them with a shared goal—which turned out to be aligned with a less Defensive and more Constructive culture.

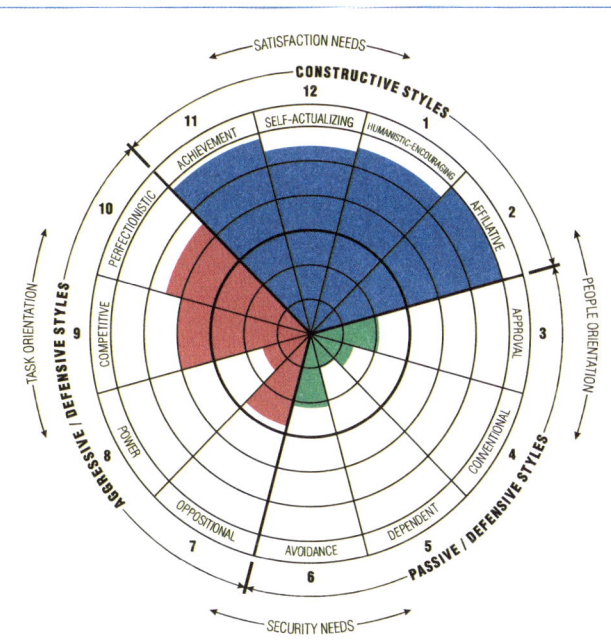

Figure 4.1. Leaders' Composite Ideal Impact Profile (2015)

Research and development by Robert A. Cooke, Ph.D. and J. Clayton Lafferty, Ph.D.
Copyright © 1987-2019 by Human Synergistics International. All Rights Reserved.

In addition, *Leadership/Impact* provided the leaders with feedback on their own leadership approaches and the extent to which their approaches influenced other people to move closer to or further away from the ideal. "It was interesting for all of them, because the results indicated that they were all having problems with their impact on peers and associates, more so than their direct reports," points out Jochen (see Figure 4.2).

The Circumplex gave the leaders a shared language that they then started using *in the course of their work* to redirect conversations and behavior—in contrast to isolated or short-lived programs that can fail to create lasting changes. "The Circumplex made it easy for them to discuss and identify behaviors," says Jochen, who recalls that during meetings some of the leaders wouldn't say a word, while others could come across as "a bit strong and undiplomatic." Using the Circumplex, the leadership team started examining examples of different statements, situations, and behaviors in terms of the style being exhibited and the impact on other people. They also discussed and identified ways that they could rephrase statements to shift situations or behavior in a more Constructive direction.

Figure 4.2. Leaders' Composite Actual Impact Profiles (2015)

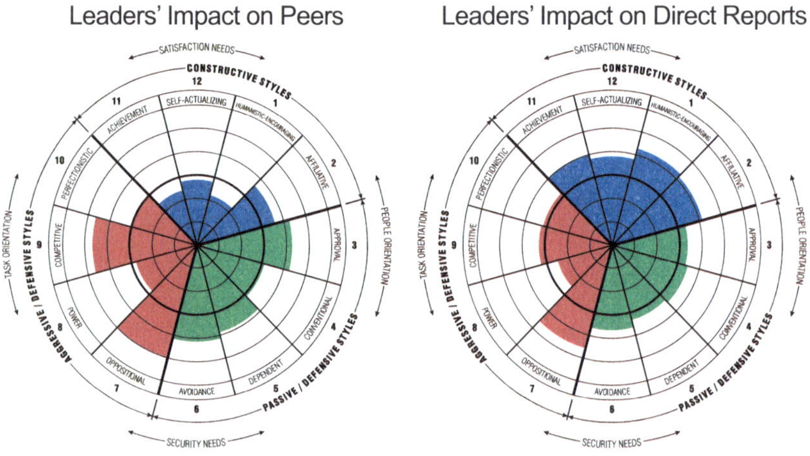

Research and development by Robert A. Cooke, Ph.D. and J. Clayton Lafferty, Ph.D. Copyright © 1987-2019 by Human Synergistics International. All Rights Reserved.

"Blue was initially viewed as weak, and that you shouldn't tell people what was going wrong," says Spreadshirt's Global HR Director, Theresa Kretzschmar. "We discovered that blue is not about being nice; it's about being realistic. Instead of shouting our concerns, we could talk about what is going wrong in a more Constructive way so that people could hear us."

The leaders started using the language during meetings. For instance, when people would start to behave more aggressively, they'd ask each other to reiterate what was said in a way that was "less red and more blue." The Circumplex and its language also helped them to become more aware of the impact they were having on others in specific situations. Says Philip,

> Everyone started to understand that when they storm into a team and say, "You must do X or you must do Y, because I say so," that's Power (red behavior), and it makes other people shout back at them (red impact) or avoid them and act like

they just don't care anymore (green impact). Up to that point, people had no awareness that their behavior was causing the red and green reactions.

This is an important point. Most often, when leaders are having a Defensive impact, it is unintentional. They are usually just trying to get something done but not going about it in the best way. Bringing attention to behavior and its impact *when it was happening* (or shortly thereafter) provided the leaders with concrete examples of the connection between their leadership approaches and impact on others—and gave them the opportunity to adjust their behavior so they could achieve results in a more effective way.

One of the realizations that came out of these discussions was that preferred solutions were often based on assumptions about customer preferences. As a result, they began testing these assumptions by referring to data from their customer target groups rather than relying exclusively on their own subjective points of view. Philip explains,

> By having everyone talk about an agreed-upon set of behaviors and, in this example, use the customer's perspective, the discussion became much more Affiliative. It's one of the ways that we've empowered teams and helped them to better understand what is to be achieved. As a result, they've been able to make more effective decisions than even we (at the C-level) would have made.

As author Deborah Schroeder-Saulnier notes in her book *The Power of Paradox: Harness the Energy of Competing Ideas to Uncover Radically Innovative Solutions*, "There is one element every strategic planning exercise needs as it gets underway, and that is a common language."[146] Her observation speaks to the enthusiasm (and smarts!) of Spreadshirt, as well as other clients who have used a shared language as part of their change process.

Clarifying Context

Within Spreadshirt, arguments often ensued when there was a lack of common understanding about the context of the problem, idea, solution, or change being discussed. This void exacerbated the old fears of failure, a sense of mistrust, and the perceived need to take control. "Most managers are afraid of making mistakes, and most CEOs and executives are afraid of mistakes happening," says Philip. "That fear drives them to try and control things and micromanage their teams. It also means they don't provide [or ask for] enough information about context."

Being explicit about the context of what you are doing or proposing is particularly important in multicultural teams, states INSEAD's international program director, Erin Meyer, because in such cases, the likelihood of misunderstanding multiplies.[147] Yet, within Spreadshirt—whose employees represent more than twenty different nationalities—problems with communication and misunderstandings didn't only occur between people from different countries. They also occurred between people with different generations of technical knowledge, as well as between those who had been with the organization a long time (and were steeped in its culture) and those who were relatively new.

The relevance of context to perceived knowledge and expertise became apparent to Philip when, a few months into the change process, he and his team went through a group problem-solving simulation. The simulation they used—*Bushfire Survival Situation*™—is set in an area where some of Philip's family members reside and have experienced bushfires. He was certain of his solution for survival, only to discover that his team's solution was better aligned with that of survival experts. He says it never occurred to him that knowledge about the best way to deal with bushfires would have changed and improved in the years since his early experiences. Philip, with his extensive experience managing, running, and setting up commercial websites, saw how the situation mirrored the way his organization operated and the incorrect contextual assumptions leaders often made. He observes,

> My experience with designing a website is out of date. I have to rely on a much younger, up-to-date team for that. We still have many people who say, "I'm the expert at this." Even the designers who think they know how best to design a website don't necessarily know how to design it to fit the needs of a particular market or customer. So, there's a lot to be learned.

Not the least of which for Spreadshirt was learning to recognize that past experiences may not be completely relevant to the current situation, given, for example, changes in technology or customer preferences.

Philip started scheduling monthly "stand-ups" where anyone in the organization could take the initiative to explain *what* they were doing and, just as importantly, provide the context for *why* they were doing it that way. For example, when one of their business teams decided to change the company's pricing model, about half of the company didn't agree with the decision. When they stood up and explained why they were doing it, Philip says the change was more widely accepted. Similarly, when the leadership team chose to restructure some of the departments and close less profitable business units to make the company more effective, Philip stood up and explained what was going on and the underlying reasons for the changes. "Spending slightly more time explaining the reasoning behind those decisions didn't necessarily lessen the emotions that people felt," says Philip. "Rather, it increased the respect and acceptance, resulting in a faster adjustment that previously would have taken twice as long."

Self-Awareness and the Three A's of Change

Recognizing and pointing out when other people are behaving in unproductive ways is often easier than seeing and correcting our own behavior. Yet this kind of self-awareness, particularly among top leaders, is essential if you want to improve your impact on people and your organization's culture.

Whereas feedback can effectively heighten awareness, it doesn't always lead to changes and improvements. What we've learned from the *Life Styles Inventory* is that how people react to feedback and their interest in self-development is related to their thinking and behavioral styles (see Table I.1). Unsurprisingly, people with more Constructive thinking and behavioral styles tend to be interested in feedback and self-development, whereas those with Aggressive/Defensive styles typically dismiss or react negatively to feedback and are usually not interested in changing. Philip recalls,

> In our first month of working with the [*Leadership/Impact*] feedback, very few people saw themselves as a problem, me included. I said, "Thank God we got this settled, because the other leaders will behave now." It took most of us six months to start recognizing when we were the problem. That was when changes really started to happen—when people began noticing when they were the problem.

His comment highlights the importance of what we call *the three A's* of development and change: Awareness, Acceptance, and Action (see box). While this may seem painfully obvious, most change efforts go awry because they are based on flawed assumptions about what change involves. According to authors Michael Papanek (grandson of organizational development founder Kurt Lewin) and Dr. Liz Alexander, "We zip through the awareness part, make a quick choice to stop doing whatever was causing the problem in the first place, and then believe we have changed"—only to find that our behavior quickly reverts back, if it even changed at all. In their book *From Breakdown to Breakthrough: Forging Resilient Business Relationships in the Heat of Change*, they point out that "change is a *process*, not an event," which is why Kurt Lewin included three phases (unfreezing-changing-freezing) in his model of change rather than one.[148]

> **The Three A's of Change**
>
> *Awareness*, or noticing how you are thinking and behaving
>
> *Acceptance* of your responsibility for your behavior and its impact on other people as well as outcomes
>
> *Action* in terms of taking steps to think and behave in a more effective way[149]

The first time Philip recognized that he was exhibiting more Aggressive/Defensive (red) than Constructive (blue) behavior and accepted the responsibility to take action to change happened quite unexpectedly—and occurred in his personal rather than his professional life:

> My wife had spent days organizing a complicated holiday in Australia, where I really wanted to dive on the Barrier Reef, attend a family wedding, and catch up with some other family members. She put together a really good schedule. However, when she showed it to me, I immediately noticed a problem with one of the flights. Frankly, she got very pissed off. She told me I was coming across as a perfectionist and, with all of the work she'd done, she felt unappreciated, because all I had focused on was the one thing that wouldn't work. We had an argument, and then my dog got stressed by the argument and threw up on the floor. Suddenly, I found myself in "green" [passive mode], cleaning up dog sick, and my wife and dog

avoiding me [behavioral impact]. As I was doing this, I realized I had acted in a really "red," aggressive manner with my wife [Awareness]. That was when I found myself for the first time thinking about how to solve this situation in a "blue" way [Acceptance]. When I re-approached my wife about it a couple days later, we had a conversation about diving, traveling, and other things, and we found the right solution very simply [Action]. I realized then that I'd also been doing this at work and that it had become routine every time we hit a problem.

Over the years, we've heard numerous leaders and managers say that they really didn't understand or accept feedback about their behavior until something happened with a spouse or a child that helped to illuminate it. Contrary to what is often assumed, in our experience, people do not act all that differently at home than they do at work. As Philip's experience illustrates, there can be a great deal of value to recognizing the impact of your behavior, whether it's inside or outside of the workplace.

Philip shared this story with his entire company to illustrate the differences between red, blue, and green behavior and their impact.

Spreadshirt production (Source: Spreadshirt)

As important, he wanted people to know that changing the culture was something of which everyone in the organization was to be a part, and that included him. "To manage change is to tell people what to do…but to lead change is to show people how to be," point out organizational change researchers Weick and Quinn.[150] This critical step helps to establish a more psychologically safe environment in which others can learn and practice new, more effective ways of behaving, which is a critical aspect of successful culture change.[151]

Early Results

Within a few months of starting their journey at Spreadshirt, Philip noticed a dramatic shift in how he was spending his time. Less than a third of it was being spent on dealing with conflicts among members of his leadership team, compared with the previous 80 percent. He specifically points out the improvements in problem solving and productivity:

> Design meetings have gone from different people shouting at each other or needing me there to sort them out, to the relevant people now being able to have a Constructive discussion and then let the rest of the organization know their decisions. The result is that we've reduced the number of people in meetings by half and get two or three times more decisions made and implemented.

Since the initial work on their own impact, team interactions, and communication, Spreadshirt's senior leaders have updated the company's strategy and structure to reflect its three different major businesses and customer groups. They extended the opportunities for feedback on impact, team building, and communication training to other levels of management. In addition, they administered the *Organizational Culture Inventory* and the *Organizational Effectiveness Inventory* to gain a better understanding of the broader culture and the various factors affecting it. Based on the survey feedback, the senior leadership team worked on clarifying the organization's values as well as people's roles and responsibilities. They also made changes to the goal-setting system and bonuses to better align them with a Constructive culture. Says HR director Theresa Kretzschmar,

> We asked people to write job descriptions, which further helped to clarify roles, set boundaries, and empower people.

For example, previously it seemed as if people at the C-level were in charge of the same things. Writing the job descriptions helped the C-suite leaders realize how much time they were spending on activities that actually were not their responsibilities, which, in turn, also helped them to empower their managers.

Because of the improvements in how their teams work together, in 2016, Spreadshirt was able to release major infrastructure changes in their technology, improve the usability of their software, and more quickly and effectively work through the unexpected problems that arose from the scale of those releases. The company's revenues, which had stalled in 2014, were once again growing—a trend that continued in 2017 (see Figure 4.3). Growth skyrocketed in key areas of the business, including the US market, where in 2017 they experienced

- an 11 percent increase in orders across all business units,
- 41 percent revenue growth from Marketplaces business unit,
- 52 percent growth in new Marketplace Sellers, and
- 35 percent growth in all Seller earnings.[152]

Spreadshirt team BBQ on the roof terrace (Source: Spreadshirt)

Figure 4.3. Spreadshirt's Revenues Over Time

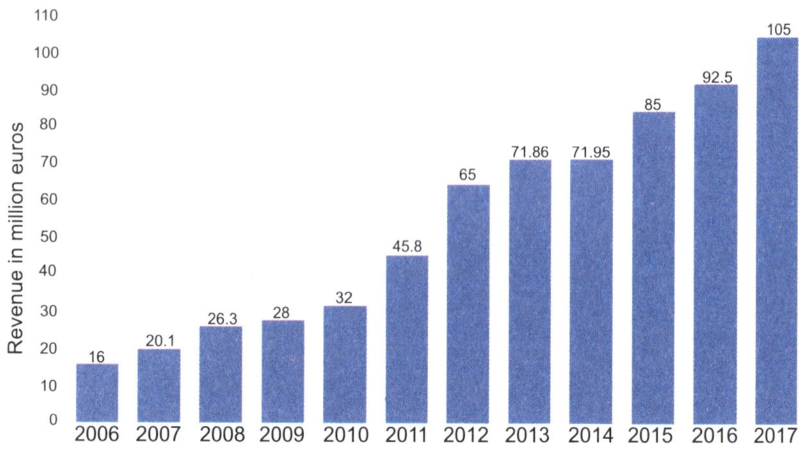

Year	Revenue (million euros)
2006	16
2007	20.1
2008	26.3
2009	28
2010	32
2011	45.8
2012	65
2013	71.86
2014	71.95
2015	85
2016	92.5
2017	105

Sources: Statista (2006-2014); Spreadshirt (2015 and 2017) and BusinessWire (2016)

Reflecting on their organization's culture journey thus far, Philip offers this critical insight:

> When things are going really well—for instance, when we have 40 percent growth, shareholders are happy, and everything seems positive—despite the behavioral problems, the organization seems very buoyant. When problems with behavior and people not being able to work together really show is when times are tough. And tough times always happen, and did happen to us several times this year. It doesn't matter whether it's a restructure as mentioned earlier, damage from a competitor, or damage from a product release that doesn't work. That's when the Constructive behavior really makes a difference and has gotten us back to a growth or a better business situation quicker. People were having to deal with a lot of problems this year, and they worked well within their teams and between their teams. I'm not claiming it was perfect, but it was certainly a lot better than I had seen in the history of Spreadshirt, and in many other companies.

Their leadership team has gone from struggling to agree about what to do in the next month or next quarter to discussing how they can be five times bigger in five years, which everyone believes they now have the capability to achieve.

And for Philip, it means waking up with excitement and optimism about the future ahead.

Key Learnings

"Culture is a critical element of any successful startup—because at the very least, you're going to be spending a great deal of time with these people, probably more than your friends and family," wrote one of Facebook's first employees, Kevin Colleran.[153] Yet culture is often the last thing that new founders think about.

While culture may not have been top-of-mind when Spreadshirt was founded, their story illustrates that it is never too late for leaders to examine their organization's culture and make changes to ensure that it guides behavior in the right direction. Self-awareness is a necessary first step to any kind of intentional change—personal or cultural—and certainly requires a shared goal (such as the vision of the ideal culture) and a shared language if people are to work together to create positive changes. Of course, self-awareness alone doesn't create change—accepting responsibility and taking action are also key and, ironically, are often overlooked, particularly when leaders are approaching change with an Aggressive/Defensive mindset rather than a more Constructive one. As a result of internalizing the three *A*'s and working on having a more Constructive impact on people and culture, people within the company are spending significantly less time arguing and more time working together to quickly and effectively solve problems and implement decisions. In turn, Spreadshirt's customer base has grown, and sales have risen.

As we'll see from the next chapter, the sooner you get started with understanding and improving your organization's culture, the better, because it only gets tougher to do so when your organization is dealing with a crisis, such as a market disruption. Let's move on now to the story of how a company headquartered in Switzerland began its culture change journey.

Key Learnings

- Make transformation both a personal and a shared responsibility at the leadership level.

- Collectively define the ideal culture (or ideal leadership impact on culture) to obtain agreement on and commitment to what the leadership team needs to work on creating.

- Practice the "Three As"—awareness, acceptance, and action—with respect to behavior and its impact.

- Use a shared language to facilitate awareness, acceptance, and action regarding behavior and its impact.

Chapter 5

Making Culture a Strategic Priority to Become More Ambidextrous and Overcome Market Disruption (Switzerland)

The fact that so many things today are completely different from how business in this industry was done ten years ago was not widely accepted due to the mindset that existed throughout the organization.
Marco Gadola, CEO, Straumann

Organization	Straumann
Headquarters	Basel, Switzerland
Industry	Manufacturer of dental implants and restorative and regenerative dental solutions
Founded	1954
Market Position	First in premium and third in nonpremium markets (2016)
Number of Employees	4,779 (2017)
Started Culture Journey	2014
Interviewees	Marco Gadola, CEO
	Guillaume Daniellot, Head of North America
	Stuart Douglas, Managing Director, Australia/New Zealand
	Eric Fromentel, Global Lean Coordinator and Director of Operational Excellence
	Dr. Ekkehard Kuppel, Sum People (Supporting Consultant)

Left to right: Marco Gadola, Eric Fromentel, Guillaume Daniellot and Stuart Douglas

With revenues, profits, operating cash flow, and share prices all plunging to their lowest levels in five years, Straumann's chairman and acting CEO started his letter to shareholders with what they probably already knew—that 2012 "was a year of rapid change, missed targets and further disappointment." The dental implant industry, which was led by Straumann for many years and represented its largest business, had been disrupted by low-cost competitors that were aggressively filling the vacuum left by Straumann and other high-end premium-priced market players. According to the chairman's letter, "rigorous cost management" and "a new style of resolute leadership" were going to be necessary to quickly stop the hemorrhaging, adapt, and move forward (see Figure 5.1).[154]

This letter undoubtedly left people wondering: How could this have happened to an organization that had been so successful for sixty years? Originally, Straumann had manufactured alloys for watches, other timing instruments, and materials testing. The company then migrated into osteosynthesis implants during the 1970s and began offering dental implants exclusively in 1990. With more than 2,500 employees in seventy countries and a product portfolio that included dental implant components and instruments, CADCAM (Computer-Aided Design/Computer-Aided Manufacturing) prosthetics, and oral tissue regeneration products, the company was still the market leader in 2012. However, as preeminent executive coach Marshall Goldsmith says, "What got you here won't get you there."[155]

Making Culture a Strategic Priority 143

Figure 5.1. Straumann's Share Price Development: 2008 to 2012

Share Price Development
(in %)

- Straumann
- SMIM index
- MSCI World Healthcare Equipment & Services index CHF

Source: Straumann, *Annual Report 2012*, 3.

Refusing to compete on price while remaining steadfast on global expansion and continuous improvements to high-quality products had worked for Straumann for a long time—until it didn't. As more low-cost competitors continued to enter the market after the 2008 economic crash, the leaders' unshakeable belief in the company's existing strategy became their Achilles' heel. Ailing economies, austerity initiatives enforced by politicians, high unemployment, and many patients' inability to pay for nonreimbursed treatments meant that more high-end dental procedures were being postponed. At the same time, the demand for cheaper alternatives throughout Europe increased. Straumann suffered financially not only when the lower-cost alternatives began swamping the Eastern European market but also as these discounters began gaining market share in the more developed economies.

It's tempting to conclude that the company's real challenge was external circumstances over which it had no control, but it wasn't. While there is little that anyone can do to stop low-cost competitors from coming into a market, you *always* have the option to take a deeper, longer look at yourself and make necessary changes.

Company leaders described Straumann's culture back then as top-down, siloed, political, compliant, and risk-averse. Problems between different departments or areas were often sent upward, and solutions were sent back down, resulting in perceived "winners and losers" and fueling the tendencies to blame, politic, and internally compete. "Proven" solutions and homegrown approaches based on the company's own experience were strongly favored over those that were new or untested, which, if considered, required extensive evidence to demonstrate minimal risk of failure. Thus, it's not surprising that, when the dental implant market was disrupted by lower-cost nonpremium providers, Straumann's leaders and managers reminded each other and their employees that the company had been challenged by low-cost competitors in the past—and that its approach of producing premium-quality (and premium-priced) products, combined with educating its customers, had always prevailed. The company stood by this decision as its market continued to be disrupted, illustrating how a Defensive culture affects problem solving and decision making, including at the top levels of the organization. The effects were costly for the company, its stockholders, and the three hundred staff members—including executive leaders—who eventually lost their jobs.

Defensive Misattribution of Success

There is a common perceptual error that leaders of successful companies often make that we call the *Defensive Misattribution of Success*.[156] It describes how Defensive cultures persist in otherwise successful organizations. Only by raising their awareness and understanding of this risky and potentially fatal tendency can leaders choose to stop the rot and reverse its deleterious effects. This was the first step in ensuring that Straumann would not just survive, but also thrive in the future.

As pointed out by Spreadshirt's CEO (chapter 4), the problems with a Defensive culture are less apparent when times are good—when the company is making money, shareholders are happy, and there are relatively few environmental pressures for innovation, adaptability, and flexibility. It's times like this, as we have repeatedly found, that organizational leaders are least likely to see the need to objectively look at their cultures. Instead, it's often assumed that whatever culture the organization has *must* be the reason for its continued success and therefore should be maintained. However, many people fail to recognize when an organization is growing and enjoying financial success not because of its culture but despite it.

For instance, current success may be due to patents, copyrights, and other proprietary assets that have made it hard for newcomers to enter the organization's industry and therefore have provided the organization with a tremendous (albeit temporary) competitive advantage—even though the organization's culture might be characterized as arrogant and aggressive. This was possibly the case with IBM until personal computers became more popular than mainframes; Motorola with mobile phones until analog technology was unseated by digital technology; and AOL until the dot-com bubble burst and the economy went into recession.[157] In addition, people sometimes attribute a company's success to its culture when, in fact, it's the size of the organization (rather than the effectiveness of its culture) that has enabled it to dominate the market and attain efficiencies not available to its competitors—as was the case with certain department store chains until Amazon disrupted the retail playing field.

Straumann Solutions (Source: Straumann)

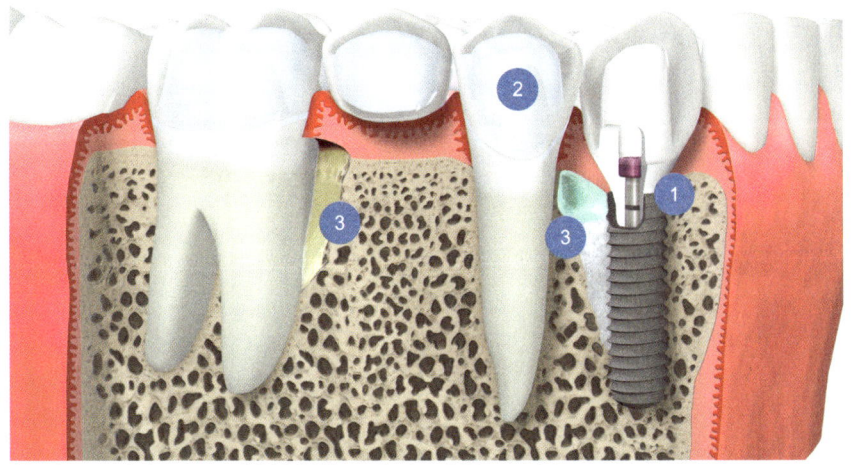

1 Implants and abutments 2 CADCAM prosthetics 3 Biomaterials

Similar to these examples, Straumann experienced a disruption in the current business model, and attempting to remain successful with a strong Defensive culture became harder and more dangerous to the business. CEO Marco Gadola, brought in to turn the company around in 2013, explains,

> We didn't understand well enough the developments in our industry and did not react fast enough to the changes in our market. The fact that so many things today are completely different from how business in this industry was done ten years ago was not widely accepted due to the mindset that existed throughout the organization.

Like many companies whose businesses have been "mature" for some time, Straumann's structures, systems, processes, and culture were designed to maximize reliability, control, and compliance rather than adaptability, risk taking, and radical or discontinuous innovation. The top-down, command-and-control mindset that had evolved as a result didn't automatically change just because the company experienced a crisis. Nor did it change after the organization was restructured in 2013 to be more customer-service focused and to forge new partnerships, agreements, and relationships with some of the low-cost manufacturers who had entered the industry. According to Straumann's 2014 annual report,

> The organizational structure that we implemented in 2013 was designed for simplicity, customer focus, agility and accountability. Only fine tuning was needed in 2014, underlining the fact that our major challenge in creating a sustainably high-performing organization is cultural rather than structural.[158]

The intense drive for personal success within Straumann was viewed as an asset rather than a liability until the company's leaders found that it got in the way of learning, solving problems, and addressing the changes that were occurring around them. Marco notes,

> Even after the financial crisis had passed, employee surveys indicated that the perception throughout the global organization was that the majority of the company was still driven by top-down leadership. It limited the amount of contribution and input that individuals throughout the organization were bringing to the table.

In *The Third Wave: An Entrepreneur's Vision of the Future*, AOL cofounder Steve Case points out that the decision-making processes in large organizations tend to afford too many people the power to stop ideas and too few the power to "green-light" them—creating environments that are strongly oriented toward "no."[159] That certainly appeared to be the case at Straumann, where conversations tended to focus on why new ideas or fresh approaches wouldn't work rather than how they could. However, we have found that cultures oriented toward rigidity and rejection are not limited to large organizations. According to corporate life cycle expert Ichak Adizes, it's self-awareness, rather than size or chronological age, that determines an organization's receptivity to change and ability to maintain both flexibility and self-control.[160]

Ambidextrous Organizations

Experts such as Adizes have pointed out the need for organizations to navigate back and forth from maximizing effectiveness to maximizing efficiency over the course of their life cycles. However, with market disruptions happening more frequently and organizations moving through life cycles much more quickly than ever before, the question of how to be *ambidextrous*—a term coined in 1976 by Robert B. Duncan of Northwestern University—has never been more important.[161]

Ambidextrous capabilities enable a single organization to simultaneously support exploitation, efficiency, and incremental improvements (often seen in mature businesses), and exploration, effectiveness, and innovation (often seen in emerging businesses).[162] One common way in which organizations might increase ambidexterity is through the implementation of dual structures, or *structural ambidexterity*, where parts of the organization focus on exploring new opportunities and adaptation, while other parts focus on exploiting the organization's current businesses and maximizing efficiency. Another approach, which some authors refer to as *contextual ambidexterity*, is to set up systems and processes to "enable and encourage individuals to make their own judgments about how to divide their time" between the two sets of conflicting demands. In other words, the organization builds the capability of ambidexterity into the norms and expectations that make up its operating culture.[163]

Regardless of which approach an organization takes, achieving ambidexterity requires building a Constructive culture. According to Stanford and Harvard professors Charles O'Reilly III and Michael Tushman, whose research has focused mainly on structural ambidexterity, managing this seemingly paradoxical situation within an organization requires a set of values and norms that provide a common identity across diverse activities and businesses. The specific values and norms they identify—"integrity, respect for people, teamwork, accountability"[164]—are consistent with aspects of each of the four Constructive styles at the top of the Circumplex (as described in the introduction to this book). Similarly, researchers who have studied contextual ambidexterity have emphasized the importance of building different aspects of what we refer to as Constructive styles (such as expectations to set challenging and realistic goals, develop others, learn, and take prudent risks).[165]

With the Constructive styles, people readily engage a larger pool of resources not only to generate more ideas and solutions but also to implement them. The notion that "two heads are better than one" is relevant, particularly when dealing with unexpected changes or unfamiliar situations. And note that it's heads, not just bodies—which is a key difference. Otherwise, people are just "showing up" rather than being genuinely engaged in the process. In contrast, Defensive cultures prevent people from being able to adapt quickly, if at all, to changes. On the passive side, Defensive norms restrict people to following orders and rules and doing what is "popular" and "safe." On the aggressive side, they limit people to considering and endorsing only their own solutions.

Thus, it's not surprising that O'Reilly and Tushman point out that building an ambidextrous organization is less about following a set of steps or phases and instead is more about cultivating an *organizational learning mindset*. Critical to this mindset is establishing an overarching vision or purpose that helps people to understand how seemingly divergent activities are complementary rather than competing.[166] Similarly, Marco recognized that the only way for Straumann to achieve its vision "to be the total solution provider for dentists and laboratories" was with the right mindset and behaviors, which reflect the culture of the organization.

Making Culture a Strategic Priority

"Culture is the way to get things done, and it drives results, which is why cultural change is our first strategic priority," stated Straumann's leaders in the company's 2015 annual report.[167] In 2014, Marco arranged for himself and the members of the executive committee, as well as the broader leadership team, to participate in a series of high-performance team workshops led by Dr. Ekkehard Kuppel. The purpose was to better understand the organization's cultural norms and what the leaders were demonstrating and promoting in their own behavior. The workshops introduced them to the basic concepts of a high-performance culture along the *It-We-I* framework used by Dr. Kuppel, and also included the *Organizational Culture Inventory* and ACUMEN® *Leadership WorkStyles* (a derivative of the *Life Styles Inventory*). He explains,

> The *Organizational Culture Inventory* was used to measure the dominant behaviors in teams and the organization—the "We" dimension—as well as support standards, conduct meetings, and have difficult conversations. On the "It" dimension, we worked on Straumann's purpose, aspirations, and the compelling story of "why change." Finally, on the "I" dimension, we used *Leadership WorkStyles* to help the executives on their personal leadership journeys, fostering Constructive mental models—from victim to player and knower to learner. Feedback sessions were an integral part of developing a high-performance culture. Straumann under Marco Gadola's leadership was very fast in adopting these tools and rolling them into the rest of the organization.

Using the *Ideal* form of the *Organizational Culture Inventory*, the leaders defined the behaviors and mindset that *should* be expected to make Straumann a sustainably high-performing organization. The predominantly Constructive ideal profile (see left side of Figure 5.2) reflects what Straumann's leaders refer to as a *player-learner* mindset. Examples of behaviors that they wanted to become more prevalent and pervasive in the organization included (in their own words): focus on customers, collaborate, take ownership, create opportunities, build trust, engage, communicate effectively, and be agile.[168]

Expectations for Constructive behaviors did exist within Straumann, particularly on the task side. However, the profile of its operating culture at that time confirmed that expectations for the Aggressive/Defensive and Passive/Defensive behaviors were even stronger, based on a sample from throughout the organization and as shown on the right side of Figure 5.2. These behaviors exemplify what Straumann's leaders referred to as the *victim-knower* mindset, which they wanted to reduce in their culture.

Figure 5.2. Straumann's Ideal and Operating Culture Profiles (2014)

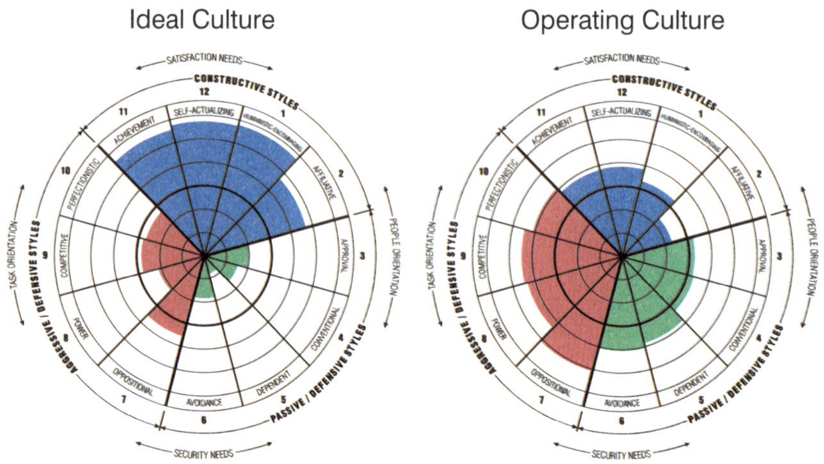

Research and development by Robert A. Cooke, Ph.D. and J. Clayton Lafferty, Ph.D. Copyright © 1987-2019 by Human Synergistics International. All Rights Reserved.

Source: Straumann, *We Love What We Do*, 88.

Changes to Systems, Structures, and Skills/Qualities

Marco became an important role model in demonstrating that everyone in Straumann must include him or herself in the change process. It is noteworthy that two years after they began their journey, he still recognized the importance of awareness, acceptance, and action (the three *A*'s). Says Marco,

> It's about becoming aware and then consciously trying to change. Sometimes I have fallen back into certain behaviors, and it helps to have people tell me, "Look, that probably wasn't the most decent reaction." So it's not a matter of "don't do this from today to tomorrow." What's important is to notice the issues and then make a genuine effort to change.

One of the key impacts was breaking down the barriers that previously generated distrust and inefficiency within the executive committee. Guillaume Daniellot, a member of the committee, explains,

> When Marco arrived, he put together a new team. While the communication was better, it was still just a bunch of individuals who wanted to perform. I was head of sales for Western Europe at the time. If I had an issue—for instance, a backorder of some very important products—I'd ask Marco

to do something because it was hurting our results. Marco would send a message to the head of production, who is also a member of the executive committee. Then the head of production would reply that they had already delivered more than what was forecasted. Then Marco would come back to me, and I'd have to justify myself because we had sold more than what was forecasted and needed some flexibility. Back and forth it went, and it was a killer in terms of efficiency. As we worked on the culture in our team, we acknowledged that we didn't have the right approach to our communications. We started to discuss things more directly with one another. If I had an issue, I'd send a message directly to the committee member, and the two of us would resolve it in two hours, whereas the previous way took two weeks of exchanges between Marco and the executive committee members.

I've learned that leading is not about being right; it's about going in the right direction with everyone, which is very different and leads to better solutions.

In addition to working on their own personal styles and interactions, the leaders involved the rest of the organization in the culture change journey. Team workshops were offered, globally and at headquarters, that incorporated one-on-one coaching tied to feedback about the culture in participants' own areas (as measured using the *Organizational Culture Inventory*) and about the behaviors that they were personally exhibiting (based on the *Life Styles Inventory*).

To promote and reinforce culture change across levels, the executive leaders organized a team of *culture change champions*. Made up of influential people from different organizational levels and functional areas, the group's members served as role models and a communication bridge across the organization. The culture change champions regularly met with Marco and the other executive committee members to discuss cultural issues and identify changes based, in part, on the feedback from the *Organizational Culture Inventory* and the *Organizational Effectiveness Inventory*, as well as on comments from town hall meetings. Among the first changes they initiated was redefining and simplifying the company's global competency model to reflect the organization's vision, core behaviors, and ideal culture. Complementary changes were then made to the organization's performance management, promotion, recruiting, onboarding development, and succession planning programs and systems to support the new culture.

Over time, teams of culture change champions were identified and organized by the leadership at different geographical locations. The local teams worked with their leaders on issues specific to their locations, as well as interacted globally by participating in a *community of practice* with the culture change champions at headquarters and other locations.

"What the cultural journey has done is brought these cross-functional groups together, and it's translated into real-life improvement opportunities for us," says Stuart Douglas, managing director of Straumann's Australia/New Zealand subsidiary. For example, shortly after being organized, the culture change champions at his subsidiary revamped their employee induction program to make it more structured, modularized, and engaging. The group's members also improved and streamlined the processing of customer data. In addition, they addressed the disconnect and conflicts between sales and logistics that were detrimentally affecting the customers' experience.

"It was great timing for me, because as a new managing director, I came in with all of this enthusiasm and fresh ideas," says Stuart. He recalls that when he first arrived at Straumann—eight months earlier to be the subsidiary's head of sales and marketing—he had naturally asked why certain things were being done in a particular way. The explanation he often received was "This is the way we've always done it," without further discussion. However, he has noticed that since embarking on their own culture change journeys, regional colleagues as well as employees are more receptive to questions and open to exploring more efficient and effective ways of doing things.

As futurist and thought leader Joel Arthur Barker points out, organizations often fail to take advantage of the unique perspectives that new employees bring, which can challenge outdated assumptions as well as foster more innovative thinking.[169] The sharing of unique perspectives is something that Straumann has started to invite and encourage more as a result of its culture change initiatives.

Using Subgroup Data to Measurably Show the Impact of Culture

Another key learning was in one of Straumann's largest plants, where the use of subgroup data helped the plant's leaders to gain insights into the connection between culture and performance, as well as the difference

Making Culture a Strategic Priority 153

between "tools and processes" and cultural norms.

Specifically, when the leaders of this plant analyzed their culture feedback in 2016, they discovered that the Lean Six Sigma management principles that had been implemented throughout Straumann back in 2011 hadn't necessarily changed the culture to be more Constructive. This might have gone unnoticed had it not been for the fact that the internal consultant who was doing their debriefing had the plant's culture results broken out by department and area. Given the opportunity to compare the operating cultures of different areas, the leaders noticed the culture profile of a department responsible for packaging. Specifically, it was significantly more Constructive and less Defensive than the culture profiles for the rest of the plant, as well as the profile for Straumann overall (see Figure 5.3). Furthermore, this department had improved its productivity by 45 percent. What were they doing differently?

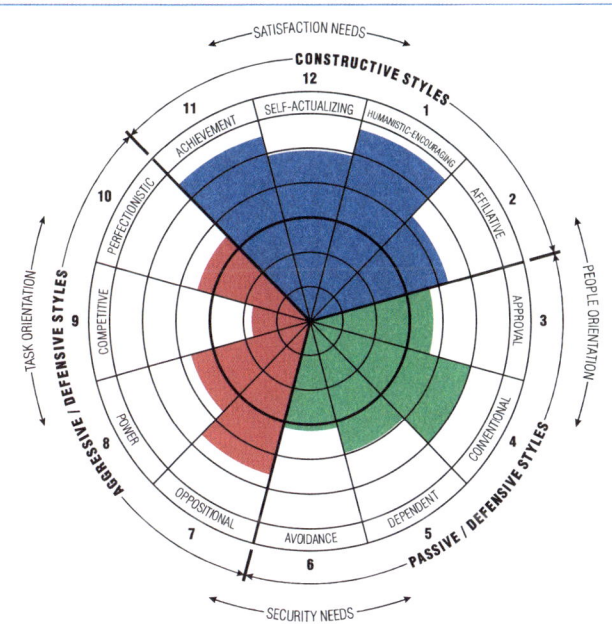

Figure 5.3. Operating Culture of Packaging Group (2016)

Research and development by Robert A. Cooke, Ph.D. and J. Clayton Lafferty, Ph.D.
Copyright © 1987-2019 by Human Synergistics International. All Rights Reserved.

The answer takes us back to 2013, when the department was struggling to solve problems with product mixing in packaging that led to incorrect shipments and, consequently, product returns. They continually tried addressing the issue through retraining, yet the problem kept recurring.

Consequently, the plant's management asked Global Lean Coordinator, Eric Fromentel, to work with the group. As Eric talked with the department manager and staff, he noticed that negativity and blaming were preventing them from identifying what they could do differently to address the issue. Eric worked with them on first learning to listen to themselves when they talked.

Eric, who is a Black Belt in Lean Six Sigma, says it's the mindset that people must develop when using Lean Six Sigma or any other tool that enables them to achieve greater effectiveness. He explains,

> Most people make the mistake of just focusing on the tool. What I've learned is that it's the mindset and the field beyond, where you use multiple things rather than rely only on the tool. I'm a fan of tools but not of using tools for tools' sake. Rather, it's about developing your thinking and maturity.

It's a key point often missed by organizations. According to *Value Stream Mapping* authors Karen Martin and Mike Osterling, topics such as leadership practices, culture, problem solving, and coaching weren't explicitly addressed by the early literature about Lean. As a result, many people today still don't understand "the core beliefs and behaviors" required in the successful implementation of Lean concepts.[170]

However, in the packaging department, the manager and staff *did* eventually develop the necessary core behaviors. Specifically, with coaching from Eric, the group learned to focus their problem-solving conversations on what they wanted to achieve (rather than avoid). They started asking each other questions to stimulate and encourage new ideas and approaches for solving whatever problem they were discussing—similar to the Prescriptive approach described in chapter 2. In doing so, they learned how to work together to more effectively resolve any problem. Not only did the department's quality dramatically improve (as evidenced by its low product return rate), its productivity improved as well. What no one in the plant had realized was that, because the packaging group continued to practice this way of interacting and approaching problems, they had developed a subculture. The group's norms were more Constructive and less Defensive than those which operated in the rest of the plant, as well as within Straumann more generally. Given this example of how developing more Constructive cultural norms substantially improved performance in one of their departments, the plant's leaders were much more eager to initiate a culture change journey in the plant.

Approaching Change with the Old Culture

Of course, not everyone within Straumann was receptive to participating in the organization's culture change journey. Few, if any, change journeys are smooth sailing—which can be a good thing, because its often the bumps along the way that provide the greatest learning.

Such was the case in 2016, when executive committee member Guillaume Daniellot arrived as the new head of Straumann's North American subsidiary keen to hear about the leaders' experiences and progress with the culture journey. The response he received was that it had been set aside because they "had to grow the business first."

"It was very telling as to what was happening," says Guillaume. When he spoke to people throughout the subsidiary about the culture journey, they told him that they didn't believe that the culture could be changed. Specifically, the subsidiary's leaders had turned responsibility for culture over to the location's human resources department. Members of the department obediently proceeded with planning the implementation of the surveys and workshops to be conducted with the directors who worked under the subsidiary's leaders and the middle managers at the next level. The implicit goal was to "check the box" so they could say they had done what they were told to do. Ironically, by approaching change with the mindset of the old culture, the subsidiary had further fueled, rather than reduced, the skepticism and Defensiveness that had been targeted for change.

"It's very difficult to be successful on this journey if you don't see any of the leaders modeling it," says Guillaume. He noted that the subsidiary's leaders were interacting in ways reminiscent of the executive committee members in Switzerland before they began working on their own mindsets and impact on culture (for example, expecting Guillaume to work out the conflicts between members of the leadership team). He decided to delay offering the workshops to the subsidiary's other levels until all members of the leadership team could fully support them. The subsidiary's human resources department said it was important learning for them, because they hadn't recognized how they were "playing out" the old culture in their initial approach.

Guillaume started holding regular meetings with the leadership team on what was and was not working in the organization and, with the help of human resources, did one-on-one coaching with the leaders in terms of their behavior and impact. He also shared stories about his experiences with the journey and its benefits. Nevertheless, after six months, he found he had to replace approximately half of the subsidiary's leadership because, as Guillaume put it, "Even if you don't take a straight path, you need to have everyone with you." It's a key point that we will explore further in the next chapter. Thus, despite the bumpy start, the subsidiary was finally ready to move forward on its culture change journey with its leadership team at the helm.

Early Results

Within two years of initiating the organization's culture change journey, over half of the people throughout Straumann's global organization had completed the *Organizational Culture Inventory* and were initiating culture journeys in their own locations. The results of the company's global perception pulse survey in 2016 indicated that the culture journey was supported by almost 90 percent of employees—and more than 60 percent reported seeing positive changes. According to Marco, people at all levels of the organization were speaking up more, offering more ideas, collaborating with one another, and working cross-functionally to address problems and implement more initiatives and projects related to the future of the company and industry than in the past.

Table 5.1. Straumann's Financial Performance: 2012 to 2016

Year	Net Revenue (in CHF million)	Net Profit (in CHF million)	Year-End Share Price (in CHF)
2012	686	38	112.00
2013	680	101	166.80
2014	710	158	250.75
2015	799	72	305.00
2016	918	230	397.50

Source: Straumann Group, *2016 Annual Report*, 4–7.

Figure 5.4. Straumann's Share Price Development: 2012 to 2016

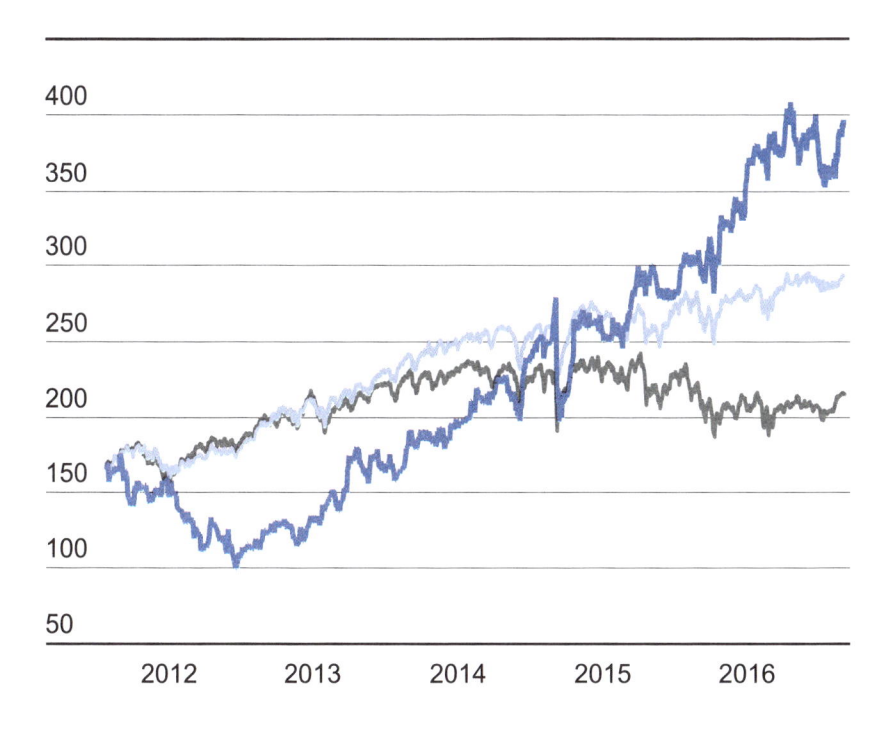

Share Price Development
(in CHF)

[Chart showing share price from 2012 to 2016, with y-axis from 50 to 400]

- Straumann
- Swiss Mid Cap index (SMIM) adjusted
- STOXX® Europe 600 index (in CHF) adjusted

Source: Straumann Group, *2016 Annual Report*, 7.

Concurrently, Straumann's financial performance steadily improved. The strategy of continued global expansion combined with expansion into new markets—including the nonpremium "value" market—paid off in terms of revenues, profits, market share, and, ultimately, share price (see Table 5.1 and Figure 5.4). By the end of 2016, Straumann had captured the third-largest share of the very competitive value market and simultaneously strengthened its dominant position in the premium market through more customer-focused practices and solutions.[171]

The strong upward trend continued to gain momentum in 2017. By end of the third quarter, the company reported 14.8 percent organic revenue growth (up from 13.1 percent in 2016 and 1 percent back in 2013) and double-digit growth in all three business segments (biomaterials, implants, and restoratives), with more than 30 percent of the group's nine-month growth generated by the North American subsidiary.[172] Its share price in 2017 soared to 700 CHF. By that time, all the company's former premium-priced competitors had been absorbed by conglomerates, leaving Straumann as the only "pure play" dental company left in the industry.[173] Said Marco in the early part of 2016,

> As I look at our industry at this point in time, I see that our key competitors focused on costs, integration, and turning their businesses into larger conglomerates. I believe that right now we're the only ones who are really working on culture.

By continuing to focus on a fundamental capability that leaders of other organizations often overlook, Straumann is better able to boldly explore new opportunities while also actively exploiting existing footholds and strengths than before its culture journey began.

Key Learnings

Culture experts point to an organization's past successes as key drivers of its current culture.[174] For Straumann, past organizational successes certainly seemed to be a key factor in shaping and sustaining the shared assumptions and behavioral norms that prevailed. However, even when those assumptions and norms were proving to no longer be valid—and the company experienced market disruption, a financial crisis, location closings, and loss of jobs—the culture still didn't change. Crises may highlight cultural issues, but they don't necessarily lead to culture change. As this case illustrates, Constructive, Passive/Defensive, and Aggressive/Defensive norms affect the way in which everyone inside the organization—including leaders—independently and collectively solves problems and makes decisions. This, in turn, affects the organization's ability to swiftly adapt to changes and be ambidextrous in how it operates. Whereas the popular literature highlights the importance of culture to strategy implementation—which we certainly see in this case—the impact of culture on leaders and the effectiveness of their strategic choices often is not recognized. In this case, it took visionary leadership to look for and crystalize a sustaining solution rather than fixate on restructuring and cost-cutting.

Making Culture a Strategic Priority 159

As in the case in the previous chapter, Straumann adopted a shared language that provided the means by which people in the organization could communicate and provide feedback to one another about thinking, behavior, and cultural norms and expectations. The executive committee members began the change process by addressing their own behavior and impact on culture, including the way in which they interacted with one another when solving problems.

In addition, Straumann made the culture journey a strategic priority and used employee involvement as a lever for change. The implementation of cross-level/cross-functional change champion teams and the community of practice, as well as individual and team development programs, led to other changes, including to systems, structures, technology, and skills/qualities. Implementation of culture change journeys at different locations led to unique learnings, including the value of using subgroup data to show the relationship between Constructive norms and productivity. However, the support of top leadership, along with the other changes made, did not necessarily eliminate the resistance to change by some of the organization's leaders and managers. This can be particularly difficult to detect when leaders and managers work in different geographical locations. When some leaders approach culture change by relying exclusively on indirect levers (such as training for other people) without addressing their own direct impact on people, it can dramatically slow down the process. Indeed, it can halt change completely or take the culture in an even more Defensive direction when the leadership qualities and skills needed to support the desired norms and expectations are not yet in place. This point is demonstrated by the initial experience of one of Straumann's subsidiaries, as well as the culture journeys of other organizations described in this book.

As shown by the next chapter, which concerns a biotechnology company based in Mexico, resistance is an impediment that can affect the implementation of any kind of change. To discover how this small niche player addressed internal resistance in order to stand up to the much larger global players in its market, we turn to the story of Agroenzymas.

Key Learnings

- Encourage Constructive (rather than Aggressive/Defensive or Passive/Defensive) thinking and behavior to attain the ambidexterity needed to simultaneously exploit and defend as well as explore and adapt.

- Make culture change a strategic priority in how leaders and managers carry out their work, solve problems, and achieve the organization's goals.

- Use subgroup breakouts and analyses to better understand the relationship between culture and outcomes within the organization.

Chapter 6

Deploying Levers for Cultural Change to Expedite Strategy Implementation (Mexico)

Without the catalyst of this feedback shaking everyone, the change in attitude would not have happened.

Sergio Acosta, Founder, Agroenzymas

Organization	Agroenzymas
Headquarters	Tlalnepantla de Baz, Edo. de México, México
Industry	Biotechnology: Manufacturer of agricultural fertilizers, biostimulants, and bioregulators
Founded	1990
Market Position	Less than 1 percent globally; higher for specific markets (for example, 85 percent of Chilean kiwi market; 48 percent of Mexican grape market; and 18 percent of Panamanian rice market)
Number of Employees	150+ (2016)
Started Culture Journey	2014
Interviewees	Sergio Acosta, Founder
	Felix Acosta, Business Uncertainty Sailor (CSO)
	Jose Eusebio Lopez, Blue Sector Group (Supporting Consultant)
	Ivette de Jacobis, Espiral Positiva (Supporting Consultant)

Agroenzymas | Turn your dreams into a success story

Left to right: Jose Eusebio Lopez, Felix Acosta, Ivette de Jacobis, and Sergio Acosta

As a visionary and the founder of Agroenzymas, a biotech company specializing in agricultural fertilizers, stimulants, and regulators for Mexican as well as Central and South American farming, Sergio Acosta recognized the need to stay ahead of impending market changes and challenges. His company was a small niche player in a sea of highly competitive biostimulant and bioregulator providers whose formulae, applied to plants and soils, enhances the quantity, quality, and stress resistance of crops. Historically, Latin America had not been a major market for plant stimulant and regulator producers. However, demand for the products had been steadily growing, and South America was now among the fastest growing markets[175]—creating both an opportunity and a challenge for Agroenzymas. Sergio knew that his company would need to become faster with innovations as well as operate more efficiently to continue to successfully compete, not only with other small local players but also large global competitors who were turning more attention toward Latin America. Sound familiar?

"Agroenzymas is like a little Chihuahua barking at a Doberman," says Sergio's son Felix, describing the challenges they faced competing against large global-market leaders based in India, Italy, the Netherlands, and other countries.

In 2013, both founder and son were championing a new customer-/market-focused business model they had crafted that included, among other things, a flatter organizational structure. You would think that implementing the new model would have been relatively easy, particularly given that, at the time, the company consisted of only 120 people. But that wasn't the case. No matter how hard Sergio and Felix tried to convince managers and employees that this was the direction that the organization needed to take, they couldn't get past the resistance to it. Most vocal were the other senior leaders who worked directly under Sergio. These senior leaders told Sergio and Felix that they couldn't understand why the company needed to change, given that it had been successful for so long—like some of the leadership team at Straumann, before they started examining their personal styles and the company's culture. But the situation faced by Agroenzymas was clearly different. Sergio points out,

> That we were still doing well made it precisely the right time to change. There would be time to recover from mistakes. However, if we waited until we *had* to change to start doing things differently, there would be no room for error, because we'd be so close to the abyss.

The real problem wasn't the company's historical success, nor was it that the leaders were trying to make a change that seemed counter to Mexican culture. Instead, the real problem was the comfort and personal success that people felt within a system they had long since mastered. Over time, the hierarchically run company, organized around functional areas and departments, had led those within it to work as if they were in almost hermetically sealed silos. Sergio described them as "power cells" that operated independently and sometimes directly against the interests of each other. Even though these silos operated in different directions, within the cells Sergio says there was "complete cohesion."

Many leaders and managers in Agroenzymas appeared to be neither concerned with nor interested in the larger organization. Challenges such as achieving greater integration or taking initiative to solve system-wide problems weren't their responsibility—that was Sergio's job. If someone had a broader issue to contend with, the typical approach was to leave it on Sergio's desk for him to deal with while they went back to focusing on their own small part of the business. And those expectations unintentionally were reinforced by Sergio, who would then solve the problem for them.

Unintended Leadership Impact

Sergio and Felix were unaware of their impact on the organization's culture. They didn't recognize how they were inadvertently strengthening the strong orientation toward protecting one's own turf and, at the same time, encouraging people to play it safe with those in higher-level positions in Agroenzymas—behaviors that were getting in the way of the ability to adapt and implement a different strategy.

Stronger organizational norms and expectations for Power-oriented and Dependent behaviors such as these might be expected in countries like Mexico that are relatively high in power distance (where less powerful members of organizations expect and accept differences in power) as compared to countries like the US, Germany, and Switzerland [176]. However, the extent to which these behaviors were expected and rewarded in Agroenzymas went beyond what other leaders in Latin America have described as ideal (see chapter 1). They also exceeded what the leaders of Agroenzymas described as necessary and appropriate for their organization to maximize its productivity and effectiveness over the long term (as will be shown in Figure 6.1).

According to business professors Fernando Bartolomé and André Laurent, most managers are "unaware of the contradictory messages they send and their motives for doing so." In their study of executives from major companies, they found that managers often expect loyalty and obedience as well as honesty and frankness from direct reports—yet fail to recognize the conflict that people would have in meeting both sets of expectations. Similarly, the managers who they studied tended to be unaware of the difficulty that direct reports have with discussing their own problems or weaknesses with someone who has significant influence over their careers.[177]

"I couldn't understand why people didn't get involved, because I had always felt that I had an open-door policy," says Sergio. "I listened, I didn't shout or get angry, and I wasn't authoritative. I thought maybe it was my personality." Consistent with what Sergio had experienced, Bartolomé and Laurent found that open-door policies were rarely effective in minimizing differences in positional power—differences that leaders in higher-level positions often unintentionally reinforce through their own behavior. Elaborating on this, Sergio says,

> I wanted people to be self-sufficient and make decisions rather than think that if I didn't say it, that it didn't have to be done. But then it got to the point where the key was for them to say to other people that they had already discussed it with me. And, oddly enough, many of those things weren't even discussed with me. So I had to start saying, "If you are told that I have authorized something, ask them to show you that in writing. If they don't have my signature, then it means we haven't discussed it."

As Sergio tried to break the Defensive, Power-oriented dynamic of people manipulating situations to their advantage, he inadvertently reinforced their dependence on him, together with the belief that "it doesn't need to be done unless Sergio says so."

Similarly, Sergio's son Felix was also unaware of his own impact on people and culture. He had come to the company's headquarters in 2013 to help craft and implement the company's new business model following his success in managing its Chilean and international operations. He describes what happened after he arrived:

> My perception when I got to Headquarters was that everyone was lying in a hammock. There was no real commitment to try new things because everyone was too protective of what they had been doing. People kept asking, "Why change?" and saying that they didn't understand what the new strategy meant. But instead of trying to understand their views and taking note of what they were feeling, I came in with an attitude of "I know how to do this because I've achieved it and you haven't." I pointed out what was wrong with the way they had done things to show them that, at least according to my thinking, this was the correct process that we needed to follow.

Felix's assumptions about the other managers and employees were consistent with what renowned author and management professor Douglas McGregor called a *Theory X* mentality. According to McGregor, managers who operate under this mentality assume that people are inherently lazy and therefore "must be coerced, controlled, directed, threatened with punishment to get them to put forth adequate effort toward the achievement of organizational objectives."[178]

Felix's attempt to prod the other leaders into action by criticizing them and pointing to his own expertise and past success didn't sway them. Instead, they became even more resistant and dependent on Sergio, putting greater pressure on him. Felix recalls,

> If we were discussing the new business model in a meeting, and Sergio was there, everyone would keep quiet and then individually catch up with him afterwards to say, "Hey, regarding what we were discussing during the meeting—here is my point of view."

Felix had unknowingly created a self-fulfilling prophecy. He expected that the other leaders would be resistant and unwilling to change. As a result, he approached the situation in a way that made it even more likely they would react as he expected. Research shows that this self-fulfilling prophecy—referred to as the *Pygmalion Effect* (named for the play *Pygmalion* by George Bernard Shaw)—can raise other people's performance when we expect that they will perform well and hurt their performance when we expect that they will perform poorly.[179] This is because how we think affects how we behave...and lead.

It isn't only verbal communications that bring self-fulfilling prophecies to fruition. According to former Harvard professor J. Sterling Livingston, "Managers often communicate most when they believe they are communicating the least." For example, when they are "cold and uncommunicative," direct reports often interpret it as a sign that their boss is "displeased" or feels that they're "hopeless."[180] Regardless of whether low expectations are communicated verbally or nonverbally, the result is lower performance. Consequently, it is not surprising that Felix's expectations about the other leaders at Agroenzymas influenced how he treated them—and that they reacted as he expected.

Although Sergio and Felix's intentions to keep the company ahead of the market were commendable, parts of their approach were incompatible with—and inadvertently worked against—the changes they wanted to make. Having a long-term focus and vision are important, but they alone do not create a culture that supports collaboratively working together to implement new strategies and adapt to change. "Because the company was doing well, the rest of the organization did not take the need for transformation seriously until the two top leaders started to align their own behavior and leadership with the culture needed to effectively implement the new strategy," says consultant Jose Eusebio Lopez. He and consultant Ivette de Jacobis worked with the leaders on changing their organization's culture and impact. In addition to making personal changes, Sergio and Felix changed the criteria for selection, placement, and promotion; made culture part of everyone's performance goals; and launched an organizational development function to monitor the culture and to support people in developing the skills and qualities that were supportive of the cultural norms and beliefs they wanted to strengthen.

Consequently, Agroenzymas was able to move forward with implementing the new business model and, most importantly, a more efficient and effective way of operating. People who had previously worked in opposition to one another—blaming each other for problems, protecting their self-interests, and relying on Sergio to settle their differences—began working together in a more integrated and self-sufficient way. The changes resulted in faster business improvements, more product innovations, and better financial performance.

As you read about how Sergio and Felix accomplished their goals, keep in mind that this case isn't just about Agroenzymas. There is a broader message: how top leaders carry out their roles on a day-to-day basis—including how they resolve disagreements, influence others, and reward certain behaviors—profoundly impacts what other people believe is required of them to be successful. This, consequently, affects their willingness to coordinate and collaborate on solving problems, implementing new strategies, and achieving goals.

Changing What It Means to Be Successful

In describing companies that transformed their performance from good to great, author Jim Collins points out that the first thing they did was make sure they had the right people on the bus and then got the wrong people off. According to Collins, identifying the right people has more to do with their character and innate capabilities than their knowledge, background, or skills.[181]

At Agroenzymas, making sure they had the right people on board began with Sergio, Felix, and the other six senior leaders each independently completing the *Organizational Culture Inventory—Ideal* by describing the behaviors necessary to maximize their organization's performance and long-term effectiveness. Their averaged responses, shown on the left side of Figure 6.1, indicated that they believed that Constructive (blue) behaviors were what people in Agroenzymas should exemplify.

Figure 6.1. Agroenzymas' Ideal and Operating Culture Profiles (2014)

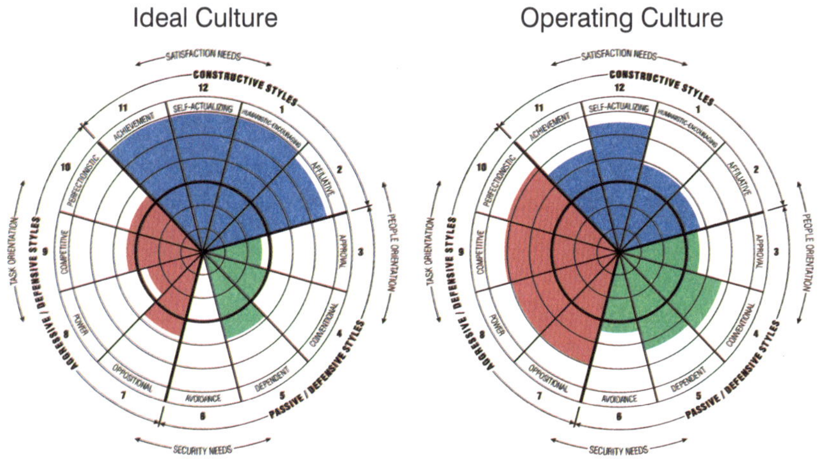

Research and development by Robert A. Cooke, Ph.D. and J. Clayton Lafferty, Ph.D. Copyright © 1987-2019 by Human Synergistics International. All Rights Reserved.

In addition, members throughout the organization were asked to complete the *Organizational Culture Inventory* by describing what was actually expected or required to fit in at Agroenzymas. Their responses (shown in the profile on the right side of Figure 6.1) confirmed much of what Sergio and Felix had experienced and observed. On the positive side, people within Argoenzymas believed that Constructive behaviors such as Self-Actualizing and Achievement were expected, particularly in terms of performing simple tasks well and enjoying their work. However, even stronger were the expectations for Aggressive/Defensive (red) behaviors in terms of working in silos, blaming, competing with one another, and narrowly focusing on their own areas rather than the company as a whole. Shared expectations for Passive/Defensive behaviors—particularly in terms of Conventional and Dependent styles—were also evident and reflected the belief that people should do only what Sergio or an immediate superior said to do.

According to consultant Ivette de Jacobis, none of the leaders seemed startled by the company's culture profiles. They were, however, taken aback by feedback about their *own* thinking styles (based on the *Life Styles Inventory Self Description*), which differed from the predominantly Constructive (blue) culture that they had identified as ideal. Sergio recounts,

> When they realized that they were red and we were advocating a culture that was preferably blue, there were people—some of whom had been with us for over ten years—who said, "I don't fit in here. I will leave." Even though I asked them to reconsider and pointed out that everything is not blue and at times we'll need your color, they still said no and left. Without the catalyst of this feedback shaking everyone, the change in attitude would not have happened.

The difference between transformative and incremental organizational changes is that the former require new ways of thinking and behaving, particularly by those in leadership roles, according to University of Michigan's Ross School of Business Professor Robert E. Quinn.[182] An ideal culture communicates to people the "right" attitude and approach for the company to be successful in the long term. The feedback that Agroenzymas' top leaders received about their own thinking and behavior made it apparent that they too would have to change to move the company toward that ideal. With the required changes specifically defined, people were explicitly given a choice as to whether they were willing to change. This was the first step in making it clear that moving toward that ideal was also a criterion for personal success. The leaders didn't have to be perfect; they did, however, need to be willing to improve.

Consistent with a major theme of this book, transformative changes within Agroenzymas began with Felix and Sergio, both in being prepared to change their own thinking and behavior and allowing people to leave who didn't want to change. Letting people go was tough for Sergio. This was at least partly because of the Mexican culture, which reveres close long-term commitments to members of "the group," be they immediate family, extended family, or long-standing relations like those at work.[183] However, doing what is comfortable is not always the same thing as doing what is effective and necessary. This is important to underscore, because people often unknowingly justify ineffective behaviors and decisions because it's the norm or "the way things are done around here" in the company, industry, or country in which they work or live. Sergio and Felix weren't focused on creating a culture for comfort. Rather, they were committed to creating a culture that would sustain the organization and those who chose to stay with it over the long term.

Aligning Bases of Power and Influence with the Right Attitude

Felix recognized how important it was to set a personal example. He disciplined himself to show others, rather than just tell them, what the new behaviors looked like. Instead of dwelling on or pressing his own position when others said no to his suggestions, Felix started taking the time to gain a better understanding of the opposing perspective. He became more curious, asked more questions about other people's views, listened to their answers, acknowledged what they had legitimately accomplished, and waited until they appeared to be ready to listen before explaining his point of view. Over time, he began to earn more respect.

He took on the role of mediator in meetings—something he says he never would have imagined—and started leading a team created to monitor the culture and help keep everyone on track. Says consultant Ivette,

> When he started to change, everyone around him also started to change. It created credibility for the changes that they wanted to make organizationally. We now see more management through asking questions than through giving orders.

Adds Sergio,

> Previously, Felix would have arrived from the airport and started to make changes to the organization. I used to say to him, "You have to learn to adjust, go down a notch, and try to understand people." I think the main achievement for him was understanding that the first person who had to change was him to promote a change in others. He is now much more empathetic.

According to the classic research of social psychologists John R. P. French and Bertram Raven,[184] there are five bases, or sources, of power that individuals typically rely on to influence the behavior, attitudes, or beliefs of others: legitimate, reward, coercive, referent, and expert. Instead of relying on his legitimate power (as the owner's son) and criticism (a form of coercive power), and reminding others of the expertise he had acquired, Felix started dealing with people from a position of understanding and appreciation. By exemplifying the ways in which he wanted other people to behave, Felix began to earn their respect and admiration, which helped to build his referent power and influence as a role model. This, in combination with his knowledge and expertise, increased Felix's influence and his effectiveness as a leader. Research shows that the combination of referent and expert power often produces the best results in terms of job performance, satisfaction, and turnover.[185] And—unlike legitimate, reward, and coercive bases of power—these more personal bases are associated with a more Constructive and less Defensive impact on people and on cultural norms.[186]

By challenging his own assumptions about people and taking the lead to change his behavior, Felix inspired others to change their behavior. That said, he points out that other people haven't forgotten how he used to react, and they don't hesitate to remind him of that when he begins to raise his voice or behave as he did in the past. "If I've been behaving like that for ten years, I can't expect to change everyone's perception of me in one year," says Felix, adding, "I am prepared to be tenacious and consistent with what I am doing for the next ten years so that people will see this is not just about keeping up appearances."

Promoting the Right Attitude in Conflicts

In addition to standing by the vision of Agroenzymas' ideal culture when long-time associates chose not to modify their behavior, one of the most important personal changes that Sergio made was to address conflict resolution and the "hub and spokes" communication network that had evolved, with him at the center. Although this dynamic is similar to that described in earlier chapters, the way Sergio redirected it in a more Constructive direction was unique. This speaks to how important it is to go with a solution that fits your personality rather than a generic solution that doesn't make sense for you or your group.[187] Felix explains,

> People were very used to coming to Sergio and leaving an issue on his desk. Now, when there is disagreement around a topic or issue, he creates mini-teams—sometimes with two people, sometimes with four—who have opposing ways of thinking. That has rendered much better outcomes, as we don't have to go back and review with Sergio the decisions and solutions that have been agreed on.

Deborah Schroeder-Saulnier, author of *The Power of Paradox*, contends that viewing conflicts as opportunities for conversation and collaboration can lead to better solutions and greater accomplishments. It also results in better relationships. The literature and research on integrative or *win-win* approaches around conflict management and negotiations, as well as that on synergistic problem solving, support this claim.[188] Sergio empowered people to resolve conflicts in small teams composed of members with different views. This moved responsibility and authority where it needed to be, creating the opportunity to work out more effective and mutually acceptable solutions. As a result, what previously took them five or six meetings to accomplish, was now accomplished in just one.

Emphasizing Attitude in HR Decisions

As Agroenzymas' leaders and managers started to change their attitudes and behavior, Sergio says they found it easier to solve problems and implement decisions. There was less "haggling" inside and outside of meetings between peers, direct reports, and leaders. Conflicts were settled by those who were directly involved in them and decisions were made by those responsible for carrying them out. There was also greater acceptance of solutions throughout the entire company, because they reflected more integrated and less one-sided views.

Research shows that most organizations continue to emphasize task-based skills, experience, and past performance when making decisions about hiring and promoting people into management positions.[189] Yet, agility, teamwork, and ambition are also necessary to effectively solve problems and adapt to the unforeseen events that inevitably occur (including in strategy execution). These remain prerequisite areas in which many executive teams still fall short, because the associated behaviors are rarely rewarded.[190]

In this regard, Agroenzymas was no different than any other company. However, having defined the right attitude in their ideal culture and having experienced what they had on their culture journey, the leaders developed a clearer idea of who they wanted to bring into the organization and promote. They now considered attitudes and behaviors when making their decisions. This helped to further break down assumptions regarding entitlement and to reinforce the importance of the Constructive behaviors that the leaders wanted embedded in the culture. Sergio reflects,

> You can acquire and learn skills by yourself. Experience you can get over time. But we have seen that behavior is very difficult to change when you don't have a positive attitude. …People who have been with the company for many years and took part in different processes are now seeing that when someone is not selected or promoted, it is because of their attitude. Those signals have helped people to realize that this is for real.

According to a 2015 survey of human resources practitioners by Human Capital Media Advisory Group, only a minority of organizations consciously hire for cultural fit.[191] However, we have found that the bigger problem for many organizations is that they *do* hire and promote for culture—specifically, they hire for the culture that is already operating in their organizations on a day-to-day basis. As Agroenzymas has experienced, hiring, promoting, and rewarding people based on the Constructive culture they want (as opposed to the more Defensive, task-oriented culture they had) is more effective. Sergio explains,

Impact on culture is linked to everyone's performance evaluations. In every commitment we make, we constantly confirm that we not only want to achieve good financial results, we also want to achieve them through the right kinds of behaviors. We don't want to leave a pile of corpses. We want to achieve the goal by building a pyramid of support that enables all of us to reach it.

Early Signs of Change and Tangible Business Outcomes

As leaders specified their ideal culture and reinforced it with changes to their own behavior, the attitudes and behavior of those who remained at Agroenzymas began to shift, and resistance to Sergio and Felix's proposed business model receded. Consequently, the company was able to retire their product-focused business model and implement the new customer-focused strategy. People now began to resolve issues directly with one another and take the initiative to do what needed to be done, rather than waiting for Sergio to ask them to take action.

Of course, it's relatively easy to behave in Constructive ways when things are going well. The challenge is maintaining the culture during difficult times. In the first two quarters of 2015—less than a year into their culture journey—Agroenzymas did not make a profit. The company had a bonus system through which employees would receive an extra 5.4 months of salary when key indicators such as profit goals were achieved. Traditionally, when the company missed its goals, members would complain that it wasn't their fault and blame other people and other departments. However, that didn't happen this time. Instead, everyone in the company started having conversations about what needed to be done to turn the situation around, and many people voluntarily took on additional responsibilities.

A remeasure of the culture later in 2015 confirmed that the norms were shifting and that people believed that thinking and acting more in terms of the whole organization (rather than only their own departments) was necessary to fit in and meet expectations (see Figure 6.2). By the end of the year, the production line staff had submitted twenty-five innovations and continuous improvement projects and had already begun implementing fifteen of them. The company's profits, which they do not publicize, nearly doubled. "We were able to pay a performance bonus," says Sergio. "For

Launching and Relaunching Change 175

people who earn 100,000 pesos a month ($5,960 USD), we are talking half a million pesos ($29,800 USD), which is significant."

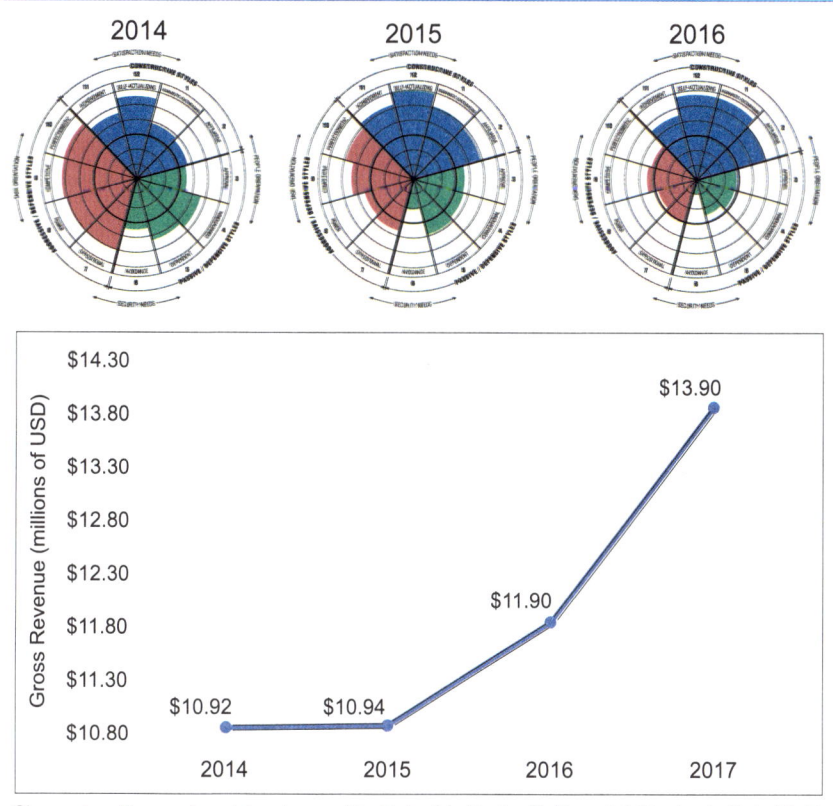

Figure 6.2. Agroenzymas' Operating Culture and Gross Revenue Over Time

Circumplex: Research and development by Robert A. Cooke Ph.D. and J. Clayton Lafferty, Ph.D. Copyright © 1987-2019 by Human Synergistics International. All Rights Reserved.

Financial performance: Mordor Intelligence.

In 2016, the company's culture and financial performance continued to improve (see Figure 6.2). Felix explains the underlying factors:

> After fourteen years without launching new products, we now have several in the market. We are focused more on improving the quality and quantity of crops while making a profit rather than making the most profit possible. An example is the market development of crops such as pineapple, rice, wheat, soybean, and coffee—which are not very lucrative from an income point of view. But by researching with the grower, we could prove

that these kinds of technological tools can also be applied to medium-low technology (income) crops. The correct use of these technological tools has helped growers make their crops more profitable and sustainable.

In 2017, Agroenzymas started working with biological synthesis to provide the market with new tools that have no environmental impact and reduce costs. Their revenues for the first half of the year were the highest they had ever been and grew to $13.9 million for the year overall. By that time, they controlled 85 percent of the Chilean kiwi market (their greatest achievement), 18 percent of the Panamanian rice market, 32 percent of the Mexican tomato market, and 48 percent of the Mexican grape market.

For a company that struggled with change and implementation of a new strategy, the adjustments they made and the results they achieved in such a short amount of time are significant. For Sergio, the investment in culture is an investment in the company's future. He explains,

> You have to invest during the first years to reap a harvest later. The length of time that you must wait depends on the type of crop. If you plant garlic, the wait is only twenty-one days. But, because you don't know what will happen after that, you must start again. If you plant grapes, you need to wait four years. For citrus crops, the wait is six years. However, if you plant a walnut tree, even though you must wait ten years until the first harvest, you know you will be able to harvest for one hundred years more. Similarly, while culture might take years to grow, we will harvest from it for many years that follow.

For Agroenzymas, it's an investment that has already begun to bear fruit.

Key Learnings

As we have seen with Agroenzymas, leaders can unknowingly fall into the trap of trying to implement strategic changes to stay ahead when much more fundamental changes to culture are prerequisite. Particularly when organizations are facing unfamiliar situations, members need to be able to communicate openly, discuss their differences constructively, and integrate their opinions and perspectives effectively to come up with high-quality solutions that people support.

Even though private or family ownership may make some of the factors that promote Defensive norms (such as emphasis on the short term) less likely, there are other factors that private ownership does not necessarily prevent (such as centralization and concentration of authority). As Sergio discovered, you might not even be intending to centralize decision making and authority—which is why feedback on your thinking and behavior as compared to what you want to strengthen in your organization's culture can be such a valuable leadership tool.

Although most leaders recognize the value of engaging in and encouraging Constructive behaviors—which they consistently describe as ideal—many inadvertently encourage and reinforce more Defensive and less Constructive cultures. They do so in the way they carry out their roles and in the decisions they make, including who to hire, promote, and reward. In their article, "Why Strategy Execution Unravels—and What to Do about It," authors Donald Sull, Rebecca Homkes, and Charles Sull point out,

> Past performance is two to three times more likely than a track record of collaboration to be rewarded. Performance is critical, of course, but if it comes at the expense of coordination, it can undermine execution.[192]

Regardless of the type of strategy companies pursue, Constructive cultures enable them to do a better job of implementing their strategies and, in turn, to achieve better performance. And this is true regardless of whether we are talking about a biotech company in Mexico trying to implement a new strategy or, as we will focus on in the next chapter, a bakery in Eastern Europe trying to sustain a strategy that was implemented some time ago. Let's move on now to Serbia, where the owner and the general manager of a local bakery found themselves struggling to keep up with solving problems, adapting to changes, and taking advantage of opportunities as their business continued to expand.

Key Learnings

- Leaders gain acceptance for strategic changes through aligning their own thinking and behavior—including how they influence others and resolve conflicts—with the Constructive culture that they collectively agree is ideal.

- Redesign HR systems—including the criteria for rewards, hiring, and performance—so that they emphasize and reinforce the behaviors and attitudes needed to achieve organizational effectiveness rather than just personal success.

Chapter 7

Trading Command and Control for Expansion and Growth (Serbia)

> There was disbelief when we first did the assessments (and saw the *Organizational Culture Inventory—Ideal* profile). They [the managers] said, "That sounds great on paper, but it's not possible in Serbia."
>
> Goran Zelenović, General Manager, Pons Bakery

Organization	PONS Bakery
Location	Čačak, Serbia
Industry	Bakery
Founded	1991
Market Position	First in regional market (Moravički district)
Number of Employees	300+
Started Culture Journey	2014
Interviewees	Ivan Matijević, Owner
	Goran Zelenović, General Manager
	Ivan Dmitrić, Human Synergistics Serbia (Supporting Consultant)

The first Le Pons opened in 2015

A story about a bakery in Serbia might be unexpected in a book like this one. But the challenges that this organization struggled with are universal, not least of which was the need to break away from command-and-control leadership in order to take advantage of opportunities to expand and grow.

What owner Ivan Matijević wanted to build was "a stable and sustainable future Pons—a well-defined organization, regardless of size," a business sufficiently geared up to "play in a completely different league." He recognized that "three years from now the bakery business would not be the same" in Serbia due to the changing needs of customers; the arrival of new, powerful, and disruptive competitors like hypermarkets; and new technologies in the baking industry. Therefore, there was no better time for his organization to create a strong foundation on which to grow.

According to Euromonitor International, the baked good market in Serbia—which includes frozen variants and packaged breads and pastries—represented a growth market at the time Pons was beginning its culture journey.[193] This was due to a market trend toward packaged foods that offer a longer shelf life and easy storage. The baked goods market in Serbia is highly competitive, with numerous local, regional, and national players. For instance, as of 2015, the market leader, Beogradska, was reported to hold just 6 percent of the market share. Despite the potential for growth offered by the market and Pons's achievements up to that point, the company's future success was anything but assured—until Pons's leaders began looking at culture and its impact on the way a company thrives.

Early Days

Back in 1991, when Pons Bakery was founded in Čačak (in west-central Serbia) by Ivan's father, Dobrivoje Matijević, the country was in the grip of runaway hyperinflation. In the midst of this turbulence, Dobrivoje hoped to create an additional source of income for his family. While this seemed like a simple undertaking, the reality turned out to be quite different. What they thought would be a part-time occupation for family members ended up meaning a twelve- or thirteen-hour daily commitment. Shortly thereafter, following time served in the obligatory Serbian army, twenty-year-old Ivan took over full responsibility for the bakery business. In 1996, backed by steady business growth and a more stable economy, Ivan built bigger facilities for Pons.

Things were looking up, at least for a while. As the number of employees increased, Ivan—at heart an entrepreneur and strategist rather than an operations-oriented type—recognized he could no longer handle a business of this size on his own. He had long wanted to introduce changes to the way the business was run but lacked the internal support and capability needed from managers and employees to implement his ideas. That was when he brought in Goran Zelenović, who had experience and success in running small businesses.

Working together, the two men diversified the market focus of the bakery so that it not only handled retail sales in its bakery shops but also supplied baked goods to other businesses, such as supermarkets, hotels, and restaurants. Their resulting business-to-business (B2B) sales service, launched in 2007, was innovative in that Pons was the first bakery in Serbia to sell its products using this model. However, even as the company grew and prospered, some major problems began to surface.

Ivan Matijević   Goran Zelenović

Command and Control

Serbia is a country whose history—at least since the end of World War II—has been marked by utilitarian practices "copied from Stalin's model" in the USSR, followed by "years of despotic and erratic rule" and extreme centralization in the form of state and municipal control.[194] Therefore, it should come as no surprise that the concepts of individual freedom, entrepreneurism, and innovation have only relatively recently become national imperatives. As with any form of culture, what occurs at the top trickles all the way down to behaviors exhibited in everyday life. Not surprisingly, given this political backdrop, people in Serbia were accustomed to being explicitly or implicitly told what to do and how to behave.

The prevailing expectation for a long period of time in Serbian organizations, including at Pons, was that senior management would operate on a "command and control" basis. However, by 2014, Ivan and Goran recognized the need to make a significant course correction in the company's culture. By this point, the day-to-day inefficiencies and stress of the old outdated approach were nearing disaster levels. As Goran reports,

> The associates who worked with me and performed a significant part of the work failed to take any initiative or responsibility. Every decision that was not common practice had to be made on the "Let me check with Goran" principle. I had to confirm their ideas if they had one and then decide whether or not to back them. Decisions were not made within the team. I made them and gave instructions for their implementation. Even though we achieved tremendous results, I was under enormous pressure. I was falling apart.

Certainly, Goran acted as a successful manager in terms of monitoring every piece of information that came across his desk and holding everything in his head. However, the effect on him as a senior leader was near-permanent exhaustion. This vital leader was not only at risk of burning out but was continually swamped by minor operational decisions in areas like production, sales, and procurement. Thus, his value as a senior leader and strategist was sorely diluted.[195]

This is an instantly recognizable scenario for any top leader tasked with rolling out new initiatives for which the underlying support structure—let alone the right cultural expectations—is not in place. The company would not be able to continue scaling up without effecting significant change in the opportunities for, as well as the willingness and ability of, middle management to embrace greater responsibility and decision making.

To be clear, this was not a situation in which the company was failing; instead, it was quite the opposite. Pons was innovative in the marketplace, but that was only because of Ivan and Goran's initiatives. They were doing reasonably well along certain criteria despite their culture, not because of it. And as we know from previous chapters, these kinds of outcomes can feed the belief that maintaining tight control must be the key to success. It wasn't until the burden on Ivan and Goran became so overwhelming that they recognized the need for things to change. Even then, it wasn't because they perceived a problem with their organization's culture. In fact, Ivan and Goran thought the reason that people weren't taking initiative and contributing new ideas was because they needed training. How often do we see leaders view training as the solution to a much bigger issue? Our affiliate in Serbia, Ivan Dmitrić, explains,

> Pons initially contacted us for assistance in training solutions to improve their sales force and basically asked if we could run field sales workshops for them. We told them that we weren't in the training business and that we could help them with other issues like behaviors, culture, and leadership. They said, "That's an even better idea!"
>
> At the time, ...they had four key managers—the heads of production, retail, wholesale, and logistics supply chain—all of whom were very dependent on them. Ivan and Goran

Sixty vans supply fresh products to more than 1,500 shops and bakeries daily wanted to change the culture in a way that people could take ownership and responsibility of their own parts of the business so that they could focus on strategy, investments, and growing the overall business. They were interested in understanding what the expected behaviors were at the various levels of the organization and the effects that they were having on others so that they could start the whole process of organizational change.

After a couple of meetings with our affiliate, the leaders decided to measure the organization's culture and the various factors related to it by using the *Organizational Culture Inventory* and the *Organizational Effectiveness Inventory*. They also initiated a leadership and team development program using *Management/Impact* and the *Group Styles Inventory*. Additionally, they asked our affiliate to assist them in some other people-related organizational changes they wanted to make. Based on the survey feedback, Pons's leaders, Ivan and Goran, saw that shifting responsibility upward was a widely held belief driven in part by decisions they had made. Such decisions included those having to do with structures, systems, technology, and skills/qualities.

The Influence of Societal Culture

For leaders to take the stern of their organization's culture firmly in hand and redirect its course is courageous in any country. It's even more daring when leaders are taking their company's culture in a direction that is not only different for their organization but also for their country. As confirmed by the research of Dr. Geert Hofstede, Serbia is relatively high in power distance, in uncertainty avoidance, and in collectivism compared to many other countries, particularly those in the Anglo and Germanic clusters (such as the US, Canada, Australia, Germany, and Switzerland).[196]

Organizational leaders in countries higher in power distance, uncertainty avoidance, and collectivism tend to place higher value on the Defensive styles (as demonstrated by the ideal profiles presented in Figure 1.8 and the correlations in Table 1.1). This certainly seemed to be the case not only with Pons but with Serbian organizations more generally, based on a study conducted by our Serbian affiliate on a sample of local organizations (most of which were randomly selected). Specifically, the results of that study showed that Serbian organizational leaders tended to place greater value on Defensive styles (particularly Perfectionistic and Competitive) than did the organizational leaders in many of the other countries we've studied. Furthermore, this translated into more Defensive (both aggressive and passive) and less Constructive operating cultures overall (see Serbian composite profiles at the top of Figure 7.1).

Figure 7.1. Serbian Organizational Culture Research Results and Pons Culture Results

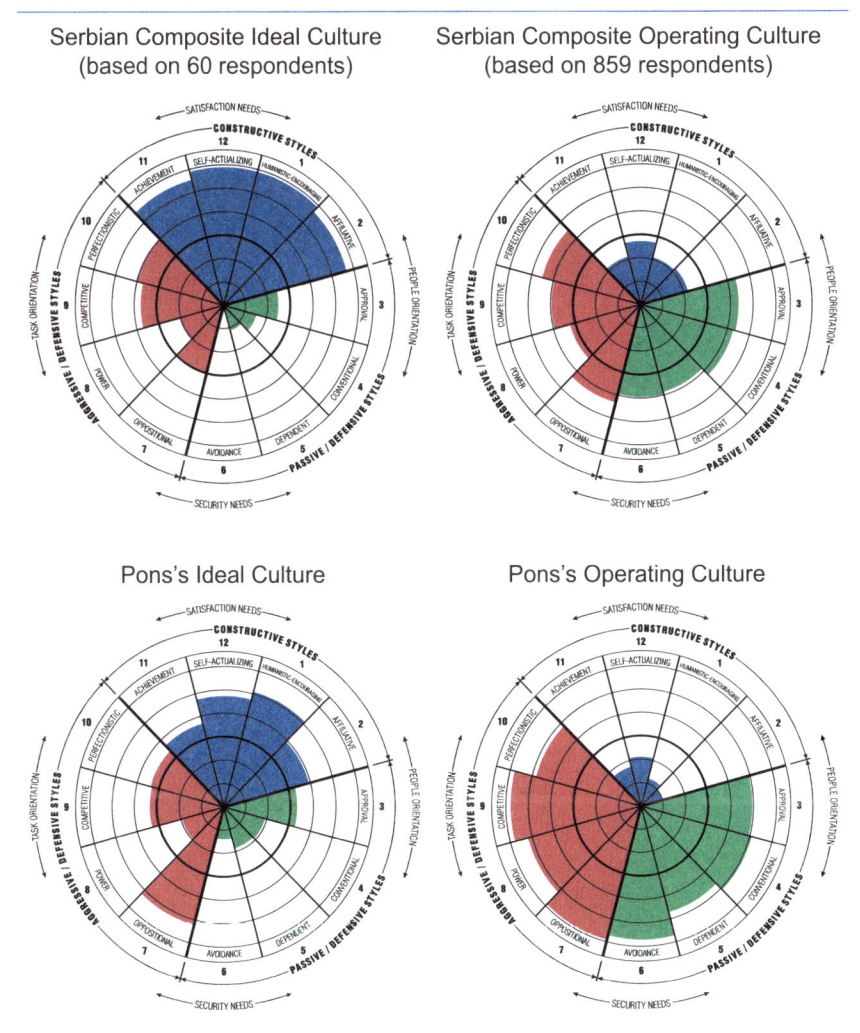

Serbian Composite Ideal Culture
(based on 60 respondents)

Serbian Composite Operating Culture
(based on 859 respondents)

Pons's Ideal Culture

Pons's Operating Culture

Research and development by Robert A. Cooke, Ph.D. and J. Clayton Lafferty, Ph.D.
Copyright © 1987-2019 by Human Synergistics International. All Rights Reserved.

Despite the value placed on certain Aggressive/Defensive styles, the ideal culture profiles of organizational leaders in Serbia indicated that they generally value Constructive styles even more. This is important, given that Defensive beliefs and values detract from leadership and organizational effectiveness, as well as world competitiveness and respect for human rights across countries.[197]

Consistent with other organizational leaders in their country, Pons's leaders placed relatively great value on Perfectionistic and Competitive styles as compared to leaders in many other countries (particularly Anglo, Germanic, Nordic, and Latin European countries). In addition, they placed greater value on Oppositional styles than most other leaders—including those in their own country (see Figure 7.1, bottom left versus top left profiles). The operating culture described by Pons employees bears some similarity to the operating cultures of other organizations in Serbia. This was the case in terms of the patterns of styles most and least extended both in the overall profile and within each of the three clusters (see Figure 7.1, bottom right versus top right profiles). In addition, the relatively high value placed on Oppositional thinking and behavior within Pons translated into even more extreme shared expectations for all the Defensive styles in the bakery's operating culture, including the passive behaviors that Ivan and Goran specifically wanted to address.

The profiles for Pons confirmed that the company's cultural norms were far more Defensive and less Constructive than their leaders viewed as ideal. Rather than continuing to practice the highly centralized form of leadership and management widely accepted and expected in Serbia, Ivan and Goran reset their course using a more empowering approach in order to create a culture in which people take more initiative to solve problems and achieve goals. This was not only novel for their bakery but for organizations in Serbia in general. Goran recalls,

> The managers were shocked by what they heard when we started to work on our company culture in 2014. There was disbelief when we first did the assessments (and saw the *Organizational Culture Inventory—Ideal* profile). They said, "That sounds great on paper, but it's not possible in Serbia."
>
> However, when they saw that we were serious about it and that this process was fully accepted by me and Ivan as the owner, they realized they had to start behaving differently too.

Levers for Change

There were many things that the leaders could have focused on to change their company's culture. Pons's *Organizational Effectiveness Inventory* results indicated that several different causal factors fell below the historical averages (see Figure 7.2). However, the factors that most stood out to the leaders were the centralized decision-making structure; lack of emphasis on goals and participation in goal setting; use of punishment; and their own leadership/management skills and qualities.

Figure 7.2. Pons's 2014 Results for Causal Factors

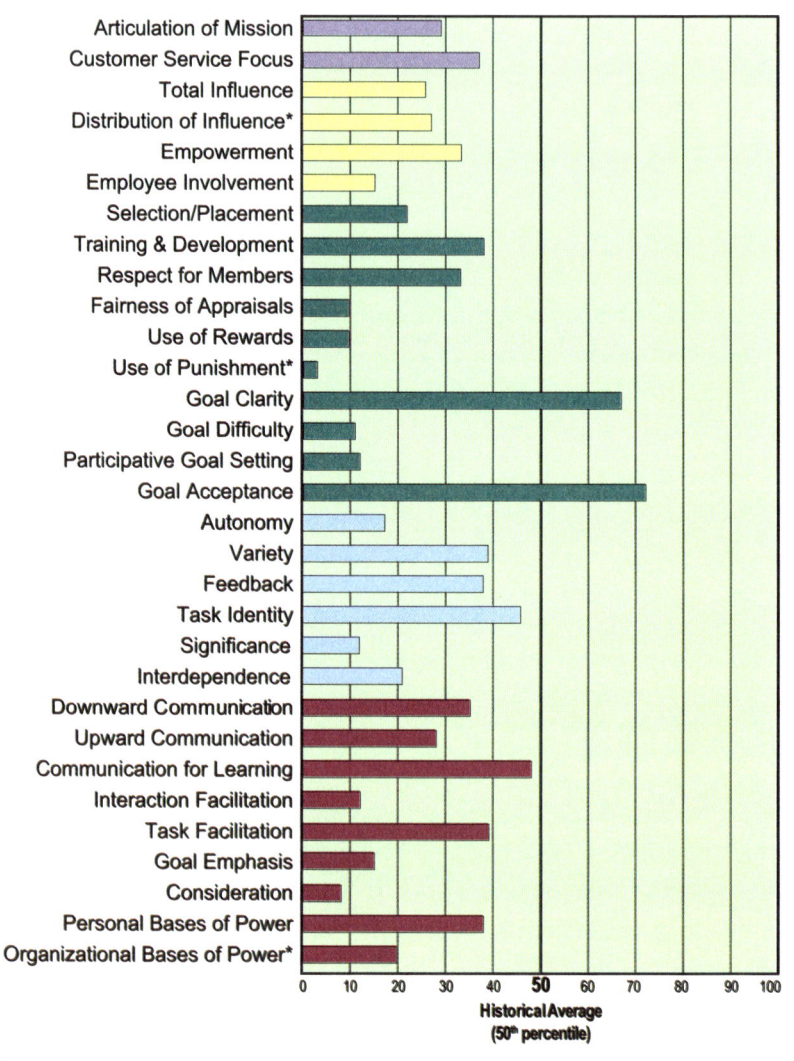

Causal Factor	Percentile
Articulation of Mission	~30
Customer Service Focus	~37
Total Influence	~25
Distribution of Influence*	~27
Empowerment	~33
Employee Involvement	~15
Selection/Placement	~22
Training & Development	~38
Respect for Members	~33
Fairness of Appraisals	~10
Use of Rewards	~10
Use of Punishment*	~3
Goal Clarity	~67
Goal Difficulty	~11
Participative Goal Setting	~13
Goal Acceptance	~73
Autonomy	~17
Variety	~38
Feedback	~37
Task Identity	~45
Significance	~12
Interdependence	~20
Downward Communication	~33
Upward Communication	~28
Communication for Learning	~47
Interaction Facilitation	~12
Task Facilitation	~38
Goal Emphasis	~15
Consideration	~8
Personal Bases of Power	~38
Organizational Bases of Power*	~20

Historical Average (50th percentile)

* In the barchart shown above, the scores for distribution of influence, use of punishment, and organizational bases of power were reversed so that higher percentile scores signify more desirable results.

From *OCI/OEI Feedback Report*.
Copyright © 2016, 2003 by Human Synergistics International.

While it would have been easy for Ivan and Goran to simply change the structure of the company and implement a new goal-setting system, these changes alone would have had little, if any, impact on the culture if the leaders continued to follow a command-and-control approach. Indeed, it was because the leaders themselves first changed that others in the organization believed that the leaders were serious about people becoming less dependent and more proactive in solving problems and achieving the organization's goals.

Goran and the other members of Pons's top team (which included the directors of production, sales, retail, logistics, and finance) participated in a development program that included *Management/Impact*. This provided them with feedback about their impact on people and culture, as well as the factors leading to that impact—specifically, the ways in which they approached their day-to-day responsibilities and interactions.

In addition, the group went through a team-building process that included the *Group Styles Inventory*. This allowed the top team members to assess the behaviors exhibited within the team as they worked on a specific problem. In turn, the team's members were able to map the Circumplex styles exhibited by their group to the styles in their personal impact profiles, as well as to the profile of their organization's operating culture. According to our Serbian affiliate, the group had recognized that they were not doing well as a team and they committed to doing something about it. They used the *Group Styles Inventory* results along with their personal feedback from *Management/Impact* to improve the way they interacted and approached problems as a team. Our affiliate, Ivan Dmitrić elaborates,

> The way they had worked together as a team was quite stressful for each of them and not particularly effective in terms of solution quality and acceptance. Therefore, they made a commitment to stick to a few principles during group meetings and discussions in order to achieve consensus decisions that better reflected their common interests. Specific behaviors they focused on included letting people express their viewpoints without interruption, listening to what is being said, encouraging passive members to speak up by asking for their opinions, and confirming that decisions were accepted by the majority. And since their personal development plans

also included tasks aimed at having a more Constructive impact on peers, the team's development plan was consistent with what they were personally as well as organizationally trying to improve.

My role as the consultant was to give them feedback on whether they were doing what they had agreed on. Of course, behaving in a more aggressive, Competitive, and Power-oriented way—including being critical of one another—was natural for them. So was behaving passively and waiting for Goran or Ivan to come up with solutions and make the decisions, because that was how they learned to work together in the first place. It had been part of the company's culture for most of its history and was the main obstacle to improving their teamwork. Thus, it was easy for them to revert and switch back to the "old way" in a moment. It was in those moments that I would help keep them focused on the positive changes that they all wanted to accomplish.

The key was that they began to understand that they were more interdependent and important to one another than they had previously realized. They recognized that if they wanted to grow as an organization—as well as grow personally, as the managers who were running it—the common goal was the most important goal, even personally!

A remeasure of the top team's group styles while working on a different problem six months later showed a significant shift in a more Constructive and less Defensive direction (see Figure 7.3).

Figure 7.3. Shift in Top Team's Group Styles (based on the *Group Styles Inventory*)

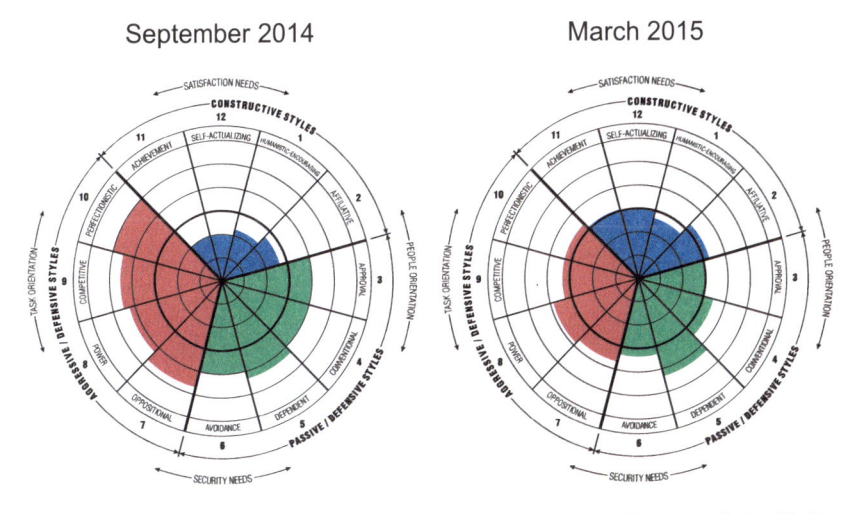

Research and development by Robert A. Cooke, Ph.D. and J. Clayton Lafferty, Ph.D. Copyright © 1987-2019 by Human Synergistics International. All Rights Reserved.

The importance of the leaders approaching culture change by starting with themselves cannot be emphasized enough. First, it was the key to overcoming some of the hesitance, resistance, and fear about change, all of which are aspects of Defensive organizational cultures. Second, even with a new structure and more challenging goals, others in the organization were not going to take initiative, make bold decisions, and test out fresh ideas if doing so meant being punished for making mistakes as they tried to learn. One of the ways in which Goran and the other top team members helped to bring about improvements was related to this point. When coworkers or direct reports came forward with ideas—even ones that might not work—they were praised for thinking innovatively about the business and their role in moving it forward, supported in their willingness to try do things differently, and guided (as opposed to criticized) so mistakes were not repeated. The changes the leaders made to their own behavior had a significant impact on what the people around them believed was actually expected, as illustrated by the changes in Goran's *Management/Impact* profile in 2014 versus 2015 (Figure 7.4).

Figure 7.4. Goran's Impact on Others

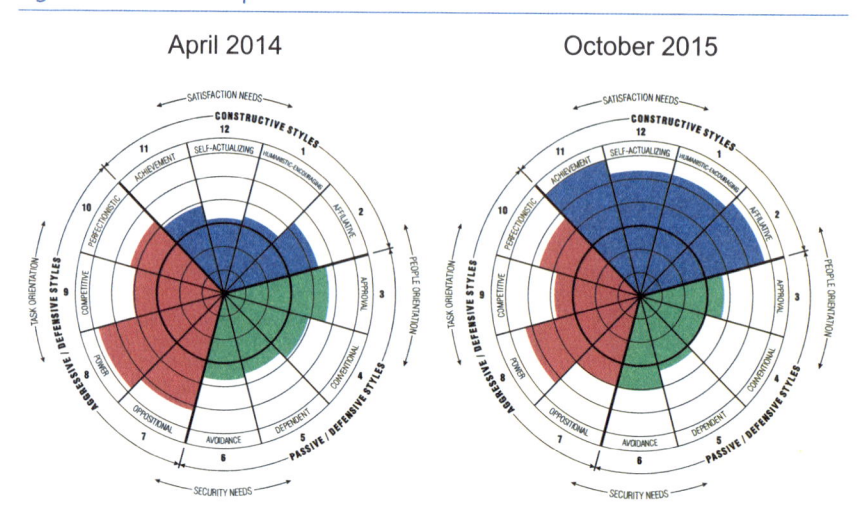

April 2014 | October 2015

Research and development by Robert A. Cooke, Ph.D. and J. Clayton Lafferty, Ph.D.
Copyright © 1987-2019 by Human Synergistics International. All Rights Reserved.

Although Goran had made significant changes in the ways he approached his role and its impact on people, learning how to give employees more autonomy—and not be afraid of the results—took time for some of the other managers. As Goran points out, many of them still needed to fully grasp that maintaining a command-and-control approach is hugely limiting.

Even with time and support, not everyone in Pons was able to learn how to effectively carry out their new responsibilities. According to our affiliate this wasn't because they were unwilling but rather because they had "hit their ceiling" in terms of how much they were able to learn and change within a reasonable amount of time. As Ivan Dmitrić points out, "We don't leave our people behind" is a norm that they have retained in the company—meaning that people in Pons are rarely fired and instead are typically moved to another position within the company. Thus, staff members who were struggling were moved to different positions, and new people were brought in who had the necessary skills, resulting in a better person/role fit overall in the company.

Tangible Gains

By the end of 2015, both Ivan and Goran reported major gains in the way the business was run. Not only had employees become much more goal- and outcome-oriented, the company as a whole had become more efficient and much quicker when implementing solutions. Reported Goran just over a year into the process,

> Currently our percentages indicate that we are experiencing organic growth. Had we not introduced these changes, it's possible we would have experienced a decline or stagnation. Considering our line of business, that is enormous success. Generally, our competitors, with some exceptions, have faced serious regression over the past several years. This means we are definitely on the right track. Pons is definitely no longer just a bakery! We are a company that wishes to grow in line with global trends.

From a personal perspective, Goran no longer carried so much stress, adding that, "We have reached the level that if Ivan and I left the firm for six months, it would stay sound and stable." He also felt he had more time to focus on the most important issues facing the company, rather than wasting time and energy on "irrelevant things, as I used to."

For both top leaders, the changes meant they were able to fully focus their attention and time on strategy and growth, something that hadn't been possible before they began their culture change journey. Thus, it's no wonder Ivan Matijević talked buoyantly regarding the future:

> I expect us to develop further in terms of the professionalism of our management and team spirit, and that will bring about the best of what Pons stands for. We should be an appealing company to first-rate people, and we cannot be such a company if we do not go through all these changes.

> I believe that changes on the global, economic, and market level are faster than the growth potential of any company owner, regardless of his age. The changes are so fast and turbulent, you simply must keep pace with them.

One of the ways in which Pons was successful at keeping pace with rapidly changing market conditions was to review its risk diversification. As a result, the company developed a new product portfolio. Instead of introducing products for which strong competition already existed, Pons began focusing on creating innovative products that offered the market greater value. In 2016, they launched a new line of frozen products, *Moderna Domaćica* ("Modern Housewife" in English), which included frozen pastry packaged and marketed in unique ways that appealed to customers. For instance, the pizza crust was shaped to easily fit in the types of rectangular pans that most of their customers already owned. For their key accounts and grocery stores, Pons provided special freezers with video monitors on top or alongside to showcase their Modern Housewife products. They also posted videos on YouTube that showed different ways of using their frozen products.[198] These approaches, which were considered novel for their market at that point in time, were just some of the ways in which Pons further differentiated themselves from competitors.

In addition, Pons was able to move innovations from idea to market more quickly with both higher- and middle-level managers working toward individually set objectives tied to organizational goals and acting on ideas for solving problems related to implementation. Whereas earlier it might have taken the company a year to implement a new idea, they began getting ideas into the market in six to nine months.

And while the company and its leaders were unable to take advantage of opportunities for further growth back in 2014, Pons was once again growing. In 2015, they opened the first Le Pons location, a premium retail establishment offering coffee, cakes, ice cream, and fresh baked goods. In 2016, they acquired the second-largest bakery in their region and then moved forward with plans to open bakeries in Belgrade. They also began exporting frozen baked goods to other countries, including Sweden and Montenegro.

The expansion of this once-small bakery was exciting, not only for Ivan and Goran but also for their community. Pons had become one of the largest employers in Čačak, with approximately four hundred people. By the beginning of 2017, it had thirty-five retail shops, produced more than two hundred different products, supplied fresh baked goods to over 1,500 shops and bakeries, and was one of the largest producers of frozen baked products in Serbia. The company was recognized by local bankers as a good investment, which is significant given that half of small and medium enterprises (SMEs) globally are unable to secure credit.[199] In addition, Pons began attracting talent from different industries, including a prominent banker in the community who changed careers to become the new CFO because he was drawn to the energy and growth ambitions of the company.

Owners and general managers of some of the other bakeries and companies in Serbia noticed the improvements that Pons had made and met with its top leaders to discuss their approach to dealing with people. Goran advises those who are considering this approach that this is a process that doesn't happen by itself. He points out,

> You need to invest a lot of your time and energy. You need to let the people make mistakes, which has a cost. And if you are not a part of it, then it will be a wasted cost. We've invested in it, and we've seen that it works.

For business owner Ivan, he remains most interested in the trends rather than the isolated numbers. And for Pons, even in the midst of an environment as turbulent as it was when the company was founded more than twenty-five years ago, that trend appears positive.

Key Learnings

This case highlights two essential points that are often overlooked when it comes to organizational culture:
- Just because certain organizational outcomes seem fine, don't assume you've got an effective culture. True leaders like Ivan and Goran have the foresight to sense when something is seriously wrong inside the organization and do something about it long

before it starts detrimentally affecting their external adaptability and successes. By addressing the root cause of the problems they were experiencing, these leaders discovered that their business could perform even better.
- Top leaders championing changes means much more than just giving their consent to change. Rather, it means having the courage to take the first steps in adjusting their *own* behaviors so that they are aligned with and reinforce the other changes being made. This helps to create an environment in which leaders can improve their own interactions and effectiveness as a team, as well as coach and support the managers under them to lead more effectively.

In addition, this case illustrates that creating a more Constructive culture is essential to the sustainability of any type of organization—including a local bakery in Serbia.

Of course, some challenges with growth have nothing to do with the top leaders being overwhelmed but instead stem from the employees being stressed and burned-out. We turn now to another country in eastern Europe, where one organization's challenge in sustaining its dominant position in the market lay in winning the war for attracting and keeping talent.

> **Key Learnings**
>
> - Assess and address cultural issues before they start affecting business performance.
> - Leaders champion change by being the first—not only in their organization but also possibly in their industry or country—to adjust their own leadership and management approaches to reinforce the other changes being made.

Chapter 8

Leveraging the Capacity of HR Directors and Middle Managers to Effect Culture Change (Hungary)

In the past, I focused mainly on the results. Now we also focus on people, coaching, and other things rather than just chasing the numbers. We've changed the focus, and the results have gotten even better.
Csaba Felföldi, HORECA[200] Channel Manager, Dreher Brewery

Organization	Dreher Brewery
Location	Kőbánya, Budapest, Hungary
Industry	Fast Moving Consumer Goods (FMCG): Beer Brewery
Founded	1854; named Dreher in 1905
Market Position	First (2012 to 2015)
Number of Employees	600+
Started Culture Journey	2012
Interviewees	Eva Kreiter, Human Resources Director
	Andrei Haret, Managing Director, 2010-2015
	Richard Szabo, Revenue Manager
	Csaba Felföldi, HORECA[200] Channel Manager
	Dr. Ildikó Magura, Flow Consulting (Supporting Consultant)

Inside Dreher Brewery

In 2012, with their market share growing and productivity increasing, Dreher Brewery appeared poised for success in the tightly competitive Hungarian beer market—which they led along with Heineken and Molson Coors[201]—when the company's new Human Resources (HR) Director, Eva Kreiter, arrived.

Upon taking over the role, Eva noticed that, despite the company's internal functional excellence, strong commitment to strategy, and best-in-class execution and technology, Dreher was losing the war for talent in the commercial part of the business. Eva explains,

> Twenty-seven percent of the freshly hired employees had left our organization in their first year and 37 percent within two years, so we were facing serious issues with retention. Over half of the departures were initiated by employees. Burnout and stress were most frequently mentioned in exit interviews as the reasons for leaving. We couldn't retain quality people.

In the commercial company's largest functional area—sales—the numbers were even more sobering. Almost a third of newly hired sales representatives had left within a year and 47 percent within two years. Interviews with employees from different departments and organizational levels revealed that enormous amounts of time and energy were being spent on internal conflicts, politicking, and micromanaging. Middle management was essentially "nonexistent," and instead there was an abundance of senior-level managers with poorly defined roles. Rewards and recognition were based mostly on the strength of a person's internal networks and relationships rather than his or her performance. "People felt that recognition was driven by their first-line manager rather than specific criteria or policies," says Eva. "Additionally, it was clear from the interviews that we tolerated poor performance and unacceptable behaviors."

With market share and production demands growing, retention of employees declining, and an internal environment that seemed focused on self-promotion and self-protection, Eva doubted if Dreher would be able to sustain its current position in the marketplace. It would also be difficult to successfully navigate the changes and challenges ahead. At the time, these included increased excise duties, smoking bans, and unfavorable shifts in weather conditions—all of which threatened to negatively impact beer consumption. After finishing with her empirical data collection, which included approximately forty interviews and an assessment of the company's existing HR data, she requested a two-hour meeting with then managing director, Andrei Haret. The purpose was to discuss her findings and ideas about a "culture-shaping program." "That will be a three-minute discussion!" he said incredulously. As it turned out, the meeting lasted for two hours and provided Andrei with insights that he eventually acted upon.

Like so many organizations that conduct exit interviews, the data were neither analyzed nor shared with Dreher's executive leadership prior to Eva's arrival. According to business professors Everett Spain and Boris Groysberg, less than a third of the companies that perform exit interviews share the results with senior leaders and use the data to guide changes. Consequently,

Top to bottom: Andrei Haret, Csaba Felföldi, Eva Kreiter, Richard Szabo

their potential as a tool for increasing employee retention is often overlooked.[202] Certainly this was at least part of the reason for Andrei's initial reaction. Eva recalls,

> Andrei and the other members of the executive committee had already sensed that there were issues. But when I presented my findings, they were surprised by the details and the size of the problem, because we had just become the market leader. The big question was "How sustainable is this success?" Hungary is a small market, and competition is very tight. We couldn't afford to let our people lose their drive and energy to win the fight. Therefore, employee burnout was a key concern, as was the fact that we had lost our power to retain quality people—especially the new ones that were hired. Even the talent that we contacted rejected us, so it was becoming more visible that our reputation in the labor market was not strong enough.

Although the data that Eva and her team had collected suggested to her that the problem was cultural, she felt that more objective findings were needed to convince the executive committee of the necessity for action. Therefore, she recommended that the company conduct a "proper assessment" of its culture, as well as the levers for reshaping it, to more concretely quantify the problem. Based on her research and recommendations, the executive committee decided to use the *Organizational Culture Inventory* and the *Organizational Effectiveness Inventory* and work with Flow Consulting (*Flow Csoport*). Dr. Ildikó Magura, the lead Flow consultant who worked with Dreher, explains,

> Dreher is the oldest Hungarian beer brand. The company has a brewery in Budapest, which employs about 180 people in manufacturing. The commercial part of the company, which is made up of about 380 people, is also located in Budapest.
>
> At the end of 2012, their executive committee decided to initiate culture development in the commercial part of the business because of the high employee turnover, as well as other related problems in that area—including work overload, the lack of opportunity for advancement, and dissatisfaction with the culture and the processes. They administered the *Organizational Culture Inventory* and *Organizational Effectiveness Inventory* to employees in the commercial side

of the business and received responses from 279 people. In addition, the executive committee members, the next level of management and a few other key talents, (forty-one people in total) completed the *Ideal* version of the *Organizational Culture Inventory*. Based on the results of those surveys, they put together a "Cultural Ambition" and implemented several initiatives, one of which was leadership development for the executive committee and middle managers, which included *Leadership/Impact* and the *Life Styles Inventory*.

Andrei and the other members of the executive committee decided to leverage the company's culture-shaping journey through their newly defined Board-1 (B-1) middle managers, who reported directly to them. "We wanted our middle managers to become the change agents of this culture shaping," explains Eva. "Without them, we wouldn't be able to reshape the culture, because they are the real operative leaders of this company and, most importantly, have a direct impact on the culture of the organization."

Middle managers were provided with extensive training, development, and coaching, along with direct support from the executive committee members (who also participated in leadership development). In addition, Dreher revamped its performance management system, including the managers' goals and the criteria for rewards and punishments.

In the course of this process, Dreher's executive committee leaders' and middle managers' definition of success changed. The company had already achieved market leadership before beginning its culture journey; what the leaders and managers discovered as they progressed in shaping the company's culture was that a truly effective organization can attain much more. In working together to create a more collaborative work environment, the company's leaders and managers further strengthened the organization's sales and financial performance, while at the same time (and possibly as a result of) dramatically improving employee retention and engagement.

As you read how Dreher prepared and supported their middle managers to direct and drive cultural change, there is a broader question for the top leaders and HR directors of any organization to consider: How are they taking care of the organization's culture and preparing and supporting their middle managers to have a Constructive impact on people and culture?

Development of Middle Managers

To prepare and support the middle managers at Dreher in their role as change agents, Eva and her team put together a comprehensive management and leadership development program that spanned almost a three-year period. The program addressed many issues and skills, including, for example,

- managers' thinking and behavioral styles and impact on culture,
- employee performance management,
- conflict management,
- coaching,
- change management,
- team dynamics,
- empowerment, and
- strategic thinking.

Most middle managers have a strong desire to advance, and this was certainly true of those at Dreher. They saw the program as invaluable to "strengthening their professional portfolios." Not only was the program comprehensive and ongoing, its application was tied to participants' performance goals and was fully supported and reinforced by the leaders to whom the managers reported. "It had the support of our managing director, which was key," attests B-1 manager Richard Szabo, who was rotated into the revenue manager role from another B-1 position in 2015.

The "Visegrad Group" and the Role of Senior Leadership

Without executive support, culture change is not going to happen or be as effective as hoped for or required. While the support at Dreher mirrors what we've recommended throughout this book, the fact that many executives do not understand what support for culture change means or entails makes the details particularly important. Especially in a case in which middle managers are taking on the role of change agents, let's be clear that executive support at Dreher meant more than just sending out an email to employees.

Over the course of the first three years of their culture journey, Dreher's executive committee leaders and B-1 managers regularly met for a few days at a time in Visegrad, a retreat away from the brewery. It was there that they got to know each other better, worked with the company's culture survey feedback, determined how they were going to reshape the culture, and discussed the progress of their initiatives and changes.

"Everything was very informal," notes then managing director Andrei Haret. "We didn't put up slides or anything like that. It didn't matter if you were the managing director, board member, or Board-1 manager. In the Visegrad Group we were all equal." The experience helped them to "come together" as team. Andrei recalls, "You could see people who had never talked to each other before starting to cooperate with one another and work in teams, which made the company's processes much more efficient."

From the perspectives of Eva and the B-1 managers, Andrei and the other executive committee members did more than just model the desired behaviors. They also allocated the necessary resources so that change initiatives were properly executed, and they ensured that decisions regarding processes, policies, and structures were aligned with the culture that they wanted to move toward. Observes B-1 manager Csaba Felföldi,

> The Visegrad Group was key to the success of the culture-shaping process, because we are the link between the executive team and the rest of the organization.
>
> The executive team practiced it in their behavior and were personally involved in this program. So, it wasn't just an email from the managing director saying, "Do this as you wish, and HR will support you." Instead, we worked with the executive committee on the culture feedback and shared thoughts about the improvements that could be made. It showed us that the culture reshaping is more than just B-1 and that the Visegrad Group could really do something.

Based on the culture feedback, the Visegrad Group identified seven behavioral principles that defined their "Cultural Ambition" (see Figure 8.1). They then organized themselves into seven "think tanks," each led by an executive committee member with volunteers from the B-1 middle managers. The groups initiated several changes to make the principles a more concrete part of the company's culture. Among the most influential were the changes made in performance management, including rewards and punishments and goal setting.

Figure 8.1. Dreher's Cultural Ambition

OUR COMPANY:

*DREHER IS A SUCCESSFUL, RESPECTED AND RESPONSIBLE COMPANY IN HUNGARY AND WITHIN SAB MILLER.
WE ARE LEADING AND SHAPING OUR MARKET
IN A SUSTAINABLE WAY.*

IN DREHER:

*IN A WINNING TEAM
WE WORK WITH PASSION AND PRIDE
TO ALWAYS BE THE BEST.*

BASED ON OUR STRENGTH IN OUR WORK WE:

1) *Constantly Exceed Expectations*
2) *Act with Innovative, Entrepreneurial Spirit*
3) *Drive & Own the Business, Take Responsibility*
4) *Work as a Team in Open & Constructive Ways*
5) *Bring the Best out of Ourselves and Each Other*
6) *Recognize Outstanding Performance, but Show No Tolerance to Poor Performers & Unacceptable Behavior*
7) *Celebrate Our Joint Successes*

AND AS A RESULT OF THAT:

- *We are Proud of Being the Best in Our Marketplace*
- *We Believe in Our Brands & Ourselves, We Think Positive*
- *We Treat Each Other with Attention and Appreciation*
- *We Enjoy the Benefits of Being Part of Dreher.*

*MORE THAN A WORKPLACE.
BEER. ENJOYMENT. TRADITION. SUCCESS.*

Breaking Down Silos with Performance Management and Job Rotation

Both the interview and survey data indicated that people perceived the organization's performance management system as subjective. Acting on the findings, one of the Visegrad task forces created a checklist based on the seven principles outlined in the company's Cultural Ambition for managers and employees to use in the performance appraisal process. The group also changed the goal-setting system so that every B-1 manager would have at least one culture-shaping goal as part of his or her performance management goals. B-1 manager Richard Szabo explains that even these "soft targets" had to be (and were) specific and measurable. For example, one of his goals was to hold regular one-on-ones with his employees and use the feedback techniques that he learned in the program. Richard observed that "You have to put it in people's goals and as part of short-term incentives (such as bonuses or cash), because that's when they really focus on it and take it seriously." Consistent with this, our research has shown that one of the strongest predictors of culture is the nature of the organization's appraisal and reinforcement systems, including the use of rewards and punishments.[203]

At Dreher, the leaders and managers not only focused on rewarding desired behaviors, they also started to address the undesired behaviors. For example, during the first three years of Dreher's journey, they let go of managers who continued to perform poorly or refused to align their behavior with the culture that the company was working toward. The necessity of doing so was something we learned from our early case studies and was also illustrated in chapter 6.

They also rotated some of the people at the B-1 level to further help in breaking down silos. Consultant Dr. Ildikó Magura explains,

> Job rotation enabled the strengthening of the empowerment-based leadership style. In contrast to their previous position, where professionally they had the most expertise, in their new positions the leaders had to rely much more on their new teams.
>
> Three managers from the finance department were selected for job rotation because they needed new challenges and development in the area of empowerment. In addition, there was a huge necessity for inspiration and motivation in the finance team at the subordinate level.

The rotation resulted in a new platform of cooperation as B-1 (middle managers) started to more vigorously share knowledge. Empowerment and the Humanistic-Encouraging style became stronger. While they were learning their new professional areas, the leaders delegated more tasks to their new teams and consulted more with the other associated departments. It got them out of their "professional ivory towers" and entered the organization's "blood circulation."

In addition, B-1 managers started collaborating on their performance goals across departments and functional areas. Within the first year, they could see the impact of the new processes, as summarized by Eva:

> Previously, a functional director would prepare his own goals and start executing them. Similarly, certain decisions would be made by department leads that would affect other departments, but they would not discuss their decisions with those other departments. Instead, the decisions would be made and pushed on other departments without asking for support or if it was okay with them. That no longer happens.
>
> Now, we collaborate on all the performance goals—not only at the Board-1 level but also at the Board-2 level—to ensure that there are no contradicting goals or interests in the organization. It's helped to break down organizational barriers. Teams have started to work together and communicate. When managers feel that they need to work together to solve a certain problem, they now voluntarily set up project teams.

This relatively simple example illustrates how even a change in performance goals—when supported by complementary changes in reinforcement systems and job design—can help to shift norms and break down silos in organizations so different groups work with, rather than against, one another to solve problems and achieve goals.

Empowering Employees

Other cases highlighted the importance of individual awareness, acceptance, and action to changing long-standing cultural beliefs and norms, and certainly this was also true at Dreher. Of particular importance was the belief that the manager is always the one who has the best solutions. For instance, B-1 manager Richard shared that he had traditionally maintained an open-door policy because his employees had insisted they didn't want something formally organized or scheduled for communicating their opinions. Consequently, he would share his expectations and how he wanted them achieved in "brief chats in the coffee room" with employees. However, when he started scheduling one-on-ones as part of the culture-change initiative and used the coaching skills that he learned in the company's new management development program, he discovered that his employees actually wanted the scheduled one-on-one sessions with him. He now regularly schedules sixty- to ninety-minute sessions with each employee that exclusively focus on them and provide them with the opportunity to decide the best way to do things and propose solutions to problems. Although he still shares his expectations, he empowers his employees to take initiative in solving problems and deciding how to meet those expectations. "Obviously, they know the solutions better than [I do]," says Richard, who now realizes that he is not the only one who can identify effective solutions.

The belief that you had to act like you had all the answers was widely shared at Dreher's managerial level, as confirmed by strong extensions in Perfectionistic, Competitive, and Power in the profile of their operating culture (see Figure 8.2). For example, B-1 manager Csaba Felföldi described how his beliefs around perfectionism and power changed as a result of the culture-reshaping process:

> I believed that…Competitive, Perfectionistic, and Power-oriented were the most important factors to being a very successful manager. I think we all realized from the feedback that we got that we had to change our perfectionism. We had to recognize that others in the group were at the same level as us. We all wanted to deliver more, and we were not the only ones who could solve the problem.
>
> We had several trainings in the last three years where we were put into different situations that demonstrated that when we cooperated and collaborated with each other the result was much better. Because we were talking more, we got to know more about each other, and our level of trust in one another increased.

This middle-manager insight is like that of executives and leaders in previous chapters and illustrates the pervasiveness with which Perfectionistic and Power styles are valued across organizational levels, industries, and societies. Even more importantly, these cases demonstrate that challenging and moderating these unproductive beliefs produces better results.

Dreher's then managing director, Andrei Haret, had also changed as a result of the culture-shaping journey. Whereas initially he was uncertain whether it would actually help to improve performance and effectiveness, over time he became a very strong advocate. Eva Kreiter recounts,

> He started to really value it, because he could feel the results and started to see the fruits of it. He saw how engaging it was for the middle management team to work on culture, so he naturally took the lead on it. He could see how advantageous it was that employees from different functions were talking and collaborating with one another. The immediate impact on efficiency was clearly visible to him.

Andrei adds,

> I had read books and heard people talking about how culture was important. This process proved it to be true. It was quite visible how the company stood in the market before the process and after the process. I could see that we had started to work in a better way internally from a cultural perspective, a process perspective, and a systems perspective.

Tangible Results

By the end of 2014, Dreher's employee turnover significantly decreased, to about 7 percent. In the sales function, which previously had experienced the greatest difficulty with retention, staff turnover dropped to around 10 percent. Burnout was no longer mentioned in exit interviews, and when the company administered a survey to assess the stress level of employees, the results were favorable. When they did their first

The company's buildings

Leveraging the Capacity of Managers 209

engagement survey with the sales department in 2015, the results came out at 92 percent, which corroborated the positive impact on employees. Annual assessments of culture at the B-1 level confirmed that norms had steadily moved in a more Constructive and less Defensive direction from 2013 to 2015 (see Figure 8.2).

Figure 8.2. Dreher's Culture Journey: 2012 to 2016

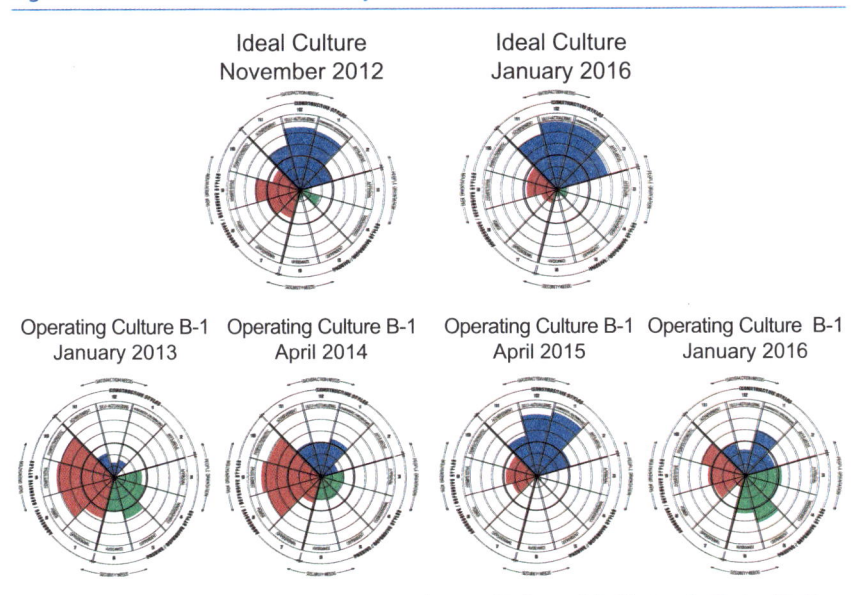

Ideal Culture November 2012

Ideal Culture January 2016

Operating Culture B-1 January 2013

Operating Culture B-1 April 2014

Operating Culture B-1 April 2015

Operating Culture B-1 January 2016

Research and development by Robert A. Cooke, Ph.D. and J. Clayton Lafferty, Ph.D.
Copyright © 1987-2019 by Human Synergistics International. All Rights Reserved.

Importantly, the company's financial results also grew stronger. Net sales revenue, which was about 46 billion Hungarian forints (179,368,000 USD) when they started the process in 2012, significantly increased to 53 billion (208,245,000 USD) by the end of 2015, and operating profit turned from negative to positive. In addition, the company maintained its market leadership with a 31 percent volume share in 2016 as compared to the 27 percent held by its closest rival, Heineken.[204]

Both Csaba and Richard talk about how being more people-focused led them to achieve even better results. Csaba notes,

> In the past, I focused mainly on the results. Now we also focus on people, coaching, and other things rather than just chasing the numbers. We've changed the focus, and the results have

gotten even better. This year we've done a fantastic job with our profit target. We are the leader in our market, and our turnover of product has increased by about 15 percent.

Similarly, because he now trusts others to take ownership of projects and choose their own "how," Richard says his employees seem more engaged, project workflow is smoother, and the financial results are better.

Unexpected and Uncontrollable Changes, "Traveling Leaders," and the Importance of Those Who Stay

In April of 2015, SABMiller (which owned Dreher at the time), promoted Andrei to managing director of Grolsch Brewery in the Netherlands. A director from another part of SABMiller arrived in July to be Dreher's new managing director. Then, in November of 2015, the world's largest brewer, AB InBev, purchased SABMiller, which was the second largest at the time. It was uncertain what would happen with management as well as with individual brands, particularly as AB InBev went to work on securing regulatory approvals around the globe. Six months later, it was announced that AB InBev was selling SABMiller's Central and Eastern European businesses, including Dreher, to gain approval from regulators. At the end of March 2017, Dreher was bought by Japanese Asahi Group Holdings.[205] And, in October of 2017, Dreher's managing director was once again replaced with someone new.

A change in leadership can disrupt a culture development initiative—particularly when the new leader has very different ideas and beliefs. In Dreher's case, however, it did not change the middle and senior managers' beliefs in the value of moving the culture in a more Constructive direction, as confirmed by reassessment of the ideal culture in 2016 (see Figure 8.2, top row). A reassessment of the operating culture at the B-1 level showed, not surprisingly given all the turbulence and uncertainty, more Defensiveness and less Constructiveness than in the previous year. Yet the culture was still more Constructive and less Defensive than when their journey had begun (see Figure 8.2, bottom row).

At all levels of the organization, people visibly tried to stay open, positive, and direct in their communications during the turbulent and uncertain period. According to Eva, "People throughout the organization asked straightforward questions and expected straightforward answers." She pointed out that the honest communication helped to reduce stress and prevented the circulation of untrue information and stories. The executive committee started to meet more frequently with the company's other leadership teams and people managers to keep them informed and answer their questions. In addition, Eva frequently met with the executive committee members to discuss engagement and retention issues and to make sure they continued to be aware of how the company and its people were doing internally as well as in relation to the market.

Though we will have to wait and see what will happen with Dreher, we know its managers were in a better position to deal with all of the turbulence and uncertainty than they would have been back in 2012. At the end of 2017, Dreher continued to lead the Hungarian market. Retention of new employees in the sales function—which had been one of the leading drivers for the culture reshaping program—remained dramatically improved over what it had been when the company began its culture journey (see Table 8.1). And, as important, they have been able to retain the HR director and the middle managers who were key to leveraging and supporting the Constructive changes to the culture.

Table 8.1. Sales Force New Hire Departures: 2012 versus 2017

	2012	2017
Within 1 year %	32%	10%
Within 2 years %	47%	15%

"We are proud of these results and happy to share them," says Eva, adding that she too has learned a lot from this journey:

> Sharing the Cultural Ambition with the middle management was essential to be successful. In our case, it was usually HR that ensured we stayed focused on the culture-shaping journey and conscious of reaching the desired phase.
>
> Through this process, I learned a lot about motivating people, how to approach different individuals, and how to read if they are supporting this process. For instance, it required a lot of persistence with the previous managing director [Andrei] to make him believe that this would have a visibly positive business impact. But after a year, he became the leader of this

whole process, and I could see that we really had his buy-in. I'm very proud of his achievement, because he changed a lot, and it impacted and motivated many of the other leaders who are still with us.

Key Learnings

Whereas the culture journeys in the previous chapters were initiated by either the CEO or owner of the business, with Dreher it was the new HR director who brought the need to redirect the culture to the attention of the other leaders. As Liza Sichon, author of *The Art of Human Resources* emphasizes, top leaders are not the only ones responsible for recognizing that they own the culture of the organization. Other senior leaders—including the top HR professional—share this responsibility. Sichon points out that, even though everything HR does directly influences culture, many HR professionals "shy away" from culture discussions with senior leaders because they don't know how to "own their part" in them.[206]

The story of Dreher uniquely illustrates how HR professionals can play a crucial role in bringing other senior leaders' attention to culture issues before they become crises and how they can support them in championing change. To help senior leaders understand how culture threatened the company's future and outcomes that were most important to them, Eva used:

a) company data on turnover,
b) exit interview results,
c) her own interview results,
d) other relevant HR data (for example, the number of vacant positions and lead times; service times in different job groups, regions, and grades; and market comparative ratios for different job groups), as well as
e) the company's sales growth, performance, and goals.

Additionally, she and the HR team used assessments to show the leaders how their own behavior and leadership approaches affected culture and could be altered to achieve even better results. She also supported their work with the middle management change agents in identifying and implementing changes in systems and structures, as well as providing all of them with ongoing coaching and feedback to help them stay aware of and improve their impact on culture.

Despite the critical role of HR in this case, the story of Dreher also illustrates how it took all of them—the HR director, senior leaders, and middle managers—to create cultural change and, in turn, a more effective organization. The value of middle managers in implementing levers for cultural change is often overlooked or misunderstood. Popular organizational change approaches have included getting rid of middle managers. However, companies such as Google have found that this approach doesn't necessarily help them to function more efficiently and solve problems more effectively.[207] As we've seen from previous chapters, leaders who have a Constructive impact actively take responsibility for culture.

Importantly, Dreher's journey shows what it really looks like when senior leaders support middle managers and HR directors in leveraging culture change. The senior leaders in this case were truly involved in the process and committed to making the necessary changes in their own behaviors and approaches to better support it. They worked on adjusting their own behavior or leadership approaches so that when they were working and interacting with middle managers, their behavior influenced and reinforced those managers to behave Constructively. This direct impact on people and culture is often overlooked by senior leaders when they hear that they should "support" and "champion" culture change.

In addition, the senior leaders at Dreher aligned their decisions (for example about budgets, systems, structures, goals, rewards, punishments, hiring, training and development, and promotions) so that their choices would encourage Constructive behavior. Most senior leaders elsewhere seem to be unaware of the impact that they have on culture and how their decisions and choices communicate and reinforce expectations for particular Constructive or Defensive behaviors. This latter point is also made by one of the leaders in the next chapter.

One question often asked is "For how long will the changes last?" Another, just as important: "What does it take to sustain culture change?" Dreher's experience shows that improved cultures have some degree of staying power even in the context of extreme turbulence. As their experience illustrates, key to lasting change is making sure that all leaders and middle managers understand the importance of culture and know how to work together in building and reinforcing Constructive norms and expectations, particularly when leaders at the top are continually being rotated.

Additional insights about growing and sustaining Constructive norms and expectations are provided by the next two chapters, which focus on organizations that have been on their culture journeys for an even longer period. We'll shift our focus to Australia, to find out how a company struggling to develop new products to meet customers' ever-changing preferences forged ahead in its market by turning unexpected challenges into opportunities to solve problems more quickly and innovatively—to the delight of their customers and the surprise of their competitors.

Key Learnings

For Senior Leaders:

- Leaders effectively involve and support others in leveraging Constructive culture change by adjusting their own behavioral styles, leadership approaches, decisions, and choices so that they encourage, elicit, and reinforce Constructive behavior and responses on the part of everyone with whom they work (including HR directors and middle managers).

- When leaders support others in this way, the organization performs even better.

For HR Directors:

- Bring attention to cultural issues before they become crises by making better use of existing HR data (such as employee retention rates and exit interviews) for initial insights and clues.

- Confirm impressions of the current culture by using valid measures to more concretely define and quantify problems and issues.

For Middle Managers:

- One-on-ones tend to be less effective when employees are simply told what to do and more effective when they are "heard," when they have a sounding board for their ideas, and when they can discuss problems that concern them.

- Focus on supporting and empowering (rather than controlling) employees to more effectively solve problems, make decisions, and achieve the organization's goals.

Chapter 9

Leading People to Think Outside the Box and Move the Organization onto the Fast Track (Australia)

The bottom line is the culture really changed the game for us in terms of our ability to be fast, and that's what triggered us to become a leader in some of the things we're doing.

Peter Hartnett, HR Director and Head of People and Culture, Sanitarium Health & Wellbeing

Organization	Sanitarium Health & Wellbeing
Location	Berkeley Vale, New South Wales, Australia
Industry	Manufacturer of Health Food
Founded	1898
Market Position	From a distant third in 2009 to a close second in 2016
Number of Employees	1,300+
Started Culture Journey	2009
Interviewees	Todd Saunders, General Manager
	Peter Hartnett, HR Director and Head of People and Culture
	Matthew Croxford, Human Synergistics Australia (Supporting Consultant)

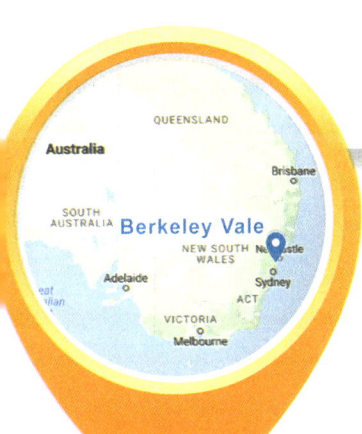

Sanitarium
health & wellbeing

Before they began their journey to redirect their culture, *agile* and *innovative* were the last words anyone would have use to describe Sanitarium Health & Wellbeing, a 116-year-old company that is owned by the Seventh-day Adventist Church and is perhaps best known in Australia for producing the breakfast cereal Weet-Bix™. Despite having considerable success in the past with dry-good breakfast products, spreads such as Marmite™, and a breakfast beverage called Up&Go™, Sanitarium found that customers' tastes, needs, and habits were dramatically changing. Consumers were showing a preference for on-the-go breakfast items that addressed health concerns, such as being higher in protein than carbohydrates; or sugar and gluten-free.[208] None of which boded well for a slow-moving company whose flagship product was a wheat-based cereal that had to be served in a bowl with milk (and perhaps some added sugar to taste).

Even when Sanitarium launched new products, they were "disasters," according to General Manager Todd Saunders. Their product development process typically took at least two years and was often ill-conceived, rushed through, or had some fundamental flaw. This was largely due to problems you've read about in previous chapters, such as leaders and managers operating in functional silos and "fiefdoms." Similarly, the quality of communication was such that much-needed conversations weren't happening that might have helped to correct these issues.

Ironically, compared to the previous chapter in which the organization had too much employee turnover, Sanitarium's extraordinarily low employee turnover—less than 0.5 percent a year—wasn't helping either. "No one ever left, because it was their whole life," notes consultant Matthew Croxford, pointing out that for Sanitarium, this was both an asset and a liability. Todd explains,

Left to right: Todd Saunders and Peter Hartnett with some of the company's well-known products

> We had a cradle-to-grave philosophy that was no different than other large manufacturers who build a factory, and a town grows up around them. We had two factories like that—one in Cooranbong and the other in Warburton.
>
> It was possible to be born in an Adventist hospital; attend an Adventist kindergarten, primary school, and high school; go to an Adventist college and get an Adventist tertiary degree; join Sanitarium; work forty or fifty years for us, then receive a pension from the company defined benefit fund; retire to an Adventist retirement village; die in an Adventist hospice; and be buried by an Adventist minister, in an Adventist graveyard, and in an Adventist-manufactured coffin. And you did all of this while attending church every week with your coworkers. The Adventist community is a fantastic community, but it did bring a sameness of thinking, particularly in the smaller towns in which we operate. Our turnover has been less than 1 percent. Even today, we have 0.5 percent voluntary termination. So, unless you retire, it takes me two hundred years to change the entire workforce.[209]

Consequently, the people who worked for Sanitarium felt little inclination to propose any unusual ideas or do anything risky. As a country, Australia is considered to have a relatively strong individualistic culture—people are generally expected to look after themselves and their immediate families, be self-reliant, and take initiative.[210] In contrast, the environment in which many of Sanitarium's employees work and live seems more collectivistic. Employees at Sanitarium usually didn't take on additional responsibilities or take the initiative to step in and offer different solutions to a problem, because their jobs and their relationships essentially were secure just as long as they showed up for work and didn't disturb the status quo.

It also hadn't helped that, since the company's inception in 1898, the breakfast cereal market had been growing every year for over a century. Thus, their leaders were confident that as long as Sanitarium continued to make good cereal, their sales would continue to rise. However, in the early 2000s, the breakfast cereal market started to stagnate. Fast-food operations were offering a variety of tasty ready-to-eat breakfast alternatives. In addition, faster-paced lifestyles were leading consumers in search of on-the-go alternatives to eating breakfast out of a bowl.[211] As a result, in 2009, Sanitarium found itself trailing behind competitors in new product introductions and in the market. They had a 21.3 percent market share, which was a distant third compared to market leader Kellogg's 40.4 percent share of the breakfast cereal market.

The need to be agile and innovative in addressing current and future changes in customer preferences, habits, and tastes is one to which any business leader can relate. As you read their story, notice how Sanitarium focused on communication to break down existing culture barriers around risk taking and to increase the speed at which they could identify more innovative approaches for successfully rolling out more new products. While good old-fashioned conversation may seem like an outmoded tool in this age of high-tech, it remains a direct and powerful means by which organizational culture is shaped and reshaped—and, just as importantly, by which problems are more readily solved.

What started as a leadership journey evolved into a cultural journey, first by the senior leadership team making themselves accountable to each other and the next level of management. They did this in terms of the changes they wanted to make to their leadership behaviors and skills. Over time, training and development opportunities like those experienced by Sanitarium's senior leaders were offered to people at all levels. In addition, they began measuring the company's culture, as well as the factors related to it, and used the feedback to make additional changes. Among the first changes they made was to raise members' awareness of the impact of their jobs on the work and lives of other people. This initial work on improving job significance—an important yet often overlooked aspect of job design and the "technology" of people's jobs—evolved into other changes. These included:

a) increased employee involvement in making improvements and problem solving (an aspect of structure);
b) greater team autonomy (another aspect of job design);
c) increased management supportiveness (a dimension of skills and qualities); and
d) recognition and celebration of accomplishments (a part of systems).

The result was that Sanitarium shortened their new product development cycle from twenty-four months to six months, first with Energize Weet-Bix and then with Gluten-Free Weet-Bix. They went to market with Gluten-Free Weet Bix in six months, even though they started from scratch without a gluten-free plant, the necessary equipment, or a recipe. Since then, the company has continued to take innovative steps, better engaging their employees, surprising and delighting their customers, and improving their market performance. Let's explore some details of their journey.

Leadership versus Management

When they administered a staff survey in 2009 to uncover what was keeping them from moving forward more quickly in their market, Sanitarium's top leaders weren't even thinking about culture. "It was all about leadership," says Todd, referring to the survey feedback and comments they received. "We had an aging group of managers and technical specialists and didn't have enough leaders."

Some people use the terms *leadership* and *management* to refer to different levels of competence. Todd, however, was referring to the fact that the senior leaders were overly focused on tactical decisions having to do with management, as opposed to activities such as surfacing, questioning, and discussing assumptions about goals and strategies, which are among the responsibilities of leadership (see Table 9.1).

Table 9.1. Leadership and Management Responsibilities

Leadership Responsibilities	Management Responsibilities
More strategic	More tactical
Focused on setting an overall agenda for the organization in terms of vision and strategies and inspiring others to achieve it	Focused on implementing strategies and turning visions into accomplishments by motivating, organizing, and guiding the efforts of other people
Examples: Envisioning, role modeling, mentoring, stimulating thinking, creating a setting	Examples: Clarifying goals, allocating resources, facilitating and supporting work activities and teamwork

Sources: *Management/Impact*® by Janet L. Szumal and Robert A. Cooke and *Leadership/Impact*® by Robert A. Cooke.

As in the other cases described in this book, Sanitarium's senior leaders took it upon themselves to change first—and they chose to do it as a group. They completed several personal assessments, including the *Life Styles Inventory*, which measured their thinking and behavioral styles. Their composite *Self Description* and *Description by Others'* profiles are shown in Figure 9.1. According to Todd, the *Life Styles Inventory* results really captured the leaders' attention because when they shared them with each other, they noticed the more effective leaders were the ones seen to have more blue in their profiles. Todd says that it didn't take long for them to realize that their behaviors were more important than the values they were espousing, and that culture went hand in hand with leadership. He describes the situation:

> There were some really tough interactions between what we were saying we valued and our egos with respect to the feedback about our own behaviors. Some of the leaders on our team had no blue in their profiles—not even a little dot that the printer cartridge puts in there to calibrate itself. It could've all fallen apart on day one, but it didn't, because the big test for us was, what was going to happen if we didn't change some of the ways in which we were behaving?

Figure 9.1. Senior Leaders' Composite *Life Styles Inventory* Profiles

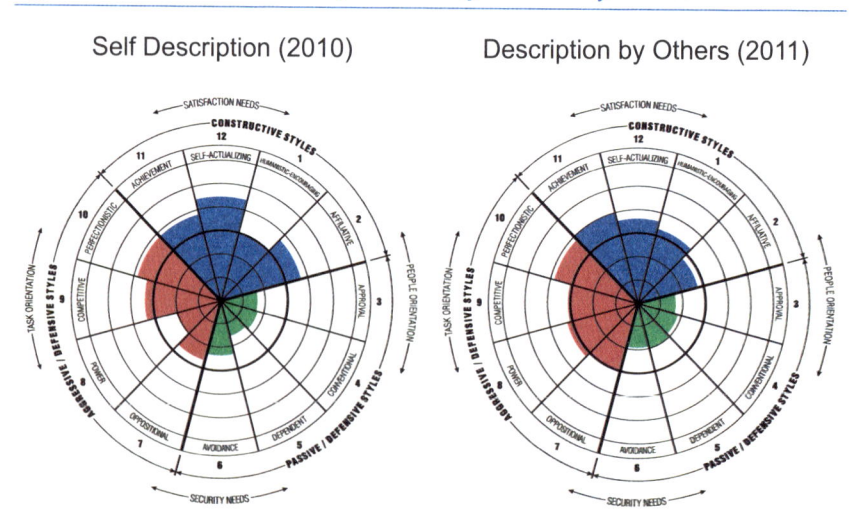

Research and development by Robert A. Cooke, Ph.D. and J. Clayton Lafferty, Ph.D.
Copyright © 1987-2019 by Human Synergistics International. All Rights Reserved.

The senior leaders organized an Extended Leadership Forum in which they explained to the middle managers what they were doing in the program, the standards to which they wanted to be held accountable, and the behaviors on which they wanted to receive feedback. Todd explains,

> We put a marker out there fairly early saying that we are going to walk the talk as far as this leadership program goes. We made it clear we wanted feedback and there would be no penalty for it. People took us up on it, which was good because it made them realize that this is real.

Most leaders assume that people know what their expectations are and that their own behavior is in line with their intentions. But as research shows, this often is not the case. Leaders frequently unknowingly behave in ways that communicate expectations that contradict what they say is desired.[212] Sanitarium is a company in which the leaders took walking the talk seriously. Communicating expectations and holding themselves and others accountable to them were among the most important levers for change they used. Sanitarium's leaders conscientiously worked on being more consistent and explicit in their own behavior and in deciding which behaviors were no longer acceptable, as well as which behaviors needed to become the norm.

Instilling Psychological Safety within the Leadership Team

Sanitarium's leaders specifically focused on the content of their communication with one another, particularly in meetings and when solving problems. This is when shared beliefs formed about how secure the leaders felt in regard to risk taking, trying new things, and proposing fresh ideas within the context of the leadership team. According to the research of Harvard Leadership and Management Professor Amy Edmondson, learning and, in turn, group performance depend on the extent to which members share a belief that they are safe with one another in taking psychological risks that might otherwise cause them to lose face.[213] Examples include admitting mistakes, acknowledging when they don't have all the answers, and asking for assistance and feedback. As Google's research on its own groups showed, shared beliefs and norms are more important in determining whether teams fail or soar than the background, technical skills, and personality characteristics of the group's members.[214]

Todd describes how they created a feeling of safety within Sanitarium's leadership team—and the importance of shared language in that process:

> We effectively banned questions about why we couldn't do things or why we shouldn't do things and started to turn the conversation to how we could do it. People were encouraged to take risks collectively and be explicit with the wider team about the fact that they were taking risks and trying to do it together.
>
> We now had a common language around blue, green, and red behaviors and attitudes. Every time people were in meetings, they would say, "How do we behave in a blue way here?" "How can we get to a solution and move forward?" There were no silent passengers or hostages. People were saying, "Let's have a shot at this," because they knew it was expected and that they weren't going to be penalized if they got it wrong.

Consistent with our own research on group problem solving, Sanitarium's senior leaders recognized the benefits of engaging in predominantly Constructive behaviors—including discussing how things could be made to work, listening, asking questions, and building on one another's ideas. When practicing these behaviors, they were able to solve problems more quickly and effectively than they had when they were engaging in Defensive behaviors that focused on avoiding risks, maintaining the status quo, and protecting their turf.

Making Culture a Strategic Priority

As Todd discovered, it is easy for leaders to make change complicated and avoidable. This was exemplified when he and the other senior leaders received the feedback from the Human Synergistics *Organizational Effectiveness Inventory* regarding the extent to which different aspects of their organization's systems, structures, technology, and skills/qualities were aligned with the Constructive behaviors they desired. Todd says it was "confronting" to realize how many factors affect culture. However, change is not inherently complicated and instead depends on how people approach it and, more specifically, the thinking and behavioral styles they use. Todd explains,

> We found out that you can't change culture overnight. If you could, everyone would have already done it.

> Like everybody else, we made huge mistakes. We had culture plans for some people that were ten pages long with bullet points on everything, and they tried to boil the ocean. If you try to do too much, people just get lost in it.
>
> It didn't take us long to realize when you are working with a team, the culture just has to be part of the strategic plan, rather than a plan by itself. If you focus on one or two causal factors that really matter, everything else comes along with it, because the program is then paramount. Culture is not difficult, but it does reward focus, discipline, and hard work."[215]

Sanitarium's leaders realized from the start that culture had to be made a part of their work activities rather than a separate undertaking. They started with communication and job significance, and they focused not only on having more Constructive conversations with each other but also with people at other levels. In addition to practicing Constructive behaviors in their conversations they started to regularly walk the factory floor; engaged in team talks; and produced sixty- to ninety-minute videos and webcasts. They also held quarterly "lunch club" meetings with all two hundred people in the head office to discuss past quarter accomplishments, agree on next quarter objectives, and plan how to Constructively work together to achieve those objectives. They continued to hold each other accountable to behaving in Constructive ways, directly calling out Defensive behavior whenever it occurred. Leaders and managers who refused to change—even after feedback and coaching—either left of their own volition or were let go.

Initially changing a few fundamental things led to other changes. For example, leaders realized they had to change the criteria for rewards and promotion so individuals and groups who exemplified desired values were recognized and promotions hinged on leadership qualities rather than technical skills. They eventually started creating cross-functional teams to work on projects and break down silos. Continuous improvement teams made up of people who worked on the factory floor were given greater autonomy and management support, allowing solutions to be implemented more readily and problems to be solved more quickly.

Culture even factored into how the company approached closing their oldest factory (located in Cooranbong, New South Wales) for business reasons in 2015. Prior to working on culture, Sanitarium simply closed factories with little notice, generating ill feelings toward the company among employees, as well as the people in the larger community. With Cooranbong, they implemented a "phased closure" over a three-year transition period. During this time, some employees were relocated to another factory, while others were given opportunities for training to move into roles in other industries or to start their own businesses. Financial and mental health counseling were also made available to employees.

Human Resources Director Peter Hartnett notes that approaching this situation in a more Constructive way meant the reactions were more positive than with past closings. He points out that the factory's culture results in late 2015 (as measured by the *Organizational Culture Inventory*) continued to show improvements. This is noteworthy, given that, in our experience, layoffs and plant closures can cause culture to go in a more Defensive direction, particularly in terms of Avoidance and Oppositional behaviors. Instead, their new approach kept people in the plant and in the rest of the organization engaged and continuing to work in a less Defensive, more Constructive mode. It's a shift that has continued, as confirmed by the remeasure of the culture in 2017 (see Figure 9.2).

The shift in culture directly corresponded with the shifts the leaders made to their own thinking, behavior, and impact. The senior leaders collectively had a fairly strong Constructive mindset and behavioral style from the start. Nevertheless, they worked on making their Constructive orientation even stronger and more consistent with the organization's values and ideal culture, through both personal development and changes to the leadership team (see Figure 9.3). They practiced thinking and behaving in more Constructive ways when approaching problems, making decisions, and carrying out their work. They also made frequent use of Prescriptive strategies and approaches (and limited their use of Restrictive strategies) in carrying out their leadership roles, as described by both self and others. As a result, they had a much stronger and more consistent Constructive impact on each other and the other people around them (see Figure 9.4) as well as on the overall operating culture of Sanitarium (see Figures 9.2 and 9.5). Not complicated, but certainly not easy. Was moving toward a more Constructive culture worth the discipline and hard work?

Leading People to Think Outside the Box 225

Figure 9.2. Sanitarium's Operating Culture Over Time

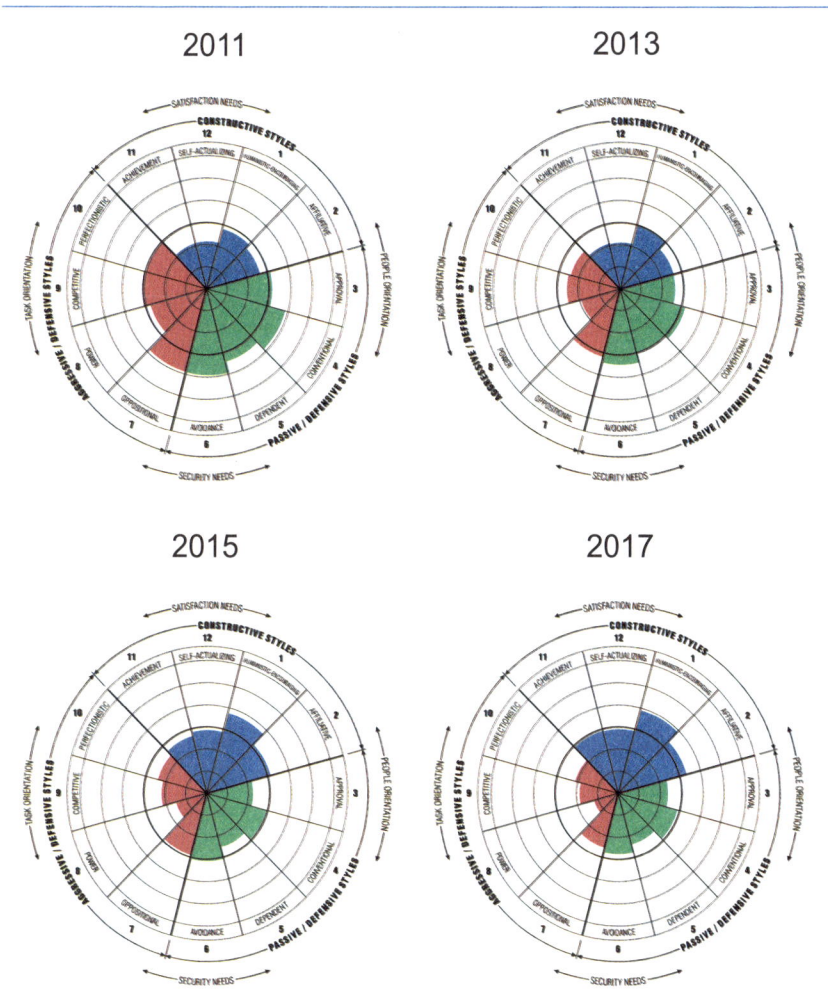

Research and development by Robert A. Cooke, Ph.D. and J. Clayton Lafferty, Ph.D.
Copyright © 1987-2019 by Human Synergistics International. All Rights Reserved.

226 Chapter 9

Figure 9.3. Senior Leaders' Composite *Life Styles Inventory* Profiles Over Time

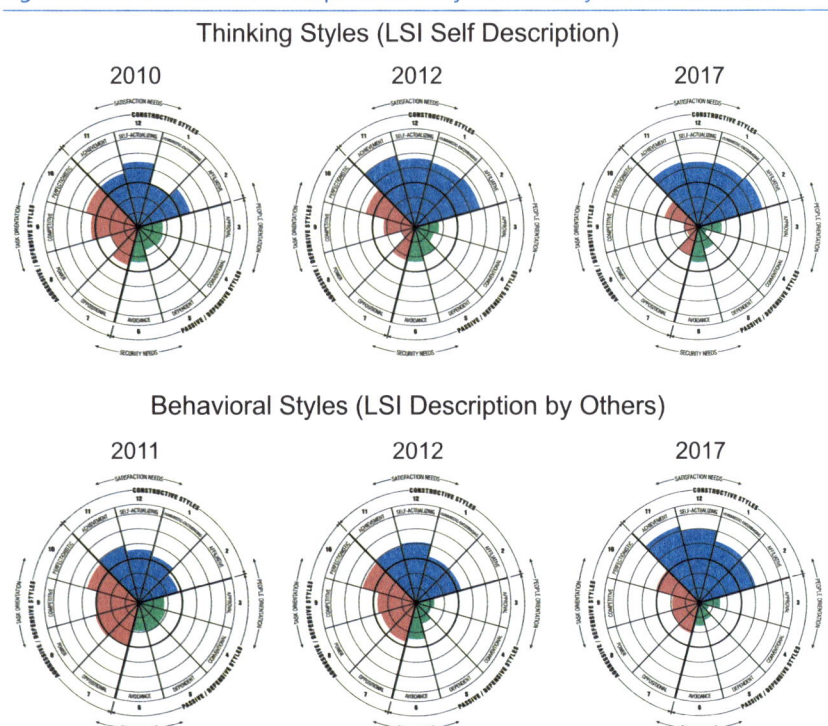

Thinking Styles (LSI Self Description)

2010   2012   2017

Behavioral Styles (LSI Description by Others)

2011   2012   2017

Research and development by Robert A. Cooke, Ph.D. and J. Clayton Lafferty, Ph.D.
Copyright © 1987-2019 by Human Synergistics International. All Rights Reserved.

Figure 9.4. Senior Leaders' Composite *Leadership/Impact* Results (2014)

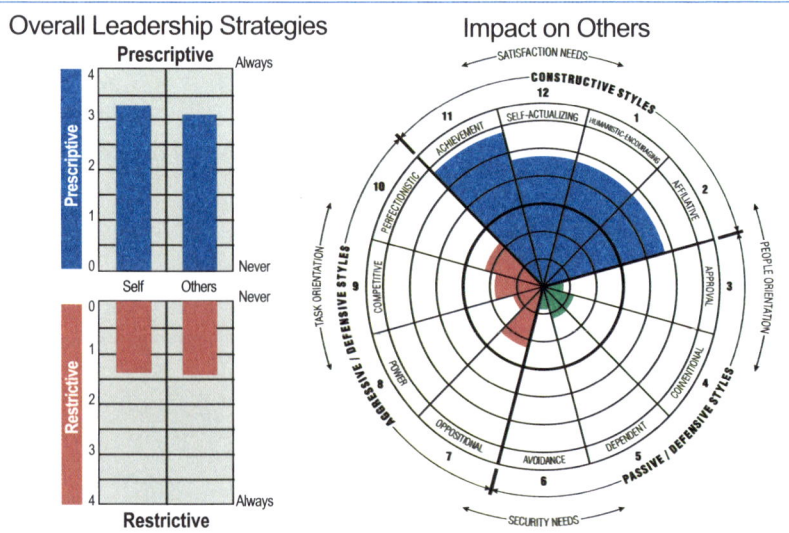

Overall Leadership Strategies

Impact on Others

From *Leadership/Impact® Composite Report* by Robert A. Cooke, Ph.D.
Copyright © 1997-2019 by Human Synergistics International. All Rights Reserved.

Leading People to Think Outside the Box   227

Figure 9.5. Changes in Senior Leaders' Thinking Styles Create Ripple Effect on Operating Culture

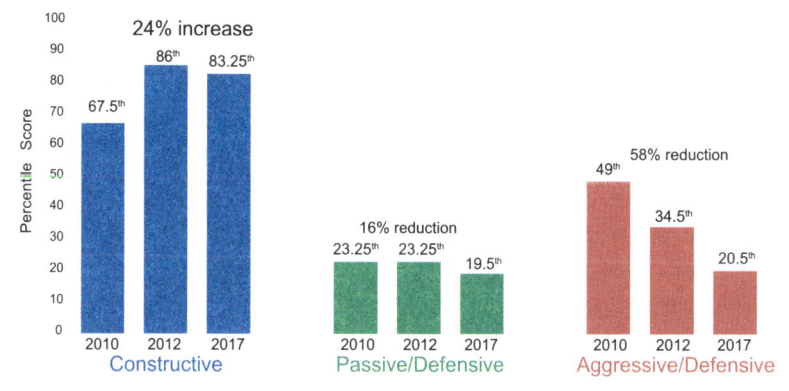

Changes in Senior Leaders' Thinking Styles
(based on *Life Styles Inventory* Self Description)

Constructive: 67.5th (2010), 86th (2012), 83.25th (2017) — 24% increase
Passive/Defensive: 23.25th (2010), 23.25th (2012), 19.5th (2017) — 16% reduction
Aggressive/Defensive: 49th (2010), 34.5th (2012), 20.5th (2017) — 58% reduction

Changes in Leaders' Behavioral Styles
(based on *Life Styles Inventory* Description by Others)

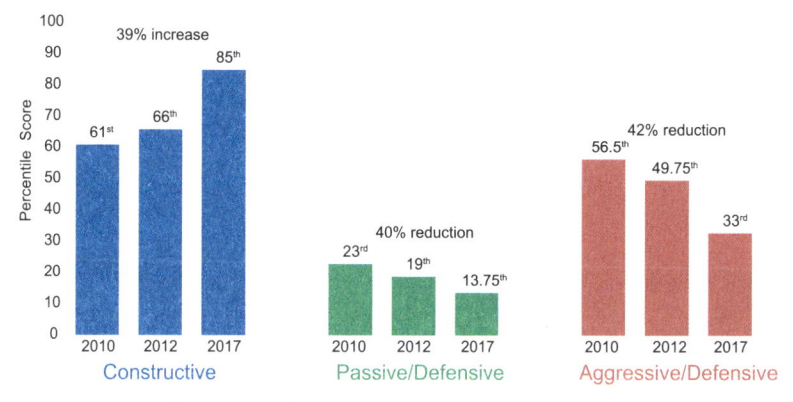

Constructive: 61st (2010), 66th (2012), 85th (2017) — 39% increase
Passive/Defensive: 23rd (2010), 19th (2012), 13.75th (2017) — 40% reduction
Aggressive/Defensive: 56.5th (2010), 49.75th (2012), 33rd (2017) — 42% reduction

Changes in Organization's Operating Culture
(based on *Organizational Culture Inventory*)

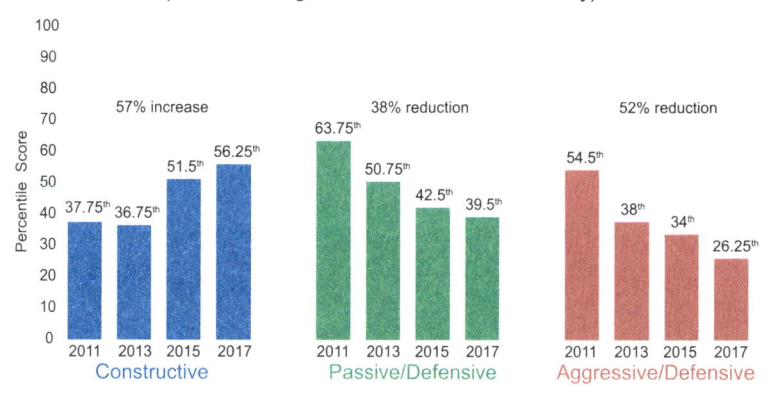

Constructive: 37.75th (2011), 36.75th (2013), 51.5th (2015), 56.25th (2017) — 57% increase
Passive/Defensive: 63.75th (2011), 50.75th (2013), 42.5th (2015), 39.5th (2017) — 38% reduction
Aggressive/Defensive: 54.5th (2011), 38th (2013), 34th (2015), 26.25th (2017) — 52% reduction

Tangible Results

At the beginning of 2013, punishing market conditions hit the company with a ferocity that they hadn't expected midway through cultural change. According to Peter Harnett,

> Everything happened at once—we got competitors into a market in which we had a monopoly, commodity prices virtually doubled overnight, and we had a decline in people eating breakfast cereal products. It was a turning point in terms of "How are we going to deal with this?" We had been doing a lot of development, but we hadn't really put it to the test in a stressful situation. There was a time when we would have sat back and pointed fingers and blamed people for the situation that we were in. But that didn't happen. The bottom line is the culture really changed the game for us in terms of our ability to be fast, and that's what triggered us to become a leader in some of the things we're doing.

Rather than revert to their old habitual ways, the leaders of Sanitarium began to apply what they had been practicing. They took risks and started partnering with their retail customers in new ways. When they ran into problems internally, they kept their conversations blue. "No tempers lost, no hissy fits, just good productive blue conversations about next steps," says Todd. These efforts resulted in a successful $2 million promotion for their Up&Go product with a major Australian retailer, among other profitable new partnerships.[216]

As a result of their efforts, the company reduced their new product development time by 75 percent, starting with their most important products, Energize Weet-Bix and Gluten-Free Weet-Bix. Then they continued to roll out that learning to other products. Todd notes,

> The important part of the culture journey was that it started to work for us. We moved to a situation where we were installing lines on time and within budget. We shortened the innovation cycle times and produced more Up&Go, which is our key product, than ever before, because we actually had people in a space where they felt more comfortable working together and getting out of the red and green behavior.[217]

Three years later, those results were sustained. Sanitarium continued to hit budget, sales, and profit targets and continued to bring new products to market quicker than ever before. In 2015, for example, they introduced two products that were completely outside of their core business: Naturally Nood, a line of whole-food bars and bites; and Weet-Bix Go, a breakfast biscuit to compete with Velveeta's. According to Todd, the breakfast biscuits helped in "building a bridge to a new pillar that's not an existing part of the core business." It is an example of something they wouldn't have considered when they began their culture journey, yet was critical because their industry is operating in some declining categories.[218] At the same time, the company managed to regain the market share that it had lost in its core business. By 2016, the shares of their largest cereal competitors, Kellogg's and Nestle, had eroded as consumers switched to healthier breakfast and snack options, as well as to protein and nutrition-rich bars, areas in which Sanitarium was well-positioned.

Independent surveys confirmed that Sanitarium was delighting their customers in a market in which their major competitors were slow to respond. In 2016, Sanitarium's Weet-Bix was voted "Most Trusted Breakfast Food" by the *Reader's Digest Most Trusted Brand* survey for a fourth year in a row.[219] Since 2010, retailers' ratings of Sanitarium have steadily increased, according to a report by an independent firm that conducts annual benchmarking and relationship analysis for over twenty suppliers to nine retailers in Australia. Whereas some of their major competitors experienced volatility and decline in their ratings from retailers during the period of 2010 to 2016, Sanitarium's net favorability ratings progressively improved.[220]

"We now see our people throughout the company changing their assumptions about process, challenging the status quo, and coming up with new ideas and ways of accelerating product development, which just didn't happen before," says Peter. For instance, on the factory floor, one group of line employees took the initiative to install a whiteboard to improve the communication of important information between shifts. They also made changes to enhance communication between operators and mechanics. Before, the operator would just leave the problem with the mechanic to figure out and fix. Now operators communicate directly with the mechanics, and they solve the problem together. As a result, production lines are up and running faster, with less downtime. Similarly, in Sanitarium's offices, the account managers used what they learned about Constructive conversations to work more effectively with retailer customers to solve problems—which was reflected in the improved customer service ratings.

"You see these touchpoints across the business where things have changed," notes Peter. "We've still got things to work on—cultural dark spots. But we know where they are and what we need to do as an organization to work through those." In 2016, Sanitarium was recognized as an innovator in Human Resource Management and as Employer of Choice for the third year in a row. And for Peter came recognition as Australia's HR Director of the Year.[221]

Reflecting on their experience thus far, Todd concludes,

> You can change the strategy very quickly with people with the right behaviors, but you can't change behaviors that easily. That is why we are succeeding in some of those areas a little further from the core. So, I think that's the tipping point for us. We can build a future now because of the change in our culture.

Key Learnings

Sanitarium's leaders learned that the Constructive behavioral styles they wanted to embed in the culture were relevant to solving all kinds of problems, from plant closings to how to go about the process of change. Making these improvements did not require the people at Sanitarium to alter their mission—nor abandon their faith-based identity and heritage—but instead required them to better honor and fulfill it. In their case, this meant continuing to share a message of health and hope for a better life. In doing so, they've gotten faster and more innovative and skyrocketed their employee engagement, customer satisfaction, and business and market performance.

Consistent with other stories in this book, Sanitarium's experience confirms the importance of making culture a strategic priority. It also highlights a few additional key points for leaders to keep in mind as they approach change:

1. Start with choosing one, two, or three things to change that really matter and that you can personally do something about. Sanitarium started with communication, personal accountability for change, and job significance. What they discovered, as many of our clients

do, is that when you understand the shared beliefs and behavioral norms that you are trying to promote and strengthen, working on just a few things will naturally lead you to align other aspects of your organization and leadership in terms of structures, systems, technology, and skills and qualities.
2. Stay focused on what it is that you decide to change and stick with it. For Sanitarium, that meant noticing what worked and what didn't, adjusting as they learned, and maintaining their commitment to change, even when they made mistakes or fell back. Leaders stayed with their commitment to change in tough times as well as in good times.
3. Recognize the wins and signs of progress along the way—big and small—to maintain the motivation and momentum. Big wins in this case included a 75 percent reduction in new product development cycle times, more frequent and numerous successes with new product introductions, increasingly rapid responsiveness to external changes, improved employee involvement and engagement, and improved market position.

The story of Sanitarium illustrates how leaders sustain their enthusiasm and commitment to culture over time and across a variety of challenging situations and events. We turn our attention now to Saskatchewan, Canada, to learn how an organization in a completely different industry has been able to sustain their commitment to a Constructive culture for more than twenty years and through two changes in leadership.

Key Learnings

- Start by changing a few specific things at a time that really matter to the organization.
- Stick with it in the most critical and difficult times.
- Recognize the wins and signs of progress along the way—big and small—to maintain motivation and momentum.

Chapter 10

Sustaining Constructive Cultures through Continuous Monitoring, Coaching, and Support (Canada)

> Our strategy has changed, our structure has changed, but our commitment to our values and our culture—that has not changed.
>
> Keith Nixon, CEO, SaskCentral

Organization	SaskCentral
Location	Regina, Saskatchewan, Canada
Industry	Financial Services
Founded	1938
Market Position	N/A
Number of Employees	80
Started Culture Journey	1996
Interviewees	Debbie Lane, Executive Vice President and Chief People Officer
	Keith Nixon, CEO, 2013-present

SaskCentral building

As the financial intermediary and trade association for forty-six credit unions in the western Canadian province of Saskatchewan, SaskCentral had much to be proud of in 2015. They had successfully emerged from the economic crisis of 2008; from the many industry, market, and technological changes in the financial services sector generally; and from changes in their own leadership. They were riding high in terms of financial metrics, having exceeded all their targets, as confirmed by CEO Keith Nixon in the organization's 2015 annual report. Deposits had increased by 7.6 percent over the previous year from $1.79 billion to $1.92 billion (Canadian dollars). And profit was $26.3 million compared to $23.6 million in 2014. In addition, SaskCentral had earned an 86 percent client satisfaction rating—their highest to date—as well as a score of 89 percent on employee engagement. Not least, SaskCentral was again ranked one of the top twenty-five Best Places to Work® in Canada,[222] making the top one hundred list for the eighth year in a row—as well as, incidentally, ranking as one of the best workplaces for women among companies of any size.

However, what Keith Nixon and Executive VP and Chief People Officer Debbie Lane were most proud of was the steadfast commitment of their people to staying Constructive during what was probably the most difficult and stressful time in the company's history. Impending transformation of

Canada's financial cooperatives into a nationally unified and internationally capable cooperative financial network. This meant that SaskCentral's leaders would be "reconfiguring the company," in ways not yet fully determined, in order to achieve greater efficiencies and reduced duplication of effort in the services provided by their organization and the other provincial centrals. Despite the uncertain future of the company, as well as their own jobs, managers and employees were collaboratively and proactively doing whatever needed to be done to move the process of transformation forward while, at the same time, continuing to deliver the high level of service that their credit union clients had grown accustomed to receiving. Indeed, SaskCentral's latest culture survey results confirmed that Constructive norms were stronger than they had ever been in the twenty years that the company has been measuring its culture.

Top to bottom: Keith Nixon and Debbie Lane

As the founders of workplace consulting firm Great Place to Work®, Milton Moskowitz and Robert Levering, pointed out in a *Fortune* magazine article, there is a virtuous circle connecting workplace culture, happy employees, and financial success. They referenced a study by the Russell Investment Group that found "The 100 best companies to work for outperform the S&P Index by a ratio of nearly 2 to 1," adding that the leaders of such companies "are focused on workplace culture as a competitive tool."[223]

As you will undoubtedly have realized from the previous chapters, establishing and maintaining the kind of culture that cultivates high employee engagement and fiscal success isn't as straightforward as many would have us believe. The story of SaskCentral's journey toward creating and maintaining a Constructive culture reinforces several of the key learnings from previous chapters. It also highlights three additional elements—continuous monitoring of culture, coaching, and support from the entire organization, including its board—that have contributed to strengthening and sustaining that culture over two decades and two changes in leadership.

Establishing the Foundation for a Long-Term Commitment to Culture

SaskCentral initiated its culture change journey back in the 1990s, during a critical time for the industry. According to Debbie Lane, the expansion of the global market, along with the rise of internet banking, had created an explosion of choices for banking consumers, changing the ways in which they wanted to do business as well as their expectations around products and services. At the same time, SaskCentral was losing touch with its credit unions, who were dissatisfied with the way in which the organization was engaging with them on important strategic projects and decisions.

Sid Bildfell, who was SaskCentral's CEO at the time, understood that the organization's long-term sustainability meant taking a critical look at operations and spending, while at the same time becoming a role model for credit unions and the community as a whole. This mindset sparked the beginning of what would eventually turn into a long-term commitment to developing and managing a more Constructive organizational culture.

Sid and Debbie recognized that to redirect and manage culture, they had to measure it. They wanted a credible and reliable assessment that could be used over the long term to help them stay on track. Debbie recalls,

> Sid said, "Find a tool that's going to help. But when you find that tool, it must be sustainable over the long term and withstand the test of time, because we aren't going to be changing how we assess our culture every other year." And I think that that was really important.

They chose the *Organizational Culture Inventory* and the *Organizational Effectiveness Inventory* because they met those criteria.

Among the cultural characteristics confirmed by the *Organizational Culture Inventory* was that members within SaskCentral believed they needed to protect themselves against one another—and particularly against those in other divisions. This "enemy within" story is one you've come across before in earlier chapters. Rather than believing they were safe to make suggestions, take risks, and show initiative—which is what the leaders described as ideal—people at all levels of SaskCentral believed they needed to protect and promote themselves by being "nice" and avoiding conflicts. At the same time, they felt they were implicitly required to deflect criticism by indirectly blaming and shifting responsibility for problems and issues to other departments and people (see Figure 10.1).

Feedback from the *Organizational Effectiveness Inventory* indicated a lack of common goals, disempowerment of lower level employees, poor communication at all levels and in all directions, and disconnection from clients. These factors were contributing to the internal competition as well as to several other Defensive norms that had become part of the organization's operating culture.

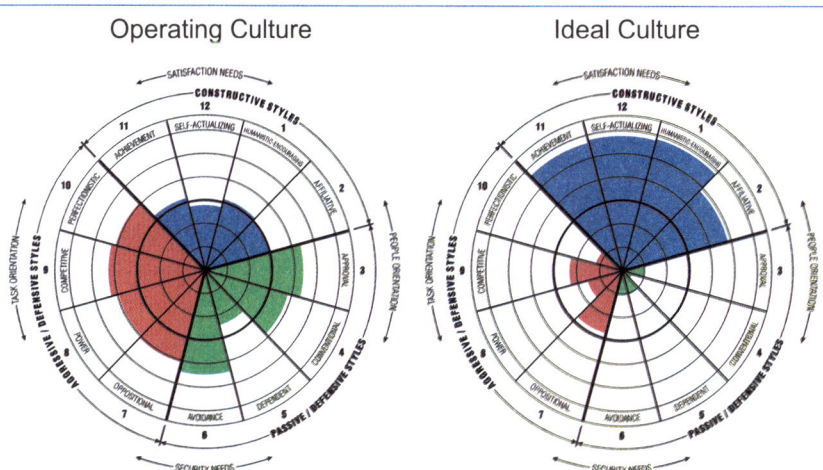

Figure 10.1. SaskCentral's Operating Culture and Ideal Culture (1996)

Research and development by Robert A. Cooke, Ph.D. and J. Clayton Lafferty, Ph.D.
Copyright © 1987-2019 by Human Synergistics International. All Rights Reserved.

The organization's leaders initially responded to the feedback by planning numerous change initiatives and programs. They also formed a Service Excellence Committee made up of employees from each of the company's divisions to act as change agents. That sounds good, doesn't it? However, two years into the process, a reassessment of their culture showed only a tiny shift toward the more Constructive norms they'd been seeking to promote. Not least, it was clear that these disappointing results were largely due to some members of the executive team being resistant to the proposed changes. Instead of changing their own attitudes and behavior, they had given the culture initiatives and programs lip service (consistent with the Approval and Avoidance aspects of SaskCentral's culture that Sid Bildfell was seeking to eliminate).

"We didn't anticipate that if the leaders were also being influenced by strong norms for Avoidance along with a lot of upward decision making, little was likely to get done," explained consultant Ken Curtis at our

Consultants' Forum in 2014. Ken worked with the organization since they began their culture change journey.[224] His observation is a good reminder that leaders not only influence culture but that culture also influences leaders, including in how they approach culture change.

As we know from examining the other cases in this book, commitment at the top is essential to changing the culture of an organization. Debbie Lane recalls,

> Sid said to me and the other leaders, "If we cannot demonstrate the behaviors that we're asking our employees to display, then we really have no business being leaders." He was really blunt about it. Performance objectives were articulated, expectations were made clear, and there were some very difficult conversations that took place.[225]

Leadership/Impact was given to the top three tiers of leadership so they would understand how they personally were contributing to the existing culture and could modify their leadership approach to have a more Constructive impact. Managers and employees were given the *Life Styles Inventory* so they were aware of the characteristics they brought to the table. Group problem-solving simulations such as the *Desert Survival Situation*, along with the *Group Styles Inventory*, were used with groups that were struggling with coming together as a team.

"Everyone in the organization started to understand and speak a common language," says Debbie. However, as was true in the other cases in this book, they wanted to achieve more than just raising awareness. People at all levels of the organization needed to accept responsibility for their behavior and take action to have a more Constructive impact (consistent with the three *A*'s). Consequently, performance objectives and reward systems were modified to be more supportive of and consistent with the ideal culture. Culture was made part of the organization's balanced scorecard and how the CEO's performance was evaluated. Personal styles became a key consideration in recruitment and selection, as well as promotions.

To further break down the silos and eliminate the competition between functions, the organization was restructured, and cross-functional goals were established. With complementary changes being made to systems, structures, and skills and qualities—including the skills and qualities of the leaders and managers—it became increasingly clear to everyone in the organization that *how* things were being achieved was just as important as *what* they achieved.

Over time, managers who realized they no longer fit with the new culture and didn't want to change self-selected out of the organization. That left SaskCentral with leaders and managers who truly believed that it was their employees that made the organization successful and would consciously check their own behavior to ensure they acted in ways that supported this belief.

Consistent with what you read in chapter 1 about ideal cultures, the movement toward creating a more Constructive culture was embraced by people of all ages within SaskCentral. Older workers and younger workers alike began demonstrating more respect and cooperation. Mentoring started working two ways, with both groups learning from each other.

As people worked together in more collaborative and synergistic ways, the organization's client satisfaction ratings began rising, as did their employee satisfaction and retention metrics. These are all authentic signs that SaskCentral really was living by the cooperative principle of working together. "Our culture allows us to support our employees so they can focus on the client," Debbie points out.

Coaching, Monitoring, and Board Support

With organizational transformation progressing much more quickly from then on, Sid Bildfell wanted to be sure his vision endured over the long term. He was therefore mindful of what could happen to the culture once he retired (which took place at the beginning of 2008) and a new leader was selected. Sid continually coached and prepared other members of the leadership team—which is important, given that you never know for certain who will eventually succeed you and others down the line. Current CEO Keith Nixon recalls that one of the things he learned from Sid was that being an executive is more than just a job:

> After Sid offered me an executive position as corporate secretary, he continually challenged me on paying attention to the impact of my leadership on people. I always appreciated what a good coach he was. When he left, I remember walking across the parking lot and thinking what a great job I had at the executive level. Then it struck me that it was much more than that. It was a responsibility to our credit unions as well as the people who work for us that we manage an excellent

company. That realization changed my thinking about what it means to be an effective leader and the impact on people and the organization. It guided the development work that I did as well as helped prepare me to be in the position of CEO when the time came. Because it's not just a job, it's a responsibility.

As we've seen in previous chapters, recognizing how culture change efforts are affecting the organization and its ability to achieve its mission and goals is essential to maintaining motivation as well as making course corrections. Since embarking on their culture change journey, SaskCentral's leadership has regularly measured and reported to the board on the state of the organization's culture. They also began regularly surveying their clients on the quality of the service that they were receiving from SaskCentral. Individual-level outcome measures from the *Organizational Effectiveness Inventory*—including employee satisfaction, motivation, and intention to stay—were used to gauge engagement. Consequently, the board's members not only understand the language of the Circumplex, they also recognize how the organization's ongoing efforts toward strengthening Constructive norms have contributed to its success as a service provider and an employer of choice. Debbie explains,

> When we did our first assessment of our service to the credit unions [shortly after they began their culture change journey], it was not that great. Now we're in the 80 percent range. What we've seen is a direct correlation between a Constructive culture and how we engage with our clients and owners.
>
> If the board didn't understand the importance of culture and instead only emphasized results, we'd probably have very high turnover, low morale, and relatively poor client service, because our people would just be delivering rather than engaging.

It's a timely point. In the wake of recent corporate culture scandals and crises, national associations of corporate directors in various countries—including the United States, Australia, the UK, and Canada—have begun working on defining the role that corporate boards should take with respect to the culture of the companies they serve.[226] In contrast, SaskCentral's board has been mindful of organizational culture for over two decades—and doing many of the things now being recommended for boards in general. This includes paying attention to:

Sustaining Constructive Cultures 241

a) the connections between the company's purpose, strategy, and culture;
b) the alignment of incentives and culture values;
c) the measurement of culture; and
d) the impact of their own behavior and decisions on the organization's culture.

Consequently, it's not surprising that SaskCentral's commitment to the original vision has been maintained through three successive CEOs, the last two of whom were selected from within. To the entire organization's credit—including its leaders, managers, employees, and board members—SaskCentral's Constructive culture has grown stronger over time (see Figure 10.2).

Figure 10.2. SaskCentral's Operating Culture Over Time

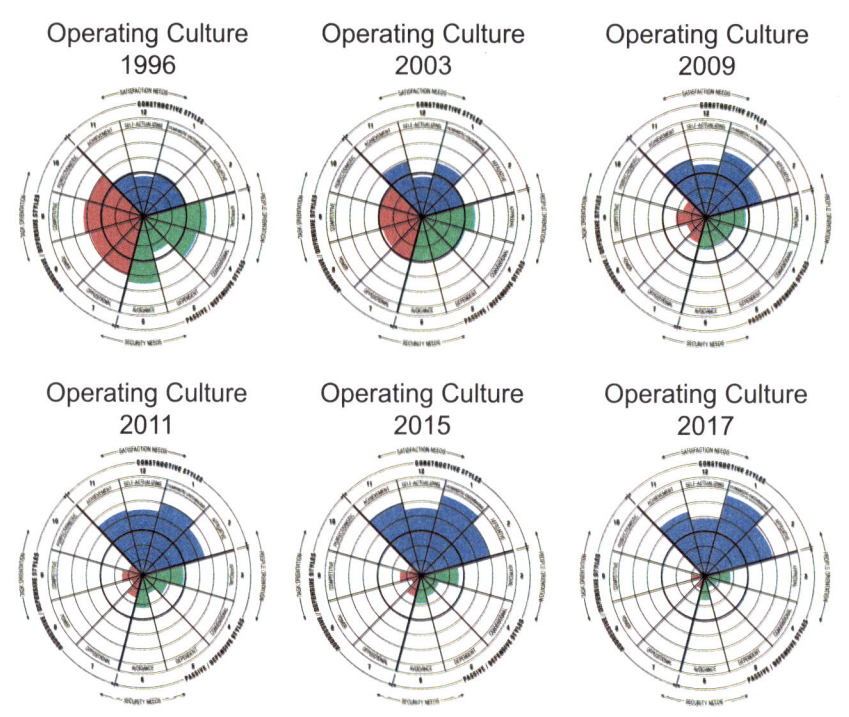

Research and development by Robert A. Cooke, Ph.D. and J. Clayton Lafferty, Ph.D.
Copyright © 1987-2019 by Human Synergistics International. All Rights Reserved.

One Thing You Can Always Control: Your Commitment to Culture

Like most organizations in the financial services industry, SaskCentral has had many rocky external—as well as internal—challenges to overcome. However, throughout the twenty years that they have been on their culture change journey, they have never strayed far from their focus on the ideal culture. Indeed, they've intentionally chosen leaders and managers who are committed to a Constructive culture. They have regularly monitored the operating culture and readily addressed any deviations from that ideal, which has been reinforced by making culture part of their organization's balanced scorecard and by monitoring the effects of culture on outcomes important to their business. And they've used the feedback to adjust their structures, systems, technology, and skills and qualities, including the way they lead, so that they continue to support and reinforce the organization's Constructive values. For instance, to make work/life balance easier for employees, they implemented a compressed workplace option before it became popular and widely used by organizations.

Their relatively long history of actively maintaining a strong, supportive culture has taught them what it takes to create a safe environment where people commit to helping one another so they can weather whatever storms they encounter. Indeed, this was one of the biggest learnings for Debbie Lane and the other leaders during the financial downturn that began in 2008.

"No one saw that coming in our industry," says Debbie. "It was something we couldn't control, but what we *can* control is keeping our focus on how we interact with one another and the culture." Even when their financial performance softened and they were unable to make any incentive payments, SaskCentral continued to invest in personal development—a stark contrast to what companies typically do during tough times. "The Constructive culture was even more important to help us get through a difficult period of performance," Debbie explains, echoing the conclusions of Spreadshirt's CEO, Philip Rooke, in chapter 4. Even when it became necessary for SaskCentral to downsize, the organization and its leaders remained resolute on their commitment to the culture. Although technical competencies were important, they continued to emphasize personal competencies when making tough decisions as to who to retain and who to let go. "If you didn't have the attitude we needed to stay positive and move forward, that certainly played into the decision," says Debbie. "You can always train technical competencies. Personal competencies and attitudes are much harder to train." Her observation is consistent with those of other leaders, including business owner Sergio Acosta in chapter 6.

In the case of SaskCentral, although their client satisfaction scores dipped slightly during the 2008 crisis, they quickly bounced back. In addition, the organization started being recognized as one of the top one hundred workplaces in Canada. It's a recognition that they have earned every year since.

As mentioned at the beginning of this chapter, more recent regulatory changes have created the opportunity for national credit unions in Canada—and, along with it, the imminent consolidation of many of the provincial centrals' trade association activities. Consequently, the SaskCentral that has traditionally existed may very well be extinct in a few years' time.

In 2013, as the industry changes began to unfold, SaskCentral's culture survey results started to show some of the silo mentality and competitiveness from earlier times. Because SaskCentral regularly monitors its culture, its leaders and managers were quick to respond when the culture started to veer off course, with Debbie and her team on hand to help. Keith Nixon had just taken over as CEO. He and Debbie knew from experience that this mentality was promoted by division barriers and boundaries. From both a cultural and business line perspective, Keith says it made sense for them to change the executive structure and realign management positions. As we know from other cases, simply deleting positions or moving them around might temporarily help the business line, but by itself such restructuring does not create a more Constructive culture. In addition to restructuring, SaskCentral's leaders modified some of the organization's human resource management practices, adjusted their own behavior and leadership approaches, and focused strongly on further improving communication and employee involvement. Now, you may be thinking, "Didn't they already do that years ago?" They most certainly did. However, as Debbie points out, "Culture just doesn't stand still because change is happening around us or to us. It's a part of who we are and how we operate."

This brings us back to a point made earlier, about the value of having employees who see SaskCentral as a great place to work—and the extent to which a Constructive culture contributes to that. You would think that with all the industry and business changes and uncertainty about their future, employees would have plenty of reason to leave. Yet that didn't happen at SaskCentral. According to Debbie,

> What we have heard through our recent surveys and the comments we've received is that even though our future is uncertain, so is the future of many other companies in the marketplace. People want to stay here and see how it plays out, because they like how they are treated and work together. They are not afraid.

Over the years, SaskCentral's leaders have made changes to HR systems, gone through downsizing and reorganizations, and changed and adapted their technology as the world, their industry, and their organization and its people have changed. Yet throughout, their Constructive culture has remained the buoy which keeps them steady. Says Keith Nixon,

> We need the good ideas of our people to get us from where we are to that new future state. We need them to feel like they are adding value, achieving things, and creating success while we're reconfiguring the company and rebuilding it in other places. We believe there will be a vibrant credit union system in the future. If our people are creating value and adding value to the organization, the credit union system will need them. It may not be the job they have now, but it could be a different or better job in a different organization. So creating a vision that we're not afraid to change, transform, merge, or redevelop, and having our Constructive culture see us through it is what is key. Because we can't do it with a protective, avoidant, competitive culture. Those Defensive behaviors will never get us to where we need to go. Our strategy has changed, our structure has changed, but our commitment to our values and our culture—that has not changed.

An Organization of Lifelong Learners

Whereas learning and adapting weren't happening at SaskCentral until they began working on their culture, it has been a part of how they

Painting of Regina by Rose Odling, given to Rob by SaskCentral's leaders

operate ever since. As SaskCentral started evolving toward a national system, a group of senior managers and employees who wanted to help the organization through the process organized themselves as a Core Change Team. Debbie points out,

> This wasn't something that the executive management team said, "We've got to strike this committee and this is what their purpose is." It happened the other way around, and they initiated this on their own. That is because of the culture.

At a time when other organizations in their position would have cut back on investments in people, SaskCentral offered a customized change and career management program to all of their managers and employees. In 2016, they attained their highest employee engagement score ever—89.7 percent. They have continued to rank as one of the top twenty-five Best Places to Work in Canada and, in 2017, they were recognized as one of Canada's top three Best Places to Work for Women.[227]

Creating a Constructive culture that encourages people to proactively adapt and expand their knowledge and skills isn't just an organizational necessity. It's also a societal imperative. As US senator Ben Sasse put it:

> We are entering an era in which we're going to have to create a society of lifelong learners. We're going to have to create a culture in which people in their 40s and 50s, who see their industry disintermediated and their jobs evaporate, get retrained and have the will and the chutzpah and the tools and the social network to get another job. Right now that doesn't happen enough.[228]

Yet at SaskCentral, people taking the initiative to adapt and continually develop themselves and each other *is* part of the culture. As their story illustrates, it's a culture in which *everyone* takes responsibility for taking care of it, regardless of position and without having to be asked. As a champion of SaskCentral's culture change journey since it began, Debbie Lane concludes,

> I started off as a really strong champion and advocate for the culture. However, as we have grown over the years, that commitment has been placed in all of our employees. We all embrace it. And so, the torch has already been passed beyond myself and HR to our organization. Because everybody recognizes that they have influence, they have accountability, and there's a strong sense of pride in this organization.

Key Learnings

What makes this story extraordinary is the unwavering commitment of SaskCentral's leaders, managers, employees, and board members to the organization's culture. With all of the relatively recent transformations and changes—including the new CEO, the new organizational structure, the changing makeup of credit unions, and the changing industry structure—the people and the culture could have been negatively affected, as we have seen happen in so many organizations. But SaskCentral has dealt with these changes in consideration of their organization's values rather than in disregard of them. By making the overall culture more Constructive, SaskCentral has maintained a highly engaged workforce; a better work environment for everyone, including women; a high level of client service; and a strong financial position (deposits in 2016 grew 4.3 percent over 2015 to $2 billion).

The insights that the organization's leaders, managers, and employees have gained through their journey has taught them quite a bit, not only about how to create a more Constructive culture but also how to maintain it. Many of their learnings were consistent with those highlighted in previous chapters—including the importance of

- tying the work on culture to outcomes relevant to the organization's purpose and goals;
- embedding transformation efforts in the day-to-day work;

- using levers for change at the individual, group, and organizational levels;
- using a shared language to communicate about behavior and culture;
- cultivating awareness, acceptance, and action with respect to everyone's own behavior and impact;
- approaching culture change with the mindset of the new culture rather than the old one;
- aligning structures, systems, technology, and skills and qualities with the ideal culture;
- collaborating with HR as a key source of support;
- purposefully making culture part of strategy; and
- nurturing an ideal culture through tough times as well as good times.

The chapter also highlighted a few additional key points, including the value of

- consistently monitoring culture;
- coaching at all levels, including at the top; and
- enlisting board support.

SaskCentral has deliberately and purposefully maintained a steady focus on exemplifying what it means for an organization to live its values. It's a rare quality indeed—not only in business organizations but, as we will see in the next chapter, in other kinds of organizations as well. We'll head back now to the United States to look at the culture change journey of an organization with the mission of inspiring and supporting people in living their values. Our next stop—the Episcopal Church.

Key Learnings

- Continually monitor culture to sustain attention and motivation as well as to signal course correction.
- Continue to coach people throughout the organization on their impact so current and future leaders know how to take care of the culture.
- Maintain the support of leaders and board members by showing how culture efforts contribute to the organization's mission, vision, and goals.

Chapter 11

From the Middle to the Top of the Organization: Making Culture a Habit of Grace (USA)

> We now have practical tools for transforming the spirit and culture of our organization. And like a spiritual practice, we have to keep going back to it so that it becomes a habit of grace.
>
> Michael Curry, Presiding Bishop of the Episcopal Church

Organization	Episcopal Church
Locations	Chicago, Illinois, and New York, New York, United States of America
Industry	Religious
Founded	1835 (Chicago Diocese); 1785 (Episcopal Church of the United States of America)
Number of Members	Over 1.9 million (as of 2016)
Number of Employees	22 in Chicago; 194 in New York central office
Started Culture Journey	2010 in Chicago; 2016 in New York
Interviewees	Jeffrey Lee, Bishop of the Diocese of Chicago
	The Reverend Gay Clark Jennings, President of the House of Deputies and former Associate Director at CREDO Institute
	Jennifer Baskerville-Burrows, Bishop of the Diocese of Indianapolis and former Director of Networking at the Diocese of Chicago
	Courtney Reid, Director of Operations at the Diocese of Chicago
	Michael Curry, Presiding Bishop of the Episcopal Church
	Tim Kuppler, Human Synergistics (Supporting Consultant)
	Scott Beilke, Brighton Leadership Group (Supporting Consultant)

THE *Episcopal* CHURCH

Left to right:
Presiding Bishop Michael Curry, The Reverend Gay Clark Jennings, and Bishop Jeffrey Lee

"Sometimes the franchise can teach the home office or parent company," points out Gay Clark Jennings, President of the Episcopal Church's House of Deputies. Her remark might not seem startling, except that she was talking about culture change—specifically, in the Episcopal Church.

The church's story illustrates that successful culture change doesn't always start at the very top of the organization—nor does it only flow top-down. In this case, the unusual flow of change was incidental rather than planned. Leaders often look outside of their organizations for ideas on how to improve effectiveness and performance. While this approach can be extremely valuable, this case shows that it can also be valuable for leaders to look *inside* their own organizations for ideas and solutions. Culture change journeys don't typically unfold the way the Episcopal Church's did. However, their experience shows what is possible when courageous visionary leaders are willing to try something that is outside the norm to more effectively carry out their organization's mission and purpose.

Although this chapter is about the experience of the Episcopal Church, keep in mind that there is a much broader message to be taken from their story—one that directly loops back to the overall message of this book and a key learning from the first example (chapter 3): Culture change in any part of an organization expands only to the extent that leaders in other parts champion the changes in their own areas by embedding transformation efforts into how they carry out their day-to-day work of running the business. Consequently, it is *always* a personal, group, and organizational journey. Let's take a closer look at the key details of the Episcopal Church's experience.

Diocese of Chicago

The Diocese of Chicago is one of the church's largest, consisting of 126 congregations located in the northern third of the state of Illinois. With more than thirty-five thousand baptized members, it is also one of the church's most economically and ethnically diverse dioceses. On any given Sunday, at least seventeen different languages may be spoken in their congregations.[229]

Jeff Lee took office as the diocese's twelfth bishop in 2008. As bishop, he has spiritual and executive oversight for the ministry in the diocese. Consequently, the clergy or head pastors of the diocese's parishes are accountable to him. However, it is critical to keep in mind that the purpose of the bishop and his or her staff is to support the congregations through provision of resources and assistance, as well as unity of focus. This is something that bishops and their staffs can sometimes forget or overlook.

Jeff had previously worked in a small diocese in northern Indiana as part of the bishop's staff, before leading a thriving congregation near Seattle, Washington. The bishops of those dioceses had high expectations and established cultures that were quite different from the one that Jeff encountered when he arrived in Chicago. He recalls:

> When I got to Chicago and visited the diocese's parishes, people would tell me, "We called the other week to ask a question and never heard back," and would point out other relatively simple things that weren't being addressed. It's a relatively steep curve going from being a parish priest to a bishop of a diocese, so there was a lot that I was trying to learn. I knew the staff wasn't responding to things. It was hard even for me to get reports from them sometimes. During staff meetings, senior staff members often criticized the congregations and complained about how bad they were.
>
> I was talking constantly throughout the diocese about excellence at every level. Regardless of whether it was pastoral care, bookkeeping, or the sermons we preached, I emphasized that we should be doing the best work that can be done and assessing it constantly. We had parishes that were exemplars of that, and I held them up as examples for everyone else to see—when the reality was the bishop's office was anything but that.

Diocesan office at St. James Commons in Chicago

Like the other organizations you've read about in this book, the Diocese of Chicago had silos. Although the silos within the bishop's office were seemingly friendly toward one another, there was still little coordination and discussion between them. Different people from the diocese would contact the same person about the same issue. Conflicting events were continually getting scheduled by different departments for the same time. There was redundancy of effort on some things, while other things—like returning phone calls and answering questions from their congregations—weren't being addressed at all.

Not only did the bishop's office operate in a siloed fashion, but so did many of its congregations. Collaboration and discussion between them on common issues were rare. An "us versus them" attitude prevailed; congregations would often refer to the staff at the diocesan office as "those people at 65 East." Several congregations had created websites that were neither tied to nor coordinated with the diocese's website, much less with each other. The behavioral norms that had evolved among the bishop's staff were preventing the diocese as a whole from efficiently and effectively responding to critical problems and changes. At the time, these included not only numerous complaints from frustrated congregation leaders but also the deteriorating state of the diocesan center's building, aging and declining church membership, and racial reconciliation. Jeff explains,

> Two years into my time here, the gulf that existed between what I was preaching and what my staff were exemplifying was widening. The problems from it were mounting, and I didn't quite know what to do. I had talked myself into thinking that it wasn't that bad and that I was running as fast as I could. Then one day, the Regional Deans, who act as my council of advice, confronted me. They said, "We really like you and the energy you've brought to the diocese. However, we have a problem. When are you going to do something about your staff?" It was like having cold water thrown in my face.

As a former faculty member of the CREDO Institute, Jeff was familiar with its wellness and renewal program for the Episcopal Church's clergy members. He called CREDO's managing director, Bill Craddock, the next day to discuss the possibility of creating a wellness and renewal program at the organizational level. That was when Bill and Gay Jennings (who, at that time, was an associate director at CREDO) suggested they start by measuring the culture and climate of the diocese.

Introducing Quantitative Measures in a Storytelling Environment

"We are really good at telling stories and anecdotes in the church, but we're not very good at measuring things," Jeff points out. Except for tracking average Sunday attendance, plate donations, and number of baptized members, the diocese didn't use any kind of objective standardized measures for gauging the quality of their service and performance over time, much less in comparison to other organizations.

With the guidance and support of CREDO, the diocesan staff and leaders described the culture and climate of the diocese using the *Organizational Culture Inventory* and the *Organizational Effectiveness Inventory*. They also defined the ideal culture of the diocese by using the *Ideal* form of the *Organizational Culture Inventory*. Working as a consulting team, Gay Jennings and Steve Smith (from the Diocese of Vermont) conducted individual and group interviews with the bishop, members of the staff, members of the standing committee, and members of the diocesan council.

The results of the *Organizational Culture Inventory* showed an operating culture that was strongly oriented toward people, as indicated by extensions predominating the right (1:00 to 6:00 positions) rather than the left side of the Circumplex (see Figure 11.1). The unusually weak extension in Achievement, reinforced by a relatively strong extension in Avoidance (11:00 and 6:00 positions), confirmed a shared belief that personal initiative and collective efforts wouldn't necessarily make a difference. Although excellence was talked about, it was clear that people within the diocese didn't believe that it was actually required to fit in and meet expectations.

Figure 11.1. Diocese of Chicago's Operating and Ideal Culture Profiles (2011)

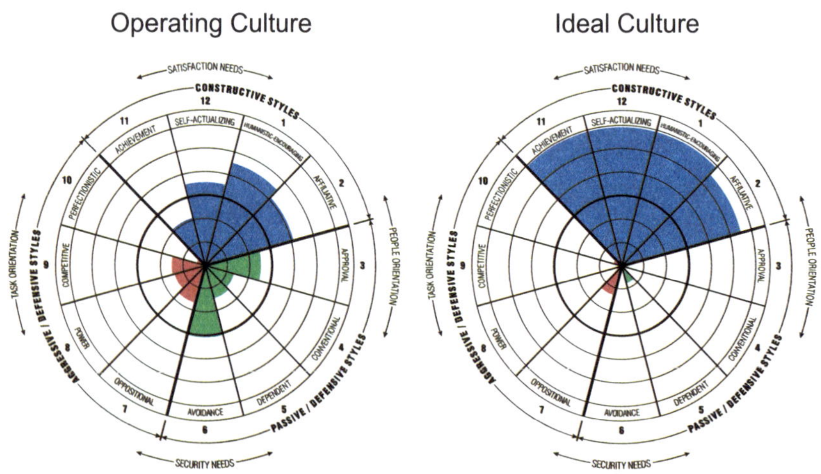

Research and development by Robert A. Cooke, Ph.D. and J. Clayton Lafferty, Ph.D.
Copyright © 1987-2019 by Human Synergistics International. All Rights Reserved.

The results of the *Organizational Effectiveness Inventory* showed that the diocese's customer service and adaptability were far below the inventory's historical average. Although the diocese was seen as doing well with fostering relationships with global partners, offering programs to strengthen and support clergy leadership, and participating in outreach efforts, it was essentially ignoring its fundamental responsibility of resourcing its congregations.[230] Both the surveys and interviews pointed to various aspects of the diocese's structure, systems, technology, and skills and qualities that were better aligned with the Defensive operating culture they had—rather than the predominantly Constructive and more Achievement-oriented ideal culture that leaders and staff described as necessary for the diocese to be effective (see profile on the right side of Figure 11.1).

Creating and Reinforcing Clarity of Purpose

The purpose of the diocese was to support the vitality of its congregations—and by all measures it was clear that the diocese was not effectively fulfilling that purpose. "We were awash in privilege, and it needed to change," Jeff points out. Based on the feedback from the surveys and interviews, he started with a complete reorganization of the diocesan office and staffing for ideal culture fit. Hiring teams that included representatives from the anti-racism commission were formed to evaluate candidates.

Rather than continue with the positions and titles traditionally used by the church (such as "Canon to the Ordinary"), new positions and titles were created to more clearly and explicitly reflect and communicate the purpose of the diocesan office and what people were responsible for doing. This included the formation of a new executive team that, in addition to the bishop, consisted of three new positions: Director of Ministry, Director of Networking, and Director of Operations.

Undoubtedly, the changes meant implementing some particularly tough decisions. Even though this case is about a church, the experiences are ones to which many leaders who have championed transformation efforts in other types of organizations can relate. Jeff recalls,

> In many ways, the hardest termination I did was one of the canons. We had just begun a large renovation project capital campaign to renovate our diocesan center. This man had cultivated some good relationships with a couple of important

lead donors. However, the existing culture at the time was embedded in his office. I knew we needed to make a change in that position and was torn because I didn't know what it was going to look like to the donors if we terminated him. After the terminations were over, I called the two donors to explain what had happened and why. They ran major organizations and understood the deficits. They both said, "You did what you had to do." It ended up increasing my credibility, and both donors made major gifts.

Consistent with one of the key learnings of this chapter, Jeff found that he didn't have to go far to find people who exemplified and knew how to reinforce the kind of culture needed to more effectively fulfill the diocese's mission and purpose. This naturally led to other changes. For instance, Jeff persuaded Jim Steen—a recently retired head of one of the diocese's best-performing churches in terms of vitality and growth—to be the new Director of Ministry. Jim's leadership style focused strongly on creating clear goals and accountability through performance management and human resource management systems, which Jeff believed would be instrumental to strengthening an Achievement orientation within the

Bishop Jeffrey Lee with executive team members Courtney Reid, the Reverend Jim Steen, and the Reverend Jennifer Baskerville-Burrows

culture. "He began articulating and enforcing these very basic levels of expectation with the staff," says Jeff. "We instituted job performance reviews for the first time ever, which was very new here."

For the Director of Networking position, Jeff recruited the Reverend Jennifer Baskerville-Burrows, with whom he had previously worked on various committees. Although the restructuring had already occurred by the time she came on board, Jennifer recalls how the effects of the old culture were still evident:

> The staff had shifted, but the culture was still coming along to believe in that shift. When I would call people back, they would spend the first five minutes expressing amazement that I had called back on the same day, because they just weren't used to having their phone call returned. Even years later, people still remembered what it was like.
>
> The networking position was designed to bring people together to collaborate and share best practices around common issues. Fairly early on, we had a summit where I called together everyone working on outreach and social justice at the local, diocesan, and national levels. There were about forty people in the room—many of whom I'd met in other parts of the church before I came to Chicago. Because they all worked for the same diocese, I assumed they were already working on issues of common concern—yet most had never met before. One person who was from a church that was growing food for the community said, "I've got a food garden and have too many seeds." Another church located on the other side of the diocese was starting a community garden and needed seeds. Right there on the spot, they started making exchanges. All this knowledge and wisdom and no one had known how to reach out within the diocese to share information about resources. So, silos operated—and still do. Our goal has been to be aware of them and try to break them down whenever possible.

Among the initiatives implemented by Jennifer and her team was the launch of *THRIVE*, a biyearly magazine that included stories of how women, men, and children promote the health and vigor of congregations throughout the diocese. They also created a biweekly email newsletter to keep clergy and lay members up to date on mission, ministry, and events at the diocese's congregations.

Courtney Reid, who was a member of another thriving and growing parish within the diocese, was hired as the new Director of Operations. She applied for the position not only because she had the necessary experience but, more importantly, she knew (from the head of her parish) that the bishop's office was undergoing restructuring and change—precisely the kind of environment that Courtney enjoyed and had experience in managing.

Like other members of the executive team, Courtney encountered silos in her new role. She described one example of a staff member who worked remotely, helping to manage a $12-million construction project on their property, as well as projects involving their missions and other properties. The staff member saw herself as separate from the rest of the staff and accountable only to the bishop and trustees.

While remote work arrangements can have benefits—including decreased real estate, utility, and travel costs, as well as greater employee satisfaction—they can also have some serious drawbacks, including a silo mentality and low engagement.[231] "Out of sight, out of mind" seems to sum up one of the key issues with employees who work entirely at home. They're not only less likely to receive feedback from coworkers, they are also less likely to interact with their managers on critical issues, such as progress on goals. Research shows that "virtual teams" (in which members telecommunicate with one another) generally have less Constructive interactions and leadership than teams in which members meet face to face—affecting group cohesion, acceptance of group decisions, synergy, and the quality of solutions.[232] These are deficits that can be overcome by using Constructive styles and Prescriptive leadership approaches. Courtney describes how she dealt with the situation:

> I had to move her to a place where she understood that we were all part of the same team and how her work related to the work of others, such as the treasurer. It was also important that she recognize how the team could support her. For example, when she left on vacation or needed time off, things would come to a standstill because no one knew how to do what she did. Being curious, working to understand what she did, and taking some things off her plate that she didn't like to do got me involved in some of her work and gave us an opportunity to work together on some things. It also helped her to realize that she was a part of our team.

Through her Constructive and more Prescriptive leadership approach, Courtney increased the employee's sense of job significance and interdependence—two important aspects of job design (technology) that are positively associated with Constructive norms and expectations.[233]

Of course, simply hiring talented new leaders is no guarantee that they will come together as an effective team. The bishop and his new executive team started regularly scheduling cross-departmental meetings and planning sessions—a practice they have continued. They also worked together on developing themselves. In addition to team building, they participated in a program titled Fierce Conversations. Techniques they've adopted from this program include tossing a beach ball around the room to quickly get different perspectives on an issue out in the open. They also practice asking people to "tell me more" to uncover and better understand the real problems, which they have learned aren't always the ones initially presented. All of this may sound unproductive, but they are quick to point out that they aren't meeting more often, gathering different perspectives, and asking people to tell them more just for the sake of having done it. For them, it's about having valuable conversations in which important information and ideas are readily shared, issues are resolved, and efforts are coordinated so they can get things done more quickly and effectively. As author Susan Scott notes in her book, *Fierce Conversations*:

> So often I've observed teams respond to what appeared to be a sincere invitation, only to be shot down by a leader's knee-jerk attempt to build a stronger case. To everyone in the room, it feels as if the leader is saying, "Apparently you haven't grasped the brilliance of my idea. Let me explain it to you one more time." When we make this mistake, we teach all of those in the room that when we encourage them to challenge our thinking, we really don't mean it.[234]

It's a great reminder that unless you are aware of how you are affecting the beliefs and behavior of other people and the culture, it is all too easy to implement new techniques, processes, strategies, structures, and systems in ways that simply reinforce the cultural norms and beliefs that already exist rather than the ones you want to strengthen and move toward. It's something the bishop and his staff have been very mindful of as they have proceeded through their journey.

A More Constructive "Service-Oriented Hub"

The Diocese of Chicago that exists today operates much differently and more effectively than it did back in 2010. The bishop's staff now act rather than wait. They go to the parishes rather than requiring the parishes to come to them. They continually evaluate and adapt their offerings to fit the current and future needs of their congregations. Previously effective programs and activities that have clearly outlived their purpose—including those that they've initiated—are retired and replaced with more relevant and timely offerings. These include Fierce Conversations workshops, which members of the executive team now lead for the church both locally and nationally.

Bishop Jeff Lee says that the number of calls they now get from the congregations has risen dramatically. Instead of frustrated congregation leaders telling him that their questions were left unanswered, he consistently hears, "Thank you. Our calls were answered within an hour."

Even their parishes have started coordinating with one another more and making better use of the resources they have. A predominantly Caucasian church located in the Chicago North Shore began working with a predominantly African American inner-city church to address issues regarding racial reconciliation. New coalitions and relationships have also formed around other community issues such as gun violence.

Thus, in 2016, it was of little surprise when consultant Gay Jennings told the diocese that they had become a "customer-service hub." Their latest culture survey results confirmed that their culture had shifted in a more Constructive and Achievement-oriented direction (see Figure 11.2). In addition, their ratings for customer service and adaptability—which in 2010 were far below average—were not only above average but also exceeded the benchmark for organizations with predominantly Constructive cultures. Says Gay,

> When I did the interviews in 2011, it was clear that when calling the bishop's staff, it was often difficult to get a timely response. When I did the interviews again in 2016, people in Chicago expected and got quality responses to calls for help. The staff are perceived by people in the diocese as being much more available and responsive. They know who the customer is. There is a clear change in attitude, in capacity, and in professionalism. Staff and leaders could clearly articulate what the mission is and how they are going about it.

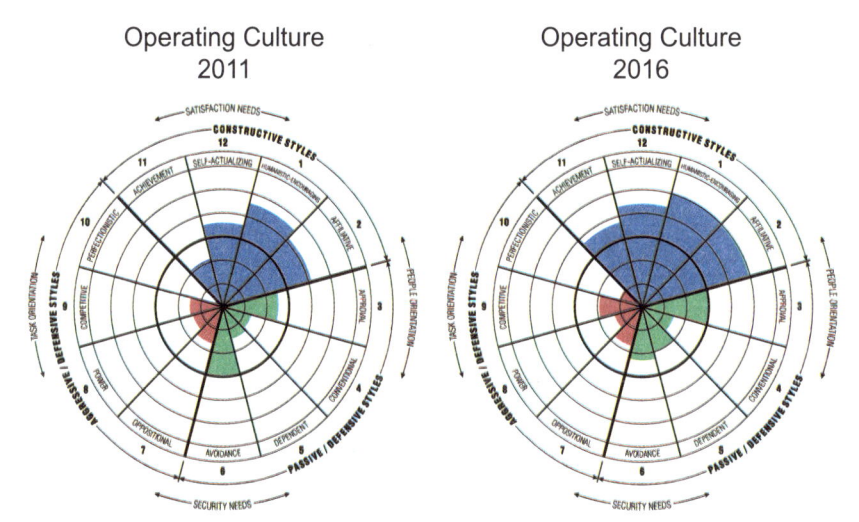

Figure 11.2. Culture Shift at the Diocese of Chicago

Operating Culture 2011

Operating Culture 2016

Research and development by Robert A. Cooke, Ph.D. and J. Clayton Lafferty, Ph.D.
Copyright © 1987-2019 by Human Synergistics International. All Rights Reserved.

At the diocese's 2016 annual convention, Bishop Jeff Lee reported,

> Nationally, since 2005, the church has reported roughly a 20 percent decline in baptized membership and a 26 percent decline in average Sunday attendance. I am happy to say that in this diocese we have been holding fairly steady over the last several years in contrast to these continuing rates of decline elsewhere.[235]

Even more impressive is that this was achieved while the population in both the city of Chicago and the state of Illinois was declining.[236] Jeff concludes,

> I see bishops getting burned out, tired, and kind of bored and hopeless because they get in and discover the system is too complex, too stuck, and there seems to be no way of changing it. I can now tell them that, "Yes, you can change it. It's hard work, but you can change it," and I think that's very big.

Because of the diocese's success in turning around their culture to more effectively carry out their mission and purpose, other leaders within the Episcopal Church have decided to undertake a similar process in their own areas, including the church's new presiding bishop, Michael Curry.

Culture Change at the Episcopal Church Center

The Episcopal Church, which has more than 1.9 million members in the United States and abroad, is led by a presiding bishop who is elected to serve a nine-year term. In November of 2015, Michael Curry became the church's twenty-seventh presiding bishop, and the first African American to hold this role. Shortly after taking office, he received reports concerning a workplace environment that Bishop Curry described as "inconsistent with the values and expectations of the Episcopal Church."[237]

Bishop Curry had grown up in a family in which there was an expectation that what you did with your work was going to change the world. He wanted to instill that kind of belief in the church center. Based on conversations with Gay Jennings (who by then was President of the church's House of Deputies) and Jeff Lee, Bishop Curry decided to undertake a process similar to that followed by the Diocese of Chicago to identify and implement changes to move the culture of the church center in a healthier direction—one that was more reflective of and consistent with the church's beliefs about the behaviors that should be embodied and modeled to support its mission of the "Jesus Movement."[238] Bishop Curry explains,

> I had been looking for something that was highlighted in one of the books by Walter Wink, a biblical scholar who had done some work on the Book of Revelation. The first three chapters of the Book of Revelation are letters to seven churches. In the letters, there is a kind of diagnosis of the spiritual condition and situation in the various churches. What Professor Walter Wink observed was how the letters were written. Instead of being written to the church, they were written to the Angel of the church, which is a way of saying that if the spirit of the church is addressed and transformed, the church will change.
>
> Culture is like the spirit of a community, organization, or group. Consequently, significant change and potential transformation happen when the spirit—the culture—is moved. This was one of the first times that I saw a very clear approach that would address the spirit of our organization in terms of its culture. Not from an anecdotal basis but from a more objective, quantifiable one.

Because Gay was now part of the national church's leadership team, Human Synergistics' Tim Kuppler was asked to lead the consulting for the project. Tim met with the presiding bishop to discuss the structure of the project and how to support the quantitative (survey) work with qualitative (interview and focus groups) approaches, similar to what had been done in Chicago. Tim also invited consultants Scott Beilke and Donna Brighton to support the subsequent debriefing and planning work.

Members of the bishop's staff, the staff of other church officers, and the executive committee were asked to complete the *Organizational Culture Inventory*, the *Organizational Culture Inventory—Ideal*, and the *Organizational Effectiveness Inventory*. In addition, the consultants interviewed key senior leaders and led separate focus group sessions with individual contributors and supervisors/managers to gather specific examples of the culture and climate in the church's own terminology.

"Though the leaders shared a commitment to working on the culture, each had a different perspective on the causes and what needed to be done differently moving forward," Tim recalls. The focus groups described an "us versus them" attitude between the church center and broader church, the existence of silos, and lack of communication. In addition, favoritism; arrogance; lack of involvement in decisions; unclear priorities and plans moving forward; fear of making mistakes; worries about potential retaliation if issues were raised; and playing it safe by "keeping heads down" and "just focusing on the work" were mentioned as problems.

The survey data highlighted some key areas of agreement. "There was amazing consistency in what people dreamed our work environment could be that also reflected the kinds of values that Christian people say we believe in," points out Bishop Curry, referring to their ideal culture profile. There was also a clear pattern in terms of the gaps identified between the ideal and the current operating culture (see Figure 11.3). Unsurprisingly, the survey results confirmed a culture that was highly Avoidant and Defensive in both passive and aggressive expectations, with relatively low expectations for the Constructive behaviors that the bishop, other leaders, and their staffs believed were necessary to maximize the church's vitality and long-term effectiveness.

"A little bit of aggressive drove a ton of passive in the broader organization, especially in Avoidance, because people didn't know where the organization was going nor how it tied to them," Tim explains. Feedback from the *Organizational Effectiveness Inventory* highlighted several aspects of the organization's climate that were misaligned with the Constructive norms and expectations described as ideal. It made it clear why gathering the perspectives of different people in a systematic way can be so valuable to identifying the changes needed to improve. As Gay discovered from her culture change work with the Diocese of Chicago, "Sometimes there's a disconnect between what people think is going on and what those who take the inventories are saying. So it's a good way to confirm or dig a little deeper into what's really going on."

Figure 11.3. Church Center's Operating and Ideal Profiles (2016)

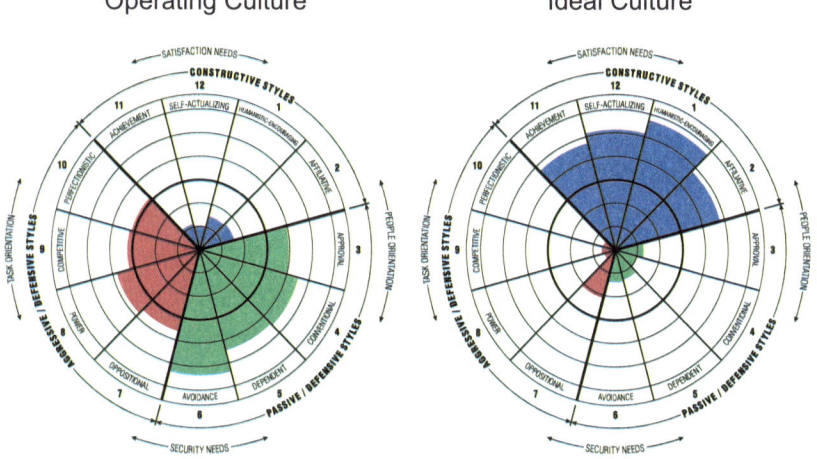

Research and development by Robert A. Cooke, Ph.D. and J. Clayton Lafferty, Ph.D.
Copyright © 1987-2019 by Human Synergistics International. All Rights Reserved.

Based on the feedback from the interviews, focus groups, and surveys, the church's senior leaders wanted to address the low level of trust and respect within the church center. This was especially important given that the last lines of the church's Baptismal Covenant are a commitment to "strive for justice and peace for all people, and respect the dignity of every human being."[239] The three major levers that the leaders chose to focus on in the first phase of change were: 1) clarity and consistency in communication about the Jesus Movement and the church's mission of fostering a world that is "loving, liberating, and life-giving"; 2) the quality of the interactions within the senior leadership team; and 3) employee engagement and involvement. Specifically, they

- coordinated their communications about the mission and vision of the Jesus Movement so they were clear and consistent;

- drafted a values statement, "The Three *E*'s" (for Esteem, Engage, and Excel), which they based on the church's ideal culture profile and verbalized using the language of scripture and their religious beliefs;
- restructured the leadership team and the rest of the organization to include new roles and people with overall skill sets and attitudes that fit the ideal culture they wanted to move toward;
- engaged themselves and the next level of management in leadership/management development to better understand how their behavior was impacting others;
- developed healthier meeting routines within the leadership team; and
- involved other leaders, managers, and staff in the culture work.

Early in the change process, the leadership team called a meeting of the members of both the House of Bishops and the House of Deputies to communicate a clear vision of the Jesus Movement; share the Three *E*'s and how they were using them to move toward that vision in their own interactions; and invite the rest of the organization to be involved in strengthening the desired norms and expectations. Meeting outside of the church's General Convention—which meets once every three years—had never been done before and, in and of itself, was a significant change from the norm. More than eight hundred people attended in person or via live webcast.[240] Says Bishop Curry:

> We shared with them the culture work—the whole thing, warts and all—and how we were moving forward. On the one hand, it modeled what we wanted to achieve. However, it also built confidence in the church community, that together we can shape a heathy, loving, liberating, and life-giving culture through the way in which we work. With Episcopal church leaders from sixteen countries in attendance, it was a big reach.
>
> We deliberately became vulnerable before the whole community and asked them to help us be accountable to do what we say we're going to do. Given that we told them what we were intending, we knew we would have to come back and tell them if we did it.

Like other leadership teams that you have read about in this book, the senior leaders made culture change part of their work, rather than a separate activity. They began meeting regularly as a team, which hadn't been done before. They established and rotated meeting roles and applied the Three *E*'s to their own behavior and interactions. Because trust was a key issue throughout the organization, including within the leadership team, addressing motives and intentions was critical. They provided each other with immediate feedback on perceived aggressive or passive behavior in their meetings by saying things like, "This is what I heard you say. Is that what you meant or intended?"

Providing that kind of feedback in a Defensive culture certainly wasn't easy and, in the beginning, there were some pretty "intense" moments, recalls consultant Scott Beilke, who helped facilitate some of the initial meetings. "The only way they were going to get through the lack of trust was to be able to call people's attention to the perceived negative behavior," he explains. Having these kinds of conversations helped the leaders to better align their own behavior with their intentions, as well as fostered a better understanding of one another's motives and intentions as they worked together on carrying out their administrative activities and achieving the mission and goals of the church.

They supplemented the ranks of the leadership team with executives who had business experience and an orientation toward connecting individual and organizational goals (consistent with the Achievement orientation that they wanted to strengthen in the culture). They also hired a new IT director and an HR director to help the organization make better use of technology by providing additional ways for employees to grow, learn, and achieve (consistent with the Self-Actualizing and Humanistic-Encouraging styles).

In addition, the leaders participated in a six-month leadership development program using *Leadership/Impact*. They involved the next level of management by engaging them in a similar development program using *Management/Impact*. The programs provided the leaders and managers with specific feedback and guidance on what they were already doing well and what they could do differently in their day-to-day roles to influence people and culture in ways more consistent with the organization's values.

A Habit of Grace

Although completely changing the culture can take a long time, substantial progress can be made in the first step when members of the leadership team agree on and are committed to the changes, points out Tim Kuppler. That is certainly consistent with the other cases in this book. When the church center remeasured their culture and climate fifteen months later, there were significant improvements (see Figure 11.4). Staff and leaders reported better communication, clarity in mission and goals, behavioral consistency among leaders, engagement and involvement of groups, listening, and asking for feedback. There was noticeably greater trust and respect. In terms of culture, people no longer felt as strongly that being self-protective and focused on position and status were necessary to survive and thrive in the church center. All twelve culture styles had shifted in the desired direction, particularly the Defensive styles. Although expectations for passive behaviors still existed, they no longer were driven by the strong expectations for Power, as reflected by the top three items in the *Organizational Culture Inventory* that decreased the most: "demand loyalty," "maintain unquestioned authority," and "lay low when things get tough."

Figure 11.4. Shift in Church Center's Operating Culture

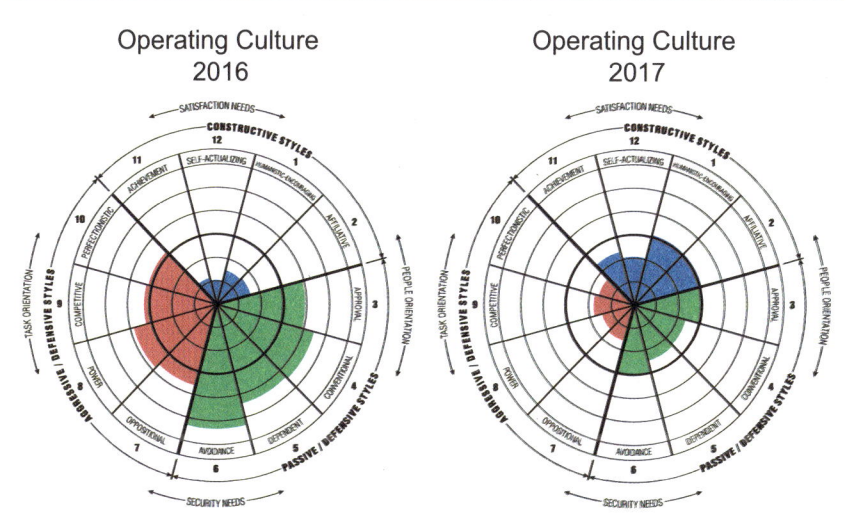

Research and development by Robert A. Cooke, Ph.D. and J. Clayton Lafferty, Ph.D. Copyright © 1987-2019 by Human Synergistics International. All Rights Reserved.

Although reducing the Defensive norms helped to reduce fear, mistrust, and resentment, this case illustrates that it doesn't necessarily mean the organization has learned a more Constructive approach. As Bishop Curry has noted, there is still more work to do in terms of moving toward a culture that is loving, liberating, and life-giving. Given the progress they've made in such a short period, the improvements that could potentially be achieved during his tenure are promising and inspiring. Says Bishop Curry,

> We now have practical tools for transforming the spirit and culture of our organization. And like a spiritual practice, we have to keep going back to it so that it becomes a habit of grace. That is what transforms us into that new way of being.

Key Learnings

The Episcopal Church's experience illustrates that successful changes to culture can transcend upward as well as outward and downward. This is more likely to happen when leaders in lateral and higher-level positions are practicing Prescriptive leadership, including in how they approach change. Both Bishop Jeff Lee and Presiding Bishop Michael Curry articulated a clear vision of what they wanted to achieve and why. Both looked within their organizations for positive examples of what they wanted to achieve, commended those examples, and learned from them.

As Bishop Curry noted, it's not what we do once that creates transformation; it's what we continue to do that shapes an organization's spirit and culture. All the cases in this book, including the Diocese of Chicago and the church center, used the same circumplicial framework to better understand their culture, received feedback about their own behavior in relation to that culture, and had the same goal of strengthening Constructive norms. Yet, each took a somewhat different path to get there. This is consistent with Professor Edgar Schein's observation that for people to internalize and integrate changes into their daily roles, they ultimately must choose for themselves how they will achieve the goals for change.[241] It's an important point to keep in mind as we turn our attention to your organization's culture change journey.

> **Key Learnings**
>
> - Successful culture change can begin anywhere in an organization and flow in any direction, particularly when leaders carry out their roles in Prescriptive ways.
>
> - Transformation happens not from what is done once, but through the new behaviors, approaches, and learnings that are practiced over and over again.

Part III

Taking the Next Step

Chapter 12

Leading Your Organization's Culture Journey

> I had read books and heard people talking about how culture was important. This process proved it to be true.
> Andrei Haret, Managing Director, Dreher Brewery, 2010–2015

We wrote this book to show you how leaders of organizations in different industries and countries have created more Constructive work environments that enable their members to take advantage of opportunities, solve a wide range of problems, and achieve their organizations' goals. Some of the leaders profiled here started out primarily focused on leadership, while others began focused on culture. They all ultimately focused on how leadership affects the operating culture of an organization and, in turn, its performance. With the shared framework and language provided by the Circumplex, these leaders were able to shift the reciprocal relationship between leadership and culture to a more Constructive trajectory by using the diverse levers directly or indirectly under their control.

In this chapter, we address how you can apply the evidence and insights from this book to creating a more Constructive culture in your own organization.

Recognizing and Changing What's Expected

"In a sense, we're all culture experts, because we've learned from an early age how to fit into our families, schools, and workplaces," notes Director of Culture and Organization Development for Human Synergistics, Tim Kuppler.[242] However, not everyone is an expert on how to intentionally change culture. Indeed, one of the biggest challenges to leaders like yourself in creating more Constructive cultures is recognizing and managing the effects of both organizational and societal norms on your own thinking and behavior. Such awareness is a prerequisite for strengthening the Constructive aspects of your organization's culture rather than inadvertently working against them.

All the Circumplex styles—Defensive as well as Constructive—have potential benefits that encourage and reinforce people to rely on them. Constructive styles are most strongly associated with effectiveness across organizations, yet Aggressive/Defensive thinking continues to be rewarded with higher salaries and promotions to higher-level positions. This persists even though the Aggressive/Defensive styles are not necessarily associated with effectiveness and in many ways detract from it. Similarly, although Passive/Defensive thinking styles are negatively related to task effectiveness as well as personal success and well-being, they can provide people with a sense of security and safety in their interpersonal relationships and lead to a genuine interest in self-improvement. The relationships between personal styles and measures of personal success have remained generally the same over time. This can be seen by comparing the results from the original *Life Styles Inventory* findings (summarized in Table I.1), which were based on data collected back in the 1970s, to the results based on recently collected *Life Styles Inventory* data (summarized in Table 12.1).

More generally, these findings suggest that *societal values* in the United States and Canada (which is where the original and the more recent data were primarily collected) haven't changed much in terms of the kinds of personal styles that tend to be rewarded across organizations. This tendency to reward and encourage styles that interfere with the effectiveness of individuals, groups, and organizations is not unique to Anglo societies. Recently collected *Life Styles Inventory* data from respondents in non-Anglo countries—including Finland, Korea, and Romania, as well as Latin American countries such as Mexico and Argentina—also show a strong tendency to reward Aggressive/Defensive styles across organizations, particularly with promotions to higher-level positions.

Our research clearly demonstrates that rewards, promotions, and the approval of others (especially superiors) signal which styles are truly expected and condoned by your organization and its leaders, and, when withheld, which are not. The implications are far reaching: the impact of your leadership on your organization's culture influences not only its overall effectiveness and long-term performance, but also the world competitiveness of the countries in which your organization operates.

Consequently, the process of improving your nation's performance begins with taking a clear look at how your leadership and your organization's operating culture currently affect one another. In turn, it also requires consideration of how the gaps between your organization's ideal culture and current culture constrain its ability to act on opportunities, solve problems, and achieve goals.

Table 12.1. Recent *Life Styles Inventory* Findings

	Personal Orientation[a]		
	Constructive	Passive/ Defensive	Aggressive/ Defensive
Salary[a]	+	--	+
Organizational Level[a]	++	--	++
Task Effectiveness[b]	++	--	0
Quality of Interpersonal Relations[b]	++	++	--
Interest in Self-Development[b]	++	++	0
Psychological Health[a]	++	--	--

Note. Results based on 7,663 individuals. Plusses and minuses denote statistically significant positive and negative relationships, respectively. Single plusses and minuses indicate $p<.05$; double plusses and minuses indicate $p<.01$. Zero indicates no statistically significant relationship.

[a] Based on *Life Styles Inventory*™ Self Description.
[b] Based on *Life Styles Inventory*™ Description By Others.

A General Process for Strengthening Constructive Norms to Improve Performance

While each situation requires specific levers for strengthening Constructive norms and addressing culture disconnects, the basic process that leaders go through to create and sustain desired changes is fundamentally the same across organizations. For instance, all the leaders described in this book had (and shared with others) clear reasons for wanting to improve the culture of their organizations. Whether it was enhancing customer experience, implementing a new strategy, attracting and retaining talent, accelerating innovation and growth, or better aligning the organization with its purpose and values, their reasons motivated and sustained their—and their coworkers'—attention to culture. These leaders each established a baseline for cultural norms against which they could gauge their progress creating the changes they wanted to see. They all used a combination of direct and indirect levers for change. In the process, they gained insights about what does and doesn't work, which helped them to refine strategies and behaviors and thus move closer to their goals. This general process, depicted in Figure 12.1, is a way to create changes in your own organization that strengthen Constructive thinking, behavior, and cultural norms.

Why Do You Want to Change Culture?

The first question that culture expert Edgar Schein asks when anyone tells him that they want to change their organization's culture or create a new one is "Why?"[243] Based on our experience, starting the change process with a clear understanding of why you want to change is beneficial for several reasons. The most critical reason is that knowing why keeps change efforts focused on *facilitating* existing priorities and projects rather than allowing change efforts to morph into a separate initiative or priority disconnected from the other things going on within the organization. This was one of the key insights shared by the Port of San Diego's leaders in chapter 3. They first applied the changes to a specific group (i.e., the Blue Team) that was working on specific organizational priorities (i.e., improved customer experience). By doing so, the leaders and core change team members were able to learn more about what worked, what didn't work, and what they needed to modify in their development plan before implementing changes across the broader organization.

Leading Your Organization's Journey   275

Figure 12.1. A Four-Phase Process for Strengthening Constructive Cultures

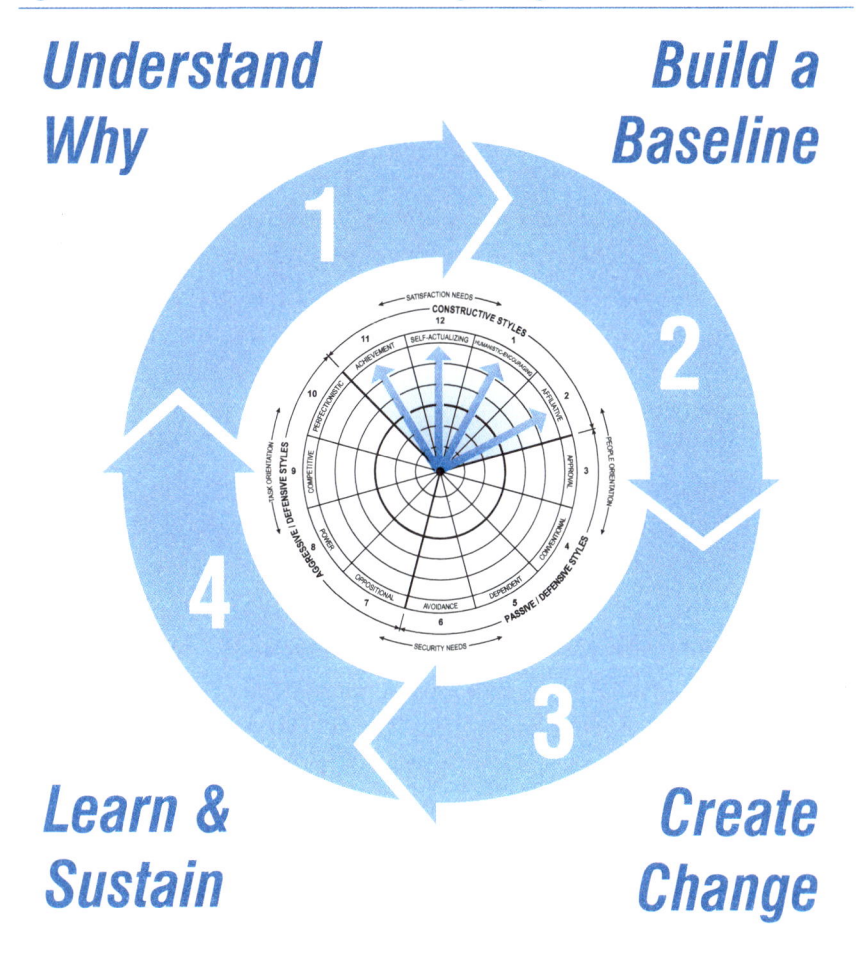

Understand Why — 1

Build a Baseline — 2

Create Change — 3

Learn & Sustain — 4

Human Synergistics Circumplex: Research and development by Robert A. Cooke, Ph.D. and J. Clayton Lafferty, Ph.D. Copyright © 1987-2019 by Human Synergistics International. All Rights Reserved.

Four-Phase Model:
Adapted from Human Synergistics' "Ultimate Culture and Performance: 90-Day Quick-Start Program," https://www.humansynergistics.com/change-solutions/culture-quick-start/.

Although most culture-related efforts, including many of those featured in this book, begin with a specific part of an organization that is ready to change, we want to be clear that the cultural changes should *not* be defined or driven by a single priority or a single group within an organization. On the one hand, you could end up with a "sales culture" (like the example at the beginning of chapter 2) or some other kind of lopsided culture that can inadvertently diminish or even destroy the organization's overall effectiveness and long-term performance. On the other hand, you could end up with an overly specialized culture change initiative that is short-lived and eventually replaced, given the more pervasive culture of the larger organization. In either case, such narrow, specialized approaches might (or might not) offer some respite from the problem(s) that an organization happens to be facing today. Regardless, they largely fail to equip the organization with the collective capability to adapt to the myriad problems, disruptions, and changes it will be confronted with in the future. The dangers of such a narrow focus are starting to be recognized. For example, safety consultant Skipper Hendricks has advised, "We don't need an add-on safety culture. We must ensure an overall culture within the organization that embraces and manages safety the same way as the rest of the business."[244] Similarly, Carl Anderson, Supreme Knight of the Knights of Columbus (ranked as one of the world's most ethical companies by the Ethisphere Institute), notes,

> Rather than solving each problem retrospectively, ideal corporate governance ultimately shapes its culture, building on what is good and discouraging what is not. It is a commitment that begins at the top and quickly becomes part of the culture as its ideals are consistently expected and applied at every level, from the board of directors to the mail room. It provides a moral compass that can be applied to any situation, rather than simply a set of rules for isolated instances.[245]

And, speaking on leadership and culture in banking, Executive Vice President of the Federal Reserve Bank of New York, Alberto G. Musalem, points out,

> A bank's culture must be consistent with public expectations and promote behavior that considers the firm's many stakeholders, including the public. Also, a positive, constructive culture can be an important pillar aligned with the execution of a firm's business strategy. ...Leadership is indispensable, and requires more than a "tone from the top." Managers of all levels must take action to promote a greater sense of personal responsibility and stewardship among employees. The next generation of financial leaders will reflect the expectations of leaders today.[246]

Consistent with this broader view, many organizations (such as SaskCentral) take a balanced scorecard approach[247], which ensures that attention to one critical aspect of the business (e.g., financial performance) isn't achieved at the expense of another (e.g., customer experience). This balanced perspective is particularly relevant when leaders are envisioning the kind of culture that they want to work toward.

A clear understanding of why you want to change culture in your organization is also important because it provides the basis for communicating with others to promote understanding and acceptance of the need for change. Thus, early in the change process, the external experts who will help in facilitating the process, as well as the key insiders who will make up the *core change team*, should be identified and brought together. The core change team is responsible for designing, coordinating, and implementing the assessments and change activities. Such activities include gathering and providing feedback; planning for change; capturing and disseminating insights and key learnings; and sustaining the changes and diffusing the process and improvements throughout the organization. As noted by Schein, although the change team might include some members of the leadership team, senior leaders usually make up the majority of the *steering committee*, which has accountability for and oversight of the change process.[248] This doesn't mean that senior leaders are in any way external to or sitting on the sidelines of this process. As shown by the examples in this book, they are very much at the center of the action and among those responsible for determining and making the changes, both direct and indirect.

The reasons for changing culture can also be helpful in determining which of the levers described in chapter 2 should initially be used to create change. The reasons for change may also point toward an area, unit, or part of the organization on which the remaining phases should initially focus (before expanding to other areas). In addition, these reasons are critical to identifying the internal metrics and key outcomes that should be monitored to ensure that efforts to change are having the desired effects. This is an activity that is often overlooked in change initiatives that, as a result, end up being short-lived.

The box below presents some questions to guide your discussions with core change team members, external experts, and other senior leaders about the work environment, the current state of your organization's operating culture, and the reasons for analyzing and improving it. If your organization is already working on culture change, you can use these questions to confirm the extent to which leaders, core team members, and other members collectively understand and agree on the reasons for assessment and change.

> **Understanding Why**
>
> Use the questions below to communicate and clarify the impetus for analyzing and improving the culture and climate at this point in time, as well as to encourage others to share their perspectives.
>
> - What priorities, opportunities, or strategies are currently being stymied by the organization's operating culture?
>
> - What metrics are currently used to determine whether the organization is making progress to effectively address the problems or take advantage of the opportunities identified above?
>
> - What have you or others in the organization already tried doing to address the problems or opportunities identified above?
>
> - Why is it personally important to you and others to address these issues with culture? How will it benefit the organization, its employees, its customers, its shareholders, and the larger society?

Building a Baseline

As with planning any kind of journey, two pieces of information are required for determining the path to take: where you are now and where you want to go. Building a baseline for your organization's culture is about defining where it currently stands so that a comparison can be made to the ideal or the optimal state. To assist you in this process, the box on the next page lists some fundamentals for building a baseline for culture.

Building a Baseline for Culture

Use the list below to identify any actions necessary to enlist and engage the relevant people in a) assessing the current culture and climate of your organization, b) identifying the ideal culture, and c) analyzing the gaps.

- Identify and bring together core change team members (if you have not already done so in the previous phase)
- Develop a communication plan
- Identify relevant subgroups (for subculture analyses)
- Define key business outcomes (and measures at the organizational and subgroup levels)
- Carry out preliminary interviews and discussions to guide measurement activities (if not already done in phase one)
- Develop protocols for observations, interviews, and focus group discussions
- Determine the strategy for selecting and surveying a representative sample of your organization's members
- Administer the *Organizational Culture Inventory*, *Organizational Effectiveness Inventory*, and supplementary items or surveys based on the preliminary interviews and discussions
- Organize and facilitate focus groups
- Conduct observations and additional interviews
- Analyze data across subgroups and identify links between levers, culture, and outcomes
- Assemble and provide qualitative and quantitative feedback on the current culture, subcultures, connections to outcomes, and potential levers for change

As illustrated by the cases in this book, effective leaders do not go through this process by themselves or exclusively rely on their own personal perspectives to guide them through. Rather, they enlist and engage other leaders and members inside the organization as well as recruit outside experts to assist in measuring and interpreting the results. Outside experts can be beneficial for several reasons, not the least of which is that they tend to bring up things going on in the organization that members overlook because they are so entrenched in the culture. As Tim Kuppler puts it, "Culture is like the water people swim in or the air they breathe. So it's no surprise that people from outside may notice some things that internal people do not think to talk about."

The activities involved in building a baseline for culture are best carried out by the members of the core change team along with the external experts you've retained. This is another reason why these individuals should be identified and brought together during phase one or at the beginning of this phase. Together, the internal teams and the external consultants should commit to building a multidimensional baseline, taking a comprehensive approach to assessment. While using a simplistic single measure might at first seem appealing, we strongly advocate the use of *triangulation* for building an accurate, unbiased, and valid baseline that you and others in your organization can trust, learn from, and act upon.

Consistent with basic geometric principles, triangulation is a strategy used to improve accuracy in research and measurement. It's also used in navigation and by the military to locate an object's exact position.[249] An excellent example of triangulation is provided in chapter 8 by Dreher Brewery's use of three types of data to establish a solid baseline for the organization's culture and climate as well as a clear direction for change:

- archival data (such as employee exit interviews and analyses of retention rates for different employee groups),
- survey data (using the *Organizational Culture Inventory* and the *Organizational Effectiveness Inventory*), and
- interviews with current employees.

Another example is provided by the Episcopal Church (chapter 11), where surveys, interviews, and focus groups were used to establish a baseline for culture and climate. The qualitative and quantitative results were combined by the consultants and fed back to the leaders to provide them with a more holistic understanding of what was going on in the organization and a clear direction for change.

Less complex triangulation methods involve gathering parallel information from multiple sources (such as self, colleagues, direct reports, and superiors). The value of such a process can readily be seen, for instance, in the story about Spreadshirt (chapter 4), where presenting each leader with survey feedback organized by respondent group (in their case, peers versus direct reports) helped them to gain a better understanding of where the greatest gaps were occurring in terms of their impact.

A triangular approach is built into the Circumplex itself. Statistical analyses confirm that the three clusters referred to throughout this book are, in fact, distinct factors. Measuring, reporting on, and discussing the three clusters separately is superior to combining the results into a single number, because individual and culture profiles that look (and are) very different can end up with the same single score. To illustrate, the three *Organizational Culture Inventory* profiles shown in Figure 12.2 all produce the same *index score* based on a formula whereby the Defensive percentile scores are subtracted from equally weighted percentile scores for the Constructive styles. Though the responses from the three organizations generate identical index scores—indicating a "neutral" culture (i.e., one that is equally strong in Constructive and Defensive cultural norms)—the profiles indicate three very different kinds of cultures with distinct issues as well as different key levers for change. Thus, while single-value indices can be appropriate for surveys measuring only one thing—such as overall satisfaction or general positive or negative affect—combining the scores on multidimensional surveys such as the *Organizational Culture Inventory* results in inferior information and misleading conclusions about culture. As illustrated by Figure 12.2, the importance of triangulation in reporting on organizational culture becomes obvious when the profiles of different organizations or units are compared to one another as well as when the profiles of a single organization or unit at different points in time are compared.

Figure 12.2. Example Culture Profiles with Equivalent Single Number Index Scores

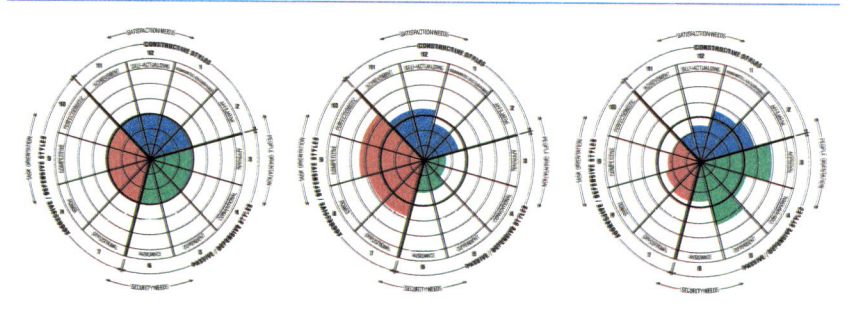

Human Synergistics Circumplex: Research and development by Robert A. Cooke, Ph.D. and J. Clayton Lafferty, Ph.D.
Copyright © 1987-2019 by Human Synergistics International. All Rights Reserved.

The cases in this book consistently underscore that, in addition to measuring your organization's current culture, it's important to establish your ideal. This profile will ensure that you, other leaders, and members throughout the organization have a clear picture of what it is you are collectively working toward. Thus, if you have not yet done so, we encourage you, your leadership team, and a sample of other members to complete the 120-item *Ideal* form of the *Organizational Culture Inventory*. You can preview the *Ideal* form online by visiting www.humansynergistics.com/culturebook. Doing so will allow you to experience a portion of the inventory, see how it works, and get a preliminary picture of your organization's ideal in terms of the Constructive, Passive/Defensive, and Aggressive/Defensive clusters based on your responses.

In building a baseline, it is recommended that you also assess at least some of the climate factors related to culture and culture disconnects. Doing so will facilitate discussion about potential levers for change. This includes an assessment of perceptions regarding leadership skills and qualities, structures, systems, technology, and mission and philosophy. If you use the Human Synergistics *Organizational Effectiveness Inventory*, your results will be presented along with the average for a thousand other organizations and units to provide context. Additionally, your change team and/or external consultants can identify (on the basis of interviews and other qualitative data) other relevant measures to add to the *Organizational Culture Inventory* and *Organizational Effectiveness Inventory*. These measures should be statistically reliable and valid, and historical benchmarks or average scores for them should be available.

The survey feedback can be used to select levers for change, for example, by focusing on the factors along which your organization's scores deviate the most, in a negative direction, from the averages. Those factors can be discussed in consideration of your culture results and may be selected by your change team to be among the first to be targeted. For example, assume that "use of rewards" (as measured by the *Organizational Effectiveness Inventory*) was among the causal factors with the greatest negative deviation from the average. Relevant levers for change could include the introduction of additional formal recognition programs, tangible rewards for team accomplishments, and the use of praise by supervisors. Alternatively, your change team might select other factors along which your organization's scores were less extreme if those factors seem more conducive to improvement and/or more directly relevant to the cultural styles of interest.

As illustrated by some of the examples in this book, subgroup analyses and comparisons (across, for example, different departments or functions, geographic locations, demographic groups, organizational levels, or high-performing versus low-performing groups) can provide further insights regarding how culture works in your organization. Because the feasibility of subgroup analysis is affected by both sampling and proper precoding of data, the subgroups of interest should be identified prior to collecting survey data. Doing so allows individual respondents' culture and climate data to be aggregated to the subgroup level and merged with data on subgroup outcomes and other relevant metrics (e.g., turnover). Correlations can then be carried out to show the relationship between the Constructive culture styles and outcomes (including satisfaction, motivation, and performance) within the organization. Alysun Johns, Director of Culture and Leadership at Human Synergistics, notes,

> Being able to make those connections back to their business measures is critical for leaders. Seeing the correlations between the culture styles and outcomes and how the cultural norms differ in areas of the organization that are performing well from those that are not performing well makes for interesting learning.[250]

After reviewing and considering the results for the overall organization, the leaders and core change team members should analyze and discuss the results across relevant subgroups. They can then visit units with relatively Constructive cultures to learn more about what they are doing that is different. The findings can then be used to identify best practices that could be emulated by other parts of the organization to improve overall effectiveness.

Directly and Indirectly Creating Change

The third phase in the process of strengthening Constructive cultures is creating change. The cases in this book confirm that culture gradually and notably changes in a Constructive direction when leaders and key members practice thinking and behaving in a more Constructive way while carrying out their roles and the work of the organization. In contrast, norms fail to change when those involved treat culture and their own impact on it as extracurricular activities. Alysun Johns points out that "culture doesn't change because people meet once a month on how to change culture." While such meetings can be valuable in planning and coordinating change efforts, the shifts in cultural norms occur when new patterns of behavior become a regular part of everything the organization's leaders are already doing.

If you've administered the *Organizational Effectiveness Inventory* in the previous phase, the survey results along with data gathered from interviews and focus groups should indicate the aspects of your organization's climate that are most inconsistent with the cultural norms that you are trying to strengthen.

Whereas engagement surveys and staff satisfaction surveys can tell you *what* to improve in terms of specific outcomes, feedback on culture (or on your impact on culture) tells you *how* to change it. For instance, improving customer service was a priority for the Chicago Diocese. The *Organizational Culture Inventory* indicated that Achievement and Avoidance were relevant issues in their culture. In addition, feedback from the *Organizational Effectiveness Inventory* indicated that mission and philosophy, structure, human resource management systems, and communication were among the key levers for changing those norms. Consistent with an Achievement orientation, the Bishop restructured the organization to make it clearer and more explicit how people's roles were tied to the mission and purpose of the diocese. He and the members of his team also developed their skills around having *productive* and *important* conversations—including about mission and philosophy and improving customer service. They also started teaching these skills to other staff members. In addition, the leaders designed and implemented a human resource management system that made expectations more explicit and held people accountable for providing customer service in a Constructive manner. Without a clear understanding of the diocese's current and ideal culture, the change efforts likely would have been different, because they would have been shaped by the organization's existing culture rather than its ideal. In turn, they would not have been as effective in improving service quality and shifting the culture itself in a direction that better supported the diocese's overall effectiveness.

Skepticism about the commitment of leaders to culture change is among the most common sources of resistance to change. As illustrated by several of the stories in this book, the most convincing ways of communicating your own commitment to making positive changes in the culture are being the first to change and being transparent about what you are doing. This is another reason why the direct impact of leaders—resulting from their behaviors, styles, strategies, and approaches—consistently is among the most important levers for creating as well as sustaining organization-wide change.

Successfully creating a more Constructive environment requires coupling *action* with *awareness* of your behavior and *acceptance* of your impact on others and the culture of your organization (the three *A*'s). Specific strategies for increasing awareness, acceptance, and action based on the examples and insights shared by leaders in the previous chapters are summarized in the Three A's boxes below.

Creating Change Using the Three A's

Use the list below to identify additional strategies to implement as part of your organization's change process moving forward.

Increase Awareness

- Ask for feedback about your behavior and impact on the behavior of others.
- Define your ideal impact on others and compare it to your organization's ideal culture profile.
- Pay more attention to your behavior and its impact (for example in meetings, when dealing with conflicts, and when handling problems at work and outside of work).
- Notice how the current cultural and subcultural norms in your organization help or hinder the formulation as well as the implementation of change strategies.
- Recognize others' efforts to improve, and use a shared language (such as that provided by the Circumplex) to help shift behaviors in a more Constructive direction.

Increase Acceptance

- Include others in identifying the ideal culture, as well as targets and levers for change.
- Notice the parallels between the organization's current culture profile and your own personal styles and/or impact styles.
- Be transparent about the changes that you personally are committed to making in your own behavior.

> **Take Action**
>
> - Carry out your leadership or management role (including the ways in which you approach change) in a manner that is consistent with the cultural norms or impact styles that you want to strengthen.
>
> - Make appropriate changes to structures, systems, technology, and skills/qualities so that they are better aligned with the organization's ideal culture as well as its purpose and goals.
>
> - Use the organization's ideal culture profile to a) recognize other leaders' behaviors and leadership styles that contribute to the kind of culture that the organization is working toward and b) identify and address behaviors and leadership styles that contribute to Defensive cultural norms.

Learn and Sustain

Managing your impact on culture is an ongoing nonlinear journey. The levers used to shift culture and improve targeted outcomes are effective only to the extent to which your own thinking, behavior, and decisions continue to support the norms and expectations that you want to strengthen. As you and your organization make progress toward the goals that originally motivated you to change, it's easy to turn your attention away from culture and your impact on it. However, as Debbie Lane from SaskCentral pointed out in chapter 10, culture doesn't stop. And neither does the impact of your own thinking, behavior, and decisions.

Three of the most common reasons that we've seen efforts to improve culture wane are

1. Lack of reinforcement and accountability for culture
2. Changes in resources or demands by stakeholders
3. Turnover at the top of the organization

We've observed leaders, along with their internal and external consultants, take a number of different actions to counter these and other threats to lasting cultural change. One of the primary methods they use to maintain momentum (and keep current on their understanding of the present state and how it is evolving) is to regularly measure norms and expectations. Closely related to this approach is a dedication to continue to receive feedback on their own behavior and impact. For instance, Sanitarium (which has been on its journey for nearly a decade) regularly monitors the relationship between culture and both employee engagement and new product development cycle times. Similarly, SaskCentral (on its journey for over two decades now) regularly remeasures its culture and tracks its relationship to their a) customer service ratings, b) Best Places to Work rankings, and c) *Organizational Effectiveness Inventory* results for individual-, group-, and organizational-level outcomes.

We recommend remeasuring culture with the *Organizational Culture Inventory* every eighteen months to two years. This interval is long enough to start to see movement, which in some cases can be dramatic, but is not so brief that remeasuring becomes overly taxing on respondents, which can result in, among other problems, contaminated responses and low response rates. Some organizations, such as SaskCentral, alternate measuring culture and causal factors as a way of monitoring both, while others, such as the Episcopal Church (chapter 11), opt to do both at the same time. Yet other organizations, including Straumann (chapter 5), also use pulse surveys to intermittently measure a few of either the causal factors, intermediate outcomes, or behavioral norms targeted for change. Finally, other organizations, such as Pons Bakery (chapter 6), use group-level surveys, like the *Group Styles Inventory* to intermittently provide leadership teams and other groups with feedback on their use of Constructive and Defensive styles during meetings.

In addition to surveys, regular discussions with organizational members can be key when these sessions focus on what is working as well as what's not working. First, regularly having these kinds of discussions is consistent with Constructive thinking and behavior (particularly Achievement and Humanistic-Encouraging). Second, by regularly sharing information and perspectives on what is and isn't working, leaders and members have more opportunities to deepen their understanding of the current situation, make adjustments and mid-course corrections, and recognize and reinforce effective behaviors and successes. For instance, the leaders at Straumann regularly meet with the organization's culture change champions for this purpose (see chapter 5). Similarly, at Sanitarium's headquarters, the leaders and approximately two hundred staff members attend a quarterly luncheon during which they review and celebrate what was accomplished in the previous quarter, collectively set goals for the next quarter, and plan how they will Constructively achieve those goals (see chapter 9).

Developing and maintaining relationships with trusted advisors—people who are knowledgeable about managing the interrelationships between leadership and culture—is yet another important way in which leaders and other members stay current in their understanding of their organization's culture and their impact on it. Trusted advisors can be internal to the organization (for example, the human resources directors at Dreher Brewery and Sanitarium). Or they can be external (as was the case with Spreadshirt and Pons Bakery, for example, where ongoing relationships were maintained with our office and accredited, independent consultants). Regardless of whether they are internal or external to the organization, these individuals can:

a) act as a sounding board;
b) informally observe and monitor culture and leaders' (as well as other members') impact on it;
c) provide feedback and coaching; and
d) offer alternative ways of approaching specific situations and opportunities.

It is also important to recognize and reinforce the smaller wins as well as medium-term achievements as a way of sustaining motivation and momentum. Doing so also demonstrates Constructive thinking and behavior, particularly Achievement and Humanistic-Encouraging. This includes recognizing and positively reinforcing individuals and teams willing to take on new challenges and make a genuine effort to approach their work and interact with one another in more Constructive ways. Such Constructive behaviors not only contribute to grander longer-term achievements but also provide the basis for solving day-to-day problems such as interunit coordination and adaptation to environmental changes.

Sharing lessons, key learnings, and results is yet another important way in which leaders sustain motivation and build upon improvements. First, this practice signals to others within the organization that culture is of personal importance to the leader. Second, it helps people both inside and outside the organization learn how to create more effective cultures. Third, by sharing their results and insights, leaders make key stakeholders aware of the *what*, *why*, and *how* of their organization's culture efforts, which helps in gaining their acceptance of and support for continuing such efforts. As a result of this kind of sharing, SaskCentral's board members, for example, came to understand why creating and maintaining a more Constructive culture is important. In turn, they began using culture as one of the factors to evaluate both the organization's and leadership's performance. Culture has even been a key consideration in selecting their CEOs. The resulting continuity has paid off considerably in terms of outcomes, given our previous assertion that top leader turnover is a common cause of the abandonment of change efforts.

Shaun McCarthy, Chairman and Director of Human Synergistics in Australia and New Zealand, notes that CEO selection—though hugely important—isn't the only way in which board members influence an organization's culture. Like the organization's leaders, they too directly and indirectly influence culture in a variety of ways, including how they

- behave as a team during Board and subcommittee meetings,
- behave toward executives who attend Board or subcommittee meetings to report to Board members,
- present and manage their own "symbols" of values and beliefs,
- manage the interplay between strategy and culture,
- monitor performance, and
- manage risk.[251]

Disruptions and cessations of culture initiatives can also result from changes in demands by clients, employees, governmental policies, or by changes in resources. Legitimately, these kinds of events capture leaders' attention and, in some cases, can cause them to forget about or set aside their interest in and impact on culture. However, when leaders continue to focus on and recognize the value of creating more Constructive cultures—not just in the best of times but also in the worst—they find it helps them avert problems and effectively deal with tough situations when they do arise. Certainly, we see this in the sustained culture change experiences at Sanitarium and SaskCentral.

The box below provides some examples of strategies and tactics shared by the leaders we interviewed that can help you learn from the process and to sustain the positive changes you make along your change journey.

Learning from the Process and Sustaining Improvements

Use the list below to stimulate ideas or identify actions to continue to improve your organization's culture and overall performance.

- Schedule regular meetings with the core change team and with staff to discuss what's working and what's not, to learn, to make adjustments, and to recognize and reinforce desired behaviors and intermediate results.

- Maintain contact with trusted advisors and discuss with them the means for sustaining and reinvigorating movement toward an improved culture and climate.

- Define the upstream and midstream indicators and other signs that signal quick wins and medium-term accomplishments—then recognize and celebrate them when they occur.

- Define and implement a plan for regularly remeasuring and linking together culture, levers for change, and performance.

- Ask about, record, and disseminate experiences, key learnings, and insights regarding the change process.

- Discuss and adjust actions and levers used to effect desired changes based on feedback.

- Plan the next four-phase cycle with members of the leadership and core change teams.

Starting with Leadership Rather Than Culture

As illustrated by the cases in chapters 4 and 9 (which focused on Spreadshirt and Sanitarium), some organizations begin their culture change journey with leadership development rather than culture. Although the basic process is essentially the same as when the initial focus is on culture, the original baseline can instead focus on leaders' personal styles, leadership strategies, and current as well as ideal impact. As exemplified by the flow of events in chapter 4, members of your executive team can complete *Leadership/Impact*. Doing so would enable each of you to generate a profile depicting the impact that you would ideally like to have on the people around you, as well as obtain feedback on your current or actual impact. In addition, the leadership strategies assessed by *Leadership/Impact* provide information on causal factors and levers for changing your impact (per Table 2.3). Data on the broader culture can be collected either simultaneously or (as in the example in chapter 4) after leaders have successfully progressed in their own development. Alternatively, if you or members of your team have never experienced an individual or leadership development assessment or would prefer to focus initially on personal styles rather than impact, then start with the *Life Styles Inventory*, like the example in chapter 9. In that example, *Leadership/Impact* as well as the *Organizational Culture Inventory* were incorporated later in the process. Whichever assessment you start with, the results from it should, in turn, be used to identify which aspects of your executive team's day-to-day behaviors, leadership strategies, or management approaches support your ideal impact and which are inconsistent with it.

The Future of Leaders' Impact on Culture

Your ability as a leader to create more Constructive and less Defensive organizational cultures will be even more critical in the future than it is now. Leaders will face new and increasingly difficult challenges because of the accelerating pace of change in, for example, societal values, climate and ecological responses, international trade patterns, competition, the political and regulatory environments, and forces within their own organizations. Focusing on advances in scientific knowledge alone, organizations are inventing, adopting, and/or extending increasingly complex and sophisticated technologies that enable them to offer products and services that go well beyond those available even a decade ago. The implementation of these technologies requires better planning, innovation, coordination, and problem-solving capabilities that are best supported by Constructive norms. Self-Actualizing and Humanistic-Encouraging styles in particular support and encourage leaders and other members within organizations to proactively think about and take steps to ensure their technologies and creations are applied in balanced ways that are ethical and beneficial not only to the organization but also to customers, the community, and the larger society.

Similarly, the convergence of changes around communication and the increased use of social media has made what goes on inside organizations increasingly transparent. Harmful behaviors such as cheating and harassment are often attributed to the "toxic" cultures of organizations, underscoring the need to decrease Defensive norms. Importantly, this includes both the aggressive norms that lead to unacceptable behavior and the resulting passive norms that allow it to continue. At the same time, strengthening and reinforcing Constructive norms is equally important, because they significantly reduce the likelihood of inappropriate or illegal behaviors occurring, being tolerated, and spreading.

As organizations continue to grow and become more global, they will have an even greater impact on the countries within which they operate, making it increasingly important to create more Constructive operating cultures. In some cases, an organization's resources are so great that they de facto represent another level in the national governing system. Constructive norms, along with enlightened missions and strategies, are therefore critical for ensuring a thoughtful, positive, and nonexploitative impact—not just for the good of the larger social system, but also for the organization's own good (for instance, in terms of averting or minimizing negative publicity, fines, and regulatory actions).

At the same time, leaders are facing increased pressures to address cultural issues so that their organizations can become more competitive in a worldwide market. Per chapter 2, the values and ideal cultures described by organizational leaders are related to their country's world competitiveness. Constructive cultural norms also support innovation and retention of talent, whereas Defensive norms work against innovation and drive talented people to leave. Consequently, the importance of understanding your organization's culture and your impact on it will continue to increase, regardless of the country or industry in which you work.

We are privileged to be able to share with you the stories of recent culture change journeys from the perspectives of their leaders, along with the evidence on the advantages of Constructive leadership and culture that has accumulated over the past forty-plus years. We hope that you have gained some insights and gathered some ideas about how you might expand your organization's capacity to solve problems and achieve goals. We also hope, above all, that we have strengthened your belief in your ability to create a more Constructive environment through your impact on people and culture.

LEARN MORE

To test-drive the *Organizational Culture Inventory*®
and get started creating a more Constructive culture in your
organization, visit www.humansynergistics.com/culturebook.

Notes

Introduction: A Different Way of Looking at Your Impact

1. Kardos, "Courage and Commitment."
2. Georgopoulos and Cooke, "Conceptual-Theoretical Framework." Also see Georgopoulos and Cooke, "Underlying Conceptual-Theoretical Framework"; and Cooke and Rousseau, *Problems of Complex Systems*.
3. See "How Corporate Culture Affects," *Duke Fuqua Insights*; and Deloitte, *Global Human Capital*, 37.
4. Kerr, "On the Folly of Rewarding A," 775.
5. Kerr, "On the Folly of Rewarding A," 778.
6. For example, see Hall, *The Hidden Dimension* (New York: Anchor, 1990).
7. Bandura, "The Self System."
8. Beer, Finnström, and Schrader, "Why Leadership Training Fails."
9. The resulting placement of the twelve styles and their association with Constructive, Passive/Defensive, and Aggressive/Defensive personal orientations, group styles, leadership impact, and organizational cultures has been validated by several studies conducted by us, our colleagues, and independent researchers who have analyzed our surveys. For example, see Cooke and Lafferty, *Level I: Life Styles Inventory*; Cooke and Rousseau, "The Factor Structure"; Cooke, Rousseau, and Lafferty, "Thinking and Behavioral Styles"; Cooke and Szumal, "The Impact of Group Interaction"; Cooke and Szumal, "Measuring Normative Beliefs"; and Ware, Leak, and Perry, "*Life Styles Inventory*."
10. *Merriam-Webster Online*, https://www.merriam-webster.com/. The remaining definitions in this chapter come from this dictionary as well.
11. See Maslow, *Motivation and Personality*; and McClelland, Atkinson, Clark, and Lowell, *The Achievement Motive*.

Chapter 1. Why Create a Constructive Culture?

12. Hinks, "Culture at Heart."
13. See Cooke and Szumal, "Using the *Organizational Culture Inventory*"; Cooke and Szumal, "Measuring Normative Beliefs"; and Balthazard, Cooke, and Potter, "Dysfunctional Culture."
14. Ain, Bailey, Bromley, Kalyta, and Cooke, *The Best of the Best*, 26.
15. Ain, Bailey, Bromley, Kalyta, and Cooke, *The Best of the Best*.

16. Glisson and James, "The Cross-Level Effects," 788.
17. Sanfilippo, Bendapudi, Rucci, and Schlesinger, "Strong Leadership."
18. Shortell, Zimmerman, Rousseau, Gillies, Wagner, Draper, Knaus, and Duffy, "The Performance of Intensive Care Units."
19. Goodspeed, "Constructive Culture Keeps Turnover."
20. Michaels, "Excellent Cultures."
21. Maier, *Problem-Solving Discussions*, 5.
22. Cooke and Szumal, "The Impact of Group Interaction Styles"; and Potter and Balthazard, "Virtual Team Interaction Styles."
23. Harvey, "The Abilene Paradox."
24. Balthazard, Waldman, Howell, and Atwater, "Shared Leadership."
25. Janis, "Groupthink," 441.
26. Keenan, Cooke, and Hillis, "Norms and Nurse Management," 66.
27. Cooke and Szumal, "The Impact of Group Interaction Styles," 432; and Potter and Balthazard, "Virtual Team Interaction Styles," 436.
28. Thompson, *Organizations in Action*, 56.
29. Minvielle, Aegerter, Dervaux, Boumendil, Retbi, Jars-Guincestre, and Guidet, "Assessing Organizational Performance," 241.
30. See Peltier, "Strategic Culture Change"; and Ephektiv, "Asco Culture Case Study."
31. See Silla, Navajas, and Koves, "Organizational Culture"; and García-Herreo, Mariscal, Gutiérrez, and Toca-Otero, "Bayesian Network Analysis."
32. Strategy&, "Culture and Culture Change."
33. Andrew Klein, "Corporate Culture: Its Value," 24–25.
34. Cooke and Szumal, "Using the *Organizational Culture Inventory*," 158.
35. See Genetzky-Haugen, "Determining the Relationship"; and Weidner, "Trust and Distrust."
36. Sull, Homkes, and Sull, "Why Strategy Execution Unravels."
37. Lafferty and Associates, *Life Styles Inventory*, Appendix C.
38. Coleman, Olverson, and Clark, "Organizational Development," 5.
39. Coleman, Olverson, and Clark, "Organizational Development," 5.
40. Puranam, "Why Even Bad Strategy."
41. Cândido and Santos, "Strategy Implementation."
42. Sprague, "Below Trend."
43. Mackintosh, "What 500 Years of Protestantism."
44. Douglas, Sindreu, and Kantchev, "The Problem with Innovation."
45. Knott, "Is R&D Getting Harder?"; and Knott, *How Innovation Really Works*, 2.
46. The Conference Board, "Global Survey of C-Suite."
47. Rogers, *Diffusion of Innovation*, 12.
48. Chadha, "Innovation as a Team."
49. Kofman, "Culture."

[50] Weber and Sorenson, "Organizational Culture and TQM."
[51] Callen, Braithwaite, Westbrook, "Cultures in Hospitals," 635.
[52] Aarons and Sawitzky, "Organizational Culture and Climate."
[53] Williams, *All Eyes Forward*.
[54] Readership Institute, "The Power to Grow Readership"; and Sanders and Cooke, "Financial Returns."
[55] Nesbitt and Lavine, "Reaching New Readers"; and Lavine, "The Readership Key."
[56] Cooke, "Culture-Performance Connection."
[57] El-Bannany and Tipu, "Culture and Other Factors."
[58] Rousseau, "Normative Beliefs," 455–456.
[59] Martin Klein, "Corporate Culture and Store Performance."
[60] Jones, Dunphy, Fishman, Larné, and Canter, *In Great Company*, 390.
[61] Murray, "Boards Need to Measure."
[62] See AXA, *2012 Activity*; and Marti "Blue Culture."
[63] Manzoni and Baillot, "Changing the Corporate Culture."
[64] AXA, *2012 Activity*, 36.
[65] AXA, *AXA Group Human Capital*, 32.
[66] Reinhardt, "Flat Hierarchy."
[67] WorldCity Staff, "Changing Corporate Culture."
[68] Hinks, "Culture at Heart."
[69] Hinks, "Culture at Heart."
[70] Straumann, *We Love What We Do,* 15, 88.
[71] House, Hanges, Javidan, Dorfman, and Gupta, *Culture, Leadership*, 76, 661, 664.
[72] Ronen and Shenkar, "Clustering Countries," 444–446.
[73] Hofstede, *Culture's Consequences*, 214–215; and Hofstede, Hofstede, and Minkov, *Cultures and Organizations*, 92.
[74] IMD, World Competitiveness Yearbook.
[75] Herciu, Ogrean, and Belascu, "Culture and National Competitiveness," 3061–62 ; and Nukić and Braje, "Considerations of National Culture's Role," 394.
[76] Fry, "Millennials Projected."
[77] Mlodzik and De Meuse, *A Scholarly Investigation*, 11.
[78] Manjoo, "Corporate America."
[79] Catalyst, "Quick Take."
[80] McCarthy, "The Share of Female CEOs."
[81] Geiger and Kent, "Number of Women Leaders."
[82] Simon, "What Type of Culture?"
[83] Shyamsunder and Emrich, "Win-Win-Win!" Also see Catalyst, "Mind Your Culture Gap."

84. Dobbin and Kalev, "Why Diversity Programs Fail."
85. Bajdo and Dickson, "Perceptions of Organizational Culture," 399, 407–410.
86. Kwantes and Kartolo, "Constructive Organizational Cultures."
87. Dwyer, Richard, and Chadwick, "Gender Diversity in Management," 1009.

Chapter 2. How Leaders Directly and Indirectly Influence and Change Culture

88. Ricardo Gil, personal interview by Janet Szumal and Robert Cooke, September 26, 2018. All quotes from this source in this chapter stem from this interview.
89. Adapted from Gluyas, "Email Trail."
90. Drucker, "The Theory."
91. Oscar Bunch, personal interview by Janet Szumal, July 25, 2016.
92. Szumal and Cooke, *Organizational Culture*.
93. Wes Bunch, personal interview by Janet Szumal, July 14, 2016.
94. Gary Thompson, personal interview by Janet Szumal, July 20, 2016.
95. United Auto Workers, *The Leadership Alliance*.
96. General Motors, "Toledo Transmission."
97. Jørgensen, Owen, and Neus, *Making Change Work*.
98. Testani and Ramakrishnan, "Sustaining a Transformation"; and "IBM Lean Best Practice Award."
99. Saha, Lam, Ramakrishnan, and Boldrin, "Lean Transformation."
100. For example, see Szumal, *An International Study*; and Szumal, *The Reliability and Validity*.
101. Andrew Klein, "Corporate Culture: Its Value."
102. Perme, "Does Culture…?"
103. Schein, *Organizational Culture and Leadership*, 56.
104. Burns and Stalker, *The Management of Innovation*.
105. The literature on learning organizations, knowledge organizations, and organizational life cycles highlights Burns and Stalker's distinction between the characteristics of structures (and systems) that promote and support adaptation, innovation, and effectiveness versus those designed to foster and optimize efficiency and reliability. For example, see Senge, *The Fifth Disciple*; and Adizes, *The Pursuit of Prime*.
106. O'Reilly and Tushman, "The Ambidextrous Organization"; and Gibson and Birkinshaw, "The Antecedents," 204.
107. Lawrence and Lorsch, "Differentiation and Integration," 40.
108. Sethia and Von Glinow, "Arriving at Four Cultures," 400–401; Kilmann, Saxton, and Serpa, "Issues in Understanding," 91; Schein, *Organizational Culture*, 91, 117.
109. Locke and Latham, *A Theory of Goal Setting*.
110. Doran, "There's a S.M.A.R.T. Way."
111. Grove, *High Output Management*.
112. Beer, Finnström, and Schrader, "Why Leadership Training Fails."

[113] Sharkey, "GE Capital." Also see Sharkey, "Leveraging HR"; and Sharpe, "Best Practice Case Study."

[114] Trist and Bamforth, "Some Social and Psychological Consequences."

[115] Hackman and Oldham, *Work Redesign*.

[116] Human Synergistics. *Improving Store Management*," iii-iv.

[117] For example, see Peltier, "Strategic Culture Change"; and Marquardt and Bonenberger; "A Personal Touch"; and Jones, Dunphy, Fishman, Larné, and Canter, *In Great Company*.

[118] Francisco Cherny, personal interview by Janet Szumal and Robert Cooke, September 26, 2018.

[119] To learn more about Axialent, visit https://www.axialent.com/. To hear more about their insights, based on fifteen years of global culture transformation and their partnership with Human Synergistics, see Zanker and Gil, "Ultimate Culture Webinar."

[120] Bowers and Seashore, "Predicting Organizational Effectiveness."

[121] Klein, Wallis, and Cooke, "The Impact of Leadership Styles."

[122] French and Raven, "The Bases of Social Power."

[123] The relationships among each of the bases of power and the total amount of influence exercised by members are identified, for example, by Tannenbaum and Cooke, "Control and Participation," 40; and Bachman, Smith, and Slesinger, "Control, Performance and Satisfaction," 133.

[124] Communication for Learning, as measured by the *Organizational Effectiveness Inventory*, is defined as "the degree to which communications reflect a system orientation that includes consideration of the 'big picture,' interdependencies, and learning."

[125] Haber and Shurberg, "Safety Culture."

[126] Haley, "The Relationship," 14.

[127] Edmondson, "Learning from Mistakes," 7-80.

[128] Silla, Navajas, and Koves, "Organizational Culture," 125.

[129] García-Herreo, Mariscal, Gutiérrez, and Toca-Otero, "Bayesian Network Analysis," 92-94.

[130] Cooke, *Leadership/Impact*, 39.

[131] Szumal, *An International Study*. Also see Szumal, "The Impact of Leaders."

[132] Fuda, *Leadership Transformed*.

[133] Szumal and Cooke, *Management/Impact*, 4.

[134] Szumal, "The Impact of Leaders," 17-18.

[135] Smith, "How to Leverage Management/Impact."

Chapter 3. Launching—and Relaunching—Constructive Cultural Change

[136] Powell, "Port District President."

[137] Port of San Diego, "Port President/CEO."

[138] Jacobson and McEntee, "What Do We Talk about...?"

Chapter 4. Using a Shared Language to Increase Self-Awareness and Reduce Conflict

[139] Statista, "Revenue of Spreadshirt."
[140] IBIS World, *Online Original Design*.
[141] IBIS World, *Online Original Design*.
[142] Bereiter and Scardamalia, *Surpassing Ourselves*, 109; 111–112.
[143] Ringel, Taylor, and Zablit, *The Most Innovative Companies 2015*.
[144] Bennis, *An Invented Life*, 57–58.
[145] Weick and Quinn, "Organizational Change," 381.
[146] Schroeder-Saulnier, *The Power of Paradox*, 29.
[147] Meyer, *The Culture Map*, 55.
[148] Papanek and Alexander, *From Breakdown to Breakthrough*, 23–24.
[149] Lafferty and Lafferty, *Perfectionism*, 118–121.
[150] Weick and Quinn, "Organizational Change," 380.
[151] Schein, *The Corporate Culture Survival Guide*, 115–117.
[152] Business Wire, "Spreadshirt Crushes 2017 Growth."
[153] Colleran, "Lessons from Facebook."

Chapter 5. Making Culture a Strategic Priority to Become More Ambidextrous and Overcome Market Disruption

[154] Straumann, *Annual Report 2012*.
[155] Goldsmith, *What Got You Here*.
[156] Cooke and Szumal, "Using the *Organizational Culture Inventory*," 160.
[157] Mills, "The Decline and Rise of IBM"; Fishman, "What Happened"; and McGrath, "15 Years Later."
[158] Straumann, *We Love What We Do*, 88.
[159] Case, *The Third Wave*, 83.
[160] Adizes, *The Pursuit of Prime*, 18–25.
[161] Duncan, "The Ambidextrous Organization," 167, 172.
[162] O'Reilly and Tushman, "The Ambidextrous Organization."
[163] Gibson and Birkinshaw, "The Antecedents," 209.
[164] O'Reilly and Tushman, *Lead and Disrupt*, 189.
[165] Gibson and Birkinshaw, "The Antecedents," 217.
[166] O'Reilly and Tushman, *Lead and Disrupt*, 217–218.
[167] Straumann, *Extraordinary Performers*, 22.
[168] Straumann Group, "About the Company."
[169] Barker, *Paradigms*, 59–60.
[170] Martin and Osterling, *Value Stream*, 5–6.

[171] Straumann Group, "2016 Full-Year Results"; and Straumann Group, "Straumann Group Posts."

[172] Straumann Group, "2017 Nine-Month and Third Quarter Sales."

[173] Cairns, "Another Dental Megamerger."

[174] Schein, *Organizational Culture and Leadership*, 260.

Chapter 6. Deploying Levers for Cultural Change to Expedite Strategy Implementation

[175] Future Market Insights, *Biostimulants*.

[176] Hofstede, Hofstede, and Minkov, *Cultures and Organizations*, 57–59.

[177] Bartolomé and Laurent, "The Manager."

[178] McGregor, *The Human Side*, 33–34.

[179] Rosenthal and Jacobson, *Pygmalion in the Classroom*; and Heroic Imagination Project, "The Pygmalion Effect." Also see Kierein and Gold, "Pygmalion in Work Organizations"; Livingston, "Pygmalion in Management"; Riggio, "Pygmalion Leadership"; and Ellison, "Being Honest."

[180] Livingston, "Pygmalion in Management."

[181] Collins, *Good to Great*, 51.

[182] Quinn, *Deep Change*, 3.

[183] Hofstede, Hofstede, and Minkov, *Cultures and Organizations*.

[184] French and Raven, "The Bases of Social Power," 155–164.

[185] Kreitner and Kinicki, *Organizational Behavior*, 444.

[186] Szumal, *An International Study*; and Cooke and Szumal, "Using the Organizational Culture Inventory." Note that similar conclusions were later drawn by Wharton professor Adam Grant in *Give and Take*.

[187] Schein, *Organizational Culture and Leadership*, 310.

[188] Savage, Blair, and Sorenson, "Consider Both Relationships"; Thomas, "Conflict and Conflict Management"; Rahim, *Managing Conflict*; Sorenson, "Conflict Management Strategies"; Kuhn and Poole, "Do Conflict Management Styles...?"; and Behfar, Peterson, Mannix, and Trochim, "The Critical Role."

[189] Beck and Harter, "Why Great Managers."

[190] Sull, Homkes, and Sull, "Why Strategy Execution Unravels."

[191] Burjek, "Firms Grapple."

[192] Sull, Homkes, and Sull, "Why Strategy Execution Unravels."

Chapter 7. Trading Command and Control for Expansion and Growth

[193] Euromonitor International, *Baked Goods in Serbia*.

[194] Šešić, with Mikić and Tomka, "Serbia/ 1. Historical Perspective."

[195] See, for example, van Dam and van der Helm, "The Organizational Cost."

[196] Hofstede, Hofstede, and Minkov, *Cultures and Organizations*, 57, 97 103, 192.

[197] Cooke, "*Organizational Culture Inventory*."

198 These videos can be seen on Pons Bakery's YouTube channel: https://www.youtube.com/watch?v=DYGYnlQjh4A&list=PLyoq7vN_hoA745IIfDZsTHRwuL6E56gOl.

199 World Bank Group. "Small and Medium Enterprises."

Chapter 8. Leveraging the Capacity of HR Directors and Middle Managers to Effect Culture Change

200 Acronym for Hotel, Restaurant, and Café.

201 *Budapest Business Journal,* "Dreher Breweries."

202 Spain and Groysberg, "Making Exit Interviews Count," 91–92.

203 Cooke and Szumal, "Using the *Organizational Culture Inventory,*" 154.

204 Registered sales results by Nielsen Hungary's retail index.

205 Jarvis and Buckley, "AB InBev Buys SABMiller"; Chaudhuri, "AB InBev Offers to Sell"; and Béni, "The Japanese to Brew Hungarian Beer."

206 Sichon, *The Art of Human Resources,* chapter 8, Kindle.

207 Garvin, "How Google Sold Its Engineers."

Chapter 9. Leading People to Think Outside the Box and Move the Organization onto the Fast Track

208 Decent, "Breakfast and Snack Habits."

209 Saunders, "Sanitarium."

210 Hofstede, Hofstede, and Minkov, *Cultures and Organizations,* 95.

211 Reference for Business, "SIC 2043: Cereal Breakfast Foods."

212 Szumal, "The Impact of Leaders and Managers."

213 Edmondson, "Psychological Safety," 367.

214 Duhigg, "What Google Learned."

215 Saunders, "Sanitarium."

216 Mitchell, "Sanitarium Launches."

217 Saunders, "Sanitarium."

218 StopPress Team. "Sanitarium Takes the Biscuit"; and Culliney. "The Least Desirable Job?"

219 Reader's Digest Australia, "Award: Winner."

220 2015 and 2016 reports by Advantage Group International.

221 Hopkins, "Revealed"; "Innovative HR Teams"; The Australian Business Awards, "Sanitarium Health and Wellbeing"; and Key Media, "The Australian HR Awards."

Chapter 10. Sustaining Constructive Cultures through Continuous Monitoring, Coaching, and Support

222 SaskCentral, *2015 Annual Report.*

223 Moskowitz and Levering, "The Best Employers."

[224] Curtis and Lane, "Creating a Top 100 Workplace."
[225] Curtis and Lane, "Creating a Top 100 Workplace."
[226] See, for example, National Association of Corporate Directors, *Culture as a Corporate Asset*; Australian Institute of Company Directors, "The Role of the Board"; and Financial Reporting Council, *Corporate Culture*.
[227] SaskCentral. "SaskCentral Named."
[228] Sasse, "The Challenge."

Chapter 11. From the Middle to the Top of the Organization: Making Culture a Habit of Grace

[229] Baskerville-Burrows, "Structural Change," chapter 11, Kindle.
[230] Baskerville-Burrows, "Structural Change," chapter 11, Kindle.
[231] Dvorak and Sasaki. "Employees at Home."
[232] Balthazard, Waldman, and Atwater, "The Mediating Effects," 6.
[233] Cooke and Szumal, "Using the *Organizational Culture Inventory*," 154–156.
[234] Scott, *Fierce Conversations*, 25.
[235] Lee, "Bishop's Address 2016." Also see The General Convention of the Episcopal Church, "Statistical Totals."
[236] *Wall Street Journal*, "Illinois: Land of Leaving"; Mahtani and Belkin, "How Bad Is the Crisis?"; and Eltagouri and Wong, "Chicago Area Leads U.S."
[237] Curry, "Presiding Bishop."
[238] Curry, "Presiding Bishop."
[239] The Episcopal Church, "What We Believe."
[240] Schjonberg, "Historic Joint Meeting."
[241] Schein, *Organizational Culture and Leadership*, 310.

Chapter 12. Leading Your Organization's Culture Journey

[242] Personal communication with the author, April 28, 2019. All quotes from this source in this chapter stem from this communication.
[243] Schein, "So You Want to Create a Culture?"
[244] "Safe[t]y Culture Controversy."
[245] Anderson, "Culture."
[246] Musalem, "Why Focus on Culture?"
[247] Kaplan and Norton. *The Balanced Scorecard*.
[248] Schein, The Corporate Culture Survival Guide, 155.
[249] Jick, "Mixing," 602.
[250] Personal communication with the author, February 22, 2019. All quotes from this source in this chapter stem from this communication.
[251] McCarthy, "The Role of the Board," 10.

Bibliography

Aarons, Gregory A., and Angelina C. Sawitzky. "Organizational Culture and Climate and Mental Health Provider Attitudes toward Evidence-Based Practice." *Psychological Services* 3, no. 1 (February 2006): 61–72. https://www.ncbi.nlm.nih.gov/pmc/articles/PMC1712666/.

Adizes, Ichak. *The Pursuit of Prime: Maximize Your Company's Success with the Adizes Program.* Santa Barbara: The Adizes Institute, 2005.

Aguirre, DeAnne, Rutger von Post, and Micah Alpern. "Why Culture Matters and How It Makes Change Stick." Infographic. Strategy&, November 19, 2013. https://www.strategyand.pwc.com/media/file/Strategyand_Infographic_Why-Culture-Matters-and-How-It-Makes-Change-Stick.pdf.

Ain, Myrna, Dara Bailey, Peter Bromley, Mark Kalyta, and Robert A. Cooke. *The Best of the Best: The Role of Leadership and Culture in Creating Canada's Best Organizations.* Toronto: First Light, 2003.

Anderson, Carl. "Culture: The Key to Corporate Governance." *Insights* (the Ethisphere Institute), May 2015. https://insights.ethisphere.com/culture-the-key-to-corporate-governance/.

The Australian Business Awards. "Sanitarium Health and Wellbeing: Employer of Choice Winner 2016." https://www.australianbusinessawards.com.au/2016-winners/australian-business-award-for-employer-of-choice/sanitarium-health-and-wellbeing-eoc/.

Australian Institute of Company Directors. "The Role of the Board in Corporate Culture." *Company Director,* August 1, 2016. https://aicd.companydirectors.com.au/membership/company-director-magazine/2016-back-editions/august/the-role-of-the-board-in-corporate-culture.

AXA. *2012 Activity and Corporate Responsibility Report.* March 20, 2013. https://cdn.axa.com/www-axa-com%2Fcb9d1279-948a-4238-ab8f-754e9e10f2a5_axa_activity_csr_report_2012b_va.pdf.

———. *AXA Group Human Capital: 2015 Social Data Report.* April 26, 2016. https://group.axa.com/en/newsroom/publications/social-data-report-2015.

Bachman Jerald, G., Clagett G. Smith, and Jonathan A. Slesinger. "Control, Performance, and Satisfaction: An Analysis of Structural and Individual Effects." *Journal of Personality and Social Psychology* 4, no. 2 (1966): 127–136.

Bajdo, Linda M., and Marcus W. Dickson. "Perceptions of Organizational Culture and Women's Advancement in Organizations: A Cross-Cultural Examination." *Sex Roles* 45, no. 5–6 (September 2001): 399–414.

Balthazard, Pierre A., Robert A. Cooke, and Richard E. Potter. "Dysfunctional Culture, Dysfunctional Organization: Capturing the Behavioral Norms That Form Organizational Culture and Drive Performance." *Journal of Managerial Psychology* 21, no. 8 (December 2006): 709–32.

Balthazard, Pierre. A., David A. Waldman, and Leanne E. Atwater. "The Mediating Effects of Leadership and Interaction Style in Face-to-Face and Virtual Teams." In *Leadership at a Distance: Research in Technologically-Supported Work*, edited by Suzanne P. Weisband, 127–50. Mahwah, NJ: Lawrence Erlbaum Associates, 2008.

Balthazard, Pierre, David Waldman, Jane Howell, and Leanne Atwater. "Shared Leadership and Group Interaction Styles in Problem-Solving Virtual Teams." *Proceedings for the Hawaii International Conference on System Sciences* 37. Big Island, HI, January 2004.

Bandura, Albert. "The Self System in Reciprocal Determinism." *American Psychologist* 33, no. 4 (April 1978): 344–58.

Barker, Joel Arthur. *Paradigms: The Business of Discovering the Future*. New York: Harper Business, 1992.

Bartolomé, Fernando, and André Laurent. "The Manager: Master and Servant of Power. *Harvard Business Review*, November 1986. https://hbr.org/1986/11/the-manager-master-and-servant-of-power.

Baskerville-Burrows, Jennifer. "Structural Change in the Diocese of Chicago." In *What We Shall Become: The Future and Structure of the Episcopal Church*, edited by Winnie Varghese. New York: Church Publishing, 2013.

Beck, Randall, and Jim Harter. "Why Great Managers Are So Rare." *Gallup Business Journal,* March 25, 2014. http://www.gallup.com/workplace/231593/167975/why-great-managers-rare.aspx.

Beer, Michael, Magnus Finnström, and Derek Schrader. "Why Leadership Training Fails—and What to Do about It." *Harvard Business Review*, October 2016. https://hbr.org/2016/10/why-leadership-training-fails-and-what-to-do-about-it.

Behfar, Kristin J., Randall S. Peterson, Elizabeth A. Mannix, and William M. K. Trochim. "The Critical Role of Conflict Resolution in Teams: A Close Look at the Link between Conflict Type, Conflict Management Strategies, and Team Outcomes." *Journal of Applied Psychology* 91, no. 1 (2008): 170–88.

Béni, Alexandra. "The Japanese to Brew Hungarian Beer." *Daily News Hungary*, December 15, 2016. https://dailynewshungary.com/japanese-brew-beer/.

Bennis, Warren. *An Invented Life: Reflections on Leadership and Change*. New York: Basic Books, 1994.

Benton, Angela. "Focus on Culture from the Beginning." *Wall Street Journal*, February 5, 2015. https://blogs.wsj.com/accelerators/2013/02/05/focus-on-culture-from-the-beginning/.

Bereiter, Carl, and Marlene Scardamalia. *Surpassing Ourselves: An Inquiry into the Nature and Implications of Expertise*. Chicago: Open Court, 1993.

Bowers, David G., and Stanley E. Seashore. "Predicting Organizational Effectiveness with a Four-Factor Theory of Leadership." *Administrative Science Quarterly* 11, no. 2 (1966): 238–63.

Budapest Business Journal. "Dreher Breweries Sees Revenue Reaching HUF 40 BLN in 2012." September 13, 2012. http://bbj.hu/business/dreher-breweries-sees-revenue-reaching-huf-40-bln-in-2012_63895.

Burjek, Andie. "Firms Grapple with Workplace Culture." *Talent Management*, December 16, 2015. http://www.talentmgt.com/2015/12/16/firms-grapple-with-workplace-culture/.

Burns, Tom, and George Stalker. *The Management of Innovation*. London: Tavistock Publications, 1961.

Business Wire. "Spreadshirt Crushes 2017 Growth Numbers." August 9, 2017. https://www.businesswire.com/news/home/20170809005174/en/Spreadshirt-Crushes-2017-Growth-Numbers.

Cairns, Elizabeth. "Another Dental Megamerger Leaves Straumann on the Shelf." *Vantage*, September 16, 2015. http://www.evaluategroup.com/Universal/View.aspx?type=Story&id=595658&sectionID=&isEPVantage=yes.

Callen, Joanne L., Jeffrey Braithwaite, and Johanna I. Westbrook. "Cultures in Hospitals and Their Influence on Attitudes to, and Satisfaction with, the Use of Clinical Information Systems." *Social Science & Medicine* 65, no. 3 (September 2007): 635–39.

Cândido, Carlos J. F., and Sérgio P. Santos. "Strategy Implementation: What Is the Failure Rate?" *Journal of Management & Organization* 21, no. 2 (March 2015): 237–62. Reprint. https://www.researchgate.net/publication/264004530_Strategy_implementation_What_is_the_failure_rate.

Case, Steve. *The Third Wave: An Entrepreneur's Vision of the Future*. New York: Simon & Schuster, 2016.

Catalyst. "Mind Your Culture Gap to Keep Your Top Talent." Infographic. Catalyst, July 7, 2015. http://www.catalyst.org/knowledge/infographic-mind-your-culture-gap-keep-your-top-talent.

———. "Quick Take: Women in the Workforce—United States." Catalyst, March 28, 2018. http://www.catalyst.org/knowledge/women-workforce-united-states.

Chadha, Janaki. "Innovation as a Team Wins, Study Finds." *Wall Street Journal*, August 9, 2018.

Chaudhuri, Saabira. "AB InBev Offers to Sell SABMiller's Central, Eastern European Brands." *Wall Street Journal*, April 29, 2016. https://www.wsj.com/articles/ab-inbev-offers-to-sell-sabmillers-central-eastern-europe-assets-1461913217.

Coleman, Garry D., Mike Olverson, and Altyn Clark. "Organizational Development as Part of a Long Term Strategic Management/Change Effort." In *Proceedings of the American Society for Engineering Management 2014 Annual Conference*, edited by S. Long, E. H. Ng, and C. Downing, Indianapolis, Indiana, June 15–18, 2014. https://transformationsystems.com/wp-content/uploads/2016/01/TSI_Article_AmericanSocietyForEngineeringManagementConf.pdf.

Colleran, Kevin. "Lessons from Facebook: How Culture Leads to Growth." *Wall Street Journal*, February 5, 2013. https://blogs.wsj.com/accelerators/2013/02/05/lessons-from-facebook-how-culture-lead-to-growth/.

Collins, Jim. *Good to Great: Why Some Companies Make the Leap…and Others Don't*. New York: HarperCollins, 2001.

The Conference Board. "Global Survey of C-Suite: Recession Fears Fade, but Talent Concerns Remain." *Cision PR Newswire*, January 18, 2018. https://www.prnewswire.com/news-releases/global-survey-of-c-suite-recession-fears-fade-but-talent-concerns-remain-300584459.html.

Cooke, Robert A. *Impact® Confidential Feedback Report*. Plymouth, MI: Human Synergistics International, 1997, 2014.

———. "*Organizational Culture Inventory*: Ideal Culture Profiles (International Management Association)." Presentation at the University of Illinois at Chicago, September 2001.

———. "Culture-Performance Connection: A Mandate for Change." Presentation at the Sixth Annual Australian Conference on Culture and Leadership, Sydney, Australia, July 2004.

Cooke, Robert A., and J. Clayton Lafferty. *Level I: Life Styles Inventory—An Instrument for Assessing and Changing the Self-Concept of Organizational Members.* Plymouth, MI: Human Synergistics, 1981.

Cooke, Robert A., and Denise M. Rousseau. *Problems of Complex Systems: A Model of System Problem Solving Applied to Schools*. Program Report No. 81-B5, Institute for Research on Educational Finance and Governance, Stanford University, May 1981.

———. "The Factor Structure of Level I: Life Styles Inventory." *Educational and Psychological Measurement* 43, no. 2 (June 1983): 449–57.

Cooke, Robert A., Denise M. Rousseau, and J. Clayton Lafferty. "Thinking and Behavioral Styles: Consistency between Self-Descriptions and Descriptions by Others." *Educational and Psychological Measurement* 47, no. 3 (September 1987): 815–23.

Cooke, Robert A., and Janet L. Szumal. "Using the *Organizational Culture Inventory* to Understand the Operating Cultures of Organizations." In *The Handbook of Organizational Culture and Climate*, edited by Neal M. Ashkanasy, Celeste P. M. Wilderom, and Mark F. Peterson, 147–62. Thousand Oaks, CA: Sage, 2000.

———. "The Impact of Group Interaction Styles on Problem-Solving Effectiveness." *Journal of Applied Behavioral Science* 30, no. 4 (1994): 415–37.

———. "Measuring Normative Beliefs and Shared Behavioral Expectations in Organizations: The Reliability and Validity of the Organizational Culture Inventory." *Psychological Reports* 72, no. 3 (1993): 1299–1330.

Culliney, Kacey. "The Least Desirable Job? Being a Breakfast Cereal Exec, Says Consultant." Bakery and Snacks.com, November 17, 2014. http://www.bakeryandsnacks.com/Markets/Breakfast-cereal-troubles-Everything-is-competition-says-consultant?utm_source=copyright&utm_medium=OnSite&utm_campaign=copyright.

Curry, Michael. "Presiding Bishop Updates Staff on Independent Investigation." *Episcopal News Service*, Episcopal Church Office of Public Affairs, April 4, 2016. http://episcopaldigitalnetwork.com/ens/2016/04/04/presiding-bishop-updates-staff-on-independent-investigation/.

Curtis, Ken, and Debbie Lane. "Creating a Top 100 Workplace through Constructive Leadership and Culture." Speech presented at the Human Synergistics' Global Consultants' Forum, Mount Prospect, IL, March 2014. Video, 01:06:09. https://www.humansynergistics.com/resources/content/2016/12/07/creating-a-top-100-workplace-through-constructive-leadership-and-culture.

Decent, Tom. "Breakfast and Snack Habits: Australians are Eating Healthier." *Sydney Morning Herald*, February 20, 2015. http://www.smh.com.au/nsw/breakfast-and-snack-habits-australians-are-eating-healthier-20150220-13kamr.html.

Deloitte. *Global Human Capital Trends 2016*. Westlake, TX: Deloitte University Press. https://www2.deloitte.com/insights/us/en/focus/human-capital-trends/2016.html.

Dobbin, Frank, and Alexandra Kalev. "Why Diversity Programs Fail." *Harvard Business Review*, July-August 2016. https://hbr.org/2016/07/why-diversity-programs-fail.

Doran, George T. "There's a S.M.A.R.T. Way to Write Management's Goals and Objectives." *Management Review* (AMA Forum) 70, no. 11 (November 1981): 35–36.

Douglas, Jason, Jon Sindreu, and Georgi Kantchev. "The Problem with Innovation: The Biggest Companies Are Hogging All the Gains." *Wall Street Journal*, July 15, 2018. https://www.wsj.com/articles/the-problem-with-innovation-the-biggest-companies-are-hogging-all-the-gains-1531680310.

Drucker, Peter F. "The Theory of the Business." *Harvard Business Review*, September-October 1994. https://hbr.org/1994/09/the-theory-of-the-business.

Duhigg, Charles. "What Google Learned from Its Quest to Build the Perfect Team." *New York Times Magazine*, February 25, 2016. http://www.nytimes.com/2016/02/28/magazine/what-google-learned-from-its-quest-to-build-the-perfect-team.html?_r=0.

Duncan, Robert B. "The Ambidextrous Organization: Designing Dual Structures for Innovation." In *The Management of Organization Design*. Vol. 1, *Strategies and Implementation*, edited by Ralph H. Kilmann, Louis R. Pondy, and Dennis P. Slevin, 167–88. New York: North-Holland Publishing, 1976.

Dvorak, Nate, and Junko Sasaki. "Employees at Home: Less Engaged." *Gallup Business Journal*, March 30, 2017. http://news.gallup.com/businessjournal/207539/employees-home-less-engaged.aspx.

Dwyer, Sean, Orlando C. Richard, and Ken Chadwick. "Gender Diversity in Management and Firm Performance: The Influence of Growth Orientation and Organizational Culture." *Journal of Business Research* 56, no. 12 (December 2003): 1009–1019.

Edmondson, Amy. "Psychological Safety and Learning Behavior in Work Teams." *Administrative Science Quarterly* 44, no. 2 (June 1999): 350–83.

———. "Learning from Mistakes Is Easier Said Than Done: Group and Organizational Influences on the Detection and Correction of Human Error." *Journal of Applied Behavioral Science* 32, no. 1 (March 1996): 5–32.

El-Bannany, Magdi, and Syed A. Tipu. "Culture and Other Factors Affecting Firm Profitability in Pakistan." *Corporate Ownership & Control* 7, no. 1 (Fall 2009): 471–76.

Ellison, Katherine. "Being Honest about the Pygmalion Effect." *Discover*, December 2015. http://discovermagazine.com/2015/dec/14-great-expectations.

Eltagouri, Marwa, and Grace Wong. "Chicago Area Leads U.S. in Population Loss, Sees Drop for 2nd Year in a Row." *Chicago Tribune*, March 23, 2017. http://www.chicagotribune.com/news/local/breaking/ct-chicago-census-population-loss-met-20170322-story.html.

Ephektiv. "Asco Culture Case Study." Accessed December 20, 2018. http://ephektiv.co/services/culture/asco-case-study/.

The Episcopal Church. "What We Believe." September 17, 2019. https://www.episcopalchurch.org/page/baptismal-covenant.

Euromonitor International. *Baked Goods in Serbia*. Country Report, November 2018.

Financial Reporting Council. *Corporate Culture and the Role of Boards*. London: Financial Reporting Council, July 2016. https://www.frc.org.uk/getattachment/3851b9c5-92d3-4695-aeb2-87c9052dc8c1/Corporate-Culture-and-the-Role-of-Boards-Report-of-Observations.pdf.

Fishman, Ted C. "What Happened to Morotola." *Chicago Magazine*, August 25, 2014. https://www.chicagomag.com/Chicago-Magazine/September-2014/What-Happened-to-Motorola/.

French, John R. P., Jr., and Bertram Raven. "The Bases of Social Power." In *Studies in Social Power*, edited by Dorwin Cartwright, 150–67. Ann Arbor, MI: University of Michigan, 1959.

Fry, Richard. "Millennials Projected to Overtake Baby Boomers as America's Largest Generation." Pew Research Center, April 25, 2016. http://www.pewresearch.org/fact-tank/2016/04/25/millennials-overtake-baby-boomers/.

Fuda, Peter. *Leadership Transformed: How Ordinary Managers Become Extraordinary Leaders*. New York: New Harvest, 2013.

Future Market Insights. *Biostimulants Market: Foliar Application to Exhibit Firm Growth during the Forecast Period: Global Industry Analysis and Opportunity Assessment 2015–2025*. http://www.futuremarketinsights.com/reports/biostimulants-market.

García-Herreo, Susana, M. A. Mariscal, J. M. Gutiérrez, and Antonio Toca-Otero. "Bayesian Network Analysis of Safety Culture and Organizational Culture in a Nuclear Power Plant." *Safety Science* 53 (March 2013): 82–95.

Garvin, David A. "How Google Sold Its Engineers on Management." *Harvard Business Review*, December 2013. https://hbr.org/2013/12/how-google-sold-its-engineers-on-management.

Geiger, A. W., and Lauren Kent. "Number of Women Leaders around the World Has Grown, but They're Still a Small Group." Pew Research Center, March 8, 2017. http://www.pewresearch.org/fact-tank/2017/03/08/women-leaders-around-the-world/.

The General Convention of the Episcopal Church. "Statistical Totals for the Episcopal Church by Province and Diocese: 2015–2016." https://extranet.generalconvention.org/staff/files/download/19547.

General Motors. "Toledo Transmission." Accessed December 28, 2018. https://plants.gm.com/Facilities/public/us/en/toledo/news.html.

Genetzky-Haugen, Mindy S. "Determining the Relationship and Influence Organizational Culture Has on Organizational Trust." MS thesis, University of Nebraska–Lincoln, 2010. https://digitalcommons.unl.edu/cgi/viewcontent.cgi?article=1005&context=aglecdiss.

Georgopoulos, Basil S., and Robert A. Cooke. "Conceptual-Theoretical Framework for the Organizational Study of Hospital Emergency Services." *Institute for Social Research Working Paper Series*, ISR Code Number 8011. University of Michigan, January 1979.

———. "Underlying Conceptual-Theoretical Framework." In *Organizational Structure, Problem Solving, and Effectiveness: A Comparative Study of Hospital Emergency Services,* edited by Basil S. Georgopoulos, 305–32. San Francisco: Jossey-Bass, 1986.

Gibson, Cristina B., and Julian Birkinshaw. "The Antecedents, Consequences, and Mediating Role of Organizational Ambidexterity." *Academy of Management Journal* 47, no. 2 (2004): 209–26.

Glisson, Charles, and Lawrence R. James. "The Cross-Level Effects of Culture and Climate in Human Service Teams." *Journal of Organizational Behavior* 23, no. 6 (September 2002): 767–94.

Gluyas, Alex. "Email Trail Sheds Light on Culture." *Australian Financial Review,* September 15–16, 2018.

Goldsmith, Marshall. *What Got You Here Won't Get You There: How Successful People Become Even More Successful.* New York: Hyperion, 2007.

Goodspeed, Scott W. "Constructive Culture Keeps Turnover Ridiculously Low and Improves Financial Quality and Team Performance." Stroudwater Associates. PowerPoint slides presented January 25, 2017. www.litmos.com/wp-content/uploads/2017/01/Constructive-Culture-PPT.pptx.

Grant, Adam. *Give and Take: Why Helping Others Drives Our Success.* New York: Penguin, 2013.

Gratzinger, Peter D., Ronald A. Warren, and Robert A. Cooke. "Psychological Orientations and Leadership: Thinking Styles That Differentiate between Effective and Ineffective Managers." In *Measures of Leadership*, edited by Kenneth E. Clark and Miriam B. Clark, 239–47. Greensboro, NC: Center for Creative Leadership, 1990.

Grove, Andrew S. *High Output Management.* New York: Random House, 1983.

Haber, Sonja B., and Deborah A. Shurberg. "Safety Culture in the Nuclear and Non-Nuclear Organization." Paper presented at the American Nuclear Society Topical Meeting on Risk Management, Boston, MA, June 1992. https://inis.iaea.org/collection/NCLCollectionStore/_Public/28/018/28018708.pdf.

Hackman, J. Richard, and Greg R. Oldham. *Work Redesign.* Reading, MA: Addison-Wesley, 1980.

Haley, Beverly R. "The Relationship of Unit Culture and RN and Client Outcomes." PhD diss., University of Illinois at Chicago, 1998.

Harvey, Jerry B. "The Abilene Paradox: The Management of Agreement." *Organizational Dynamics* 3, no. 1 (Summer 1974): 63–80.

Herciu, Mihaela, Claudia Ogrean, and Lucian Belascu. "Culture and National Competitiveness." *African Journal of Business Management* 5, no. 8 (May 2011): 3056–62.

Heroic Imagination Project. "The Pygmalion Effect: Robert Rosenthal's Study on the Power of Positive Expectations." *YouTube*. Video, 5:59. https://www.youtube.com/watch?v=EjbL7zW-Wig.

Hinks, Gaven. "Culture at Heart: Steven Baert, Novartis." *Board Agenda*, May 21, 2018. https://boardagenda.com/2018/05/21/culture-heart-steven-baert-novartis/.

Hofstede, Geert. *Culture's Consequences: International Differences in Work-Related Values*. Newbury Park, CA: Sage, 1980.

Hofstede, Geert, Gert Jan Hofstede, and Michael Minkov. *Cultures and Organizations: Software of the Mind*. 3rd ed. New York: McGraw-Hill, 2010.

Hopkins, Iain. "Revealed: Australia's Best Employers." *Human Resources Director*, May 19, 2015. http://www.hcamag.com/hr-news/revealed-australias-best-employers-200460.aspx.

House, Robert J., Paul J. Hanges, Mansour Javidan, Peter W. Dorfman, and Vipin Gupta. *Culture, Leadership, and Organizations: The GLOBE Study of 62 Societies*. Thousand Oaks, CA: Sage, 2004.

"How Corporate Culture Affects the Bottom Line." *Duke Fuqua Insights*, Duke University Fuqua School of Business, November 12, 2015. https://www.fuqua.duke.edu/duke-fuqua-insights/corporate-culture.

Human Synergistics. *Improving Store Management Effectiveness*. Atlanta, GA: Coca-Cola Retailing Research Council, 1986.

IBIS World. *Online Original Design T-Shirt Sales Industry in the US—Market Research Report*. IBIS World, February 2019. http://www.ibisworld.com/industry/online-original-design-t-shirt-sales.html?partnerid=prweb.

"IBM Lean Best Practice Award: Sustaining a Lean Transformation in Complex Server Assembly and Test Organization." Slides presented at ISC Poughkeepsie, Manufacturing Operations, 2010. http://www1.humansynergistics.com/docs/default-source/2013-affiliate-meeting/sustaining-a-lean-transformation.pdf?sfvrsn=2.

IMD. *World Competitiveness Yearbook*. Annual Report. Lausanne, Switzerland: IMD. https://www.imd.org/wcc/products/eshop-world-competitiveness-yearbook/.

"Innovative HR Teams." *Human Resources Director* 14, no. 3 (March 2016): 16–28. https://issuu.com/keymedia/docs/hrd14.03_emag-ipad.

Jacobson, Michael, and Jeffrey B. McEntee. "What Do We Talk about When We Talk about Performance? The Uses of Performance Information." Presentation at 2009 Government Finance Officers Association (GFOA) 103rd Annual Conference, Seattle Washington, June 28–July 1, 2009.

Janis, Irving L. "Groupthink." In *Readings in Managerial Psychology*. 4th ed. Edited by Harold J. Leavitt, Louis R. Pondy, and David M. Boje, 439–449. Chicago: University of Chicago Press, 1989.

Jarvis, Paul, and Thomas Buckley. "AB InBev Buys SABMiller for $107 Billion as U.S. Deal Agreed." *Bloomberg*, November 11, 2015. http://www.bloomberg.com/news/articles/2015-11-11/ab-inbev-to-buy-sabmiller-for-107-billion-as-u-s-deal-agreed.

Jick, Todd D. "Mixing Qualitative and Quantitative Methods: Triangulation in Action." *Administrative Science Quarterly* 24, no. 4 (December 1979): 602–11.

Jones, Quentin, Dexter Dunphy, Rosalie Fishman, Margherita Larné, and Corrine Canter. *In Great Company: Unlocking the Secrets of Cultural Transformation*. 2nd ed. Wellington, New Zealand and Sydney, Australia: Human Synergistics New Zealand and Australia, 2011.

Jørgensen, Hans Henrik, Lawrence Owen, and Andreas Neus. *Making Change Work*. IBM, 2008. https://demo.idg.com.au/cw/cw_howard_MakingChangeWork.pdf.

Kaplan, Robert S., and David P. Norton. *The Balanced Scorecard: Translating Strategy into Action*. Cambridge, MA: Harvard Business School Press, 1996.

Kardos, Rebecca. "Courage and Commitment: That's Culture." Speech presented at the 20th Annual Human Synergistics Culture and Leadership Conference, Sydney, Australia, September 12, 2018. Video, 24:21. https://www.youtube.com/watch?v=J4IH6rhW2RQ.

Keenan, Gail M., Robert Cooke, and Stephen L. Hillis. "Norms and Nurse Management of Conflicts: Keys to Understanding Nurse-Physician Collaboration." *Research in Nursing & Health* 21 (1998): 59–72.

Kerr, Steven. "On the Folly of Rewarding A, while Hoping for B." *Academy of Management Journal* 18 (December 1975): 769–83.

Key Media. "The Australian HR Awards 2016 Winners." Australian HR Awards. http://www.hrawards.com.au/index.php/winners/2016-winners.

Kierein, Nicole M., and Michael A. Gold. "Pygmalion in Work Organizations: A Meta-Analysis." *Journal of Organizational Behavior* 21, no. 8 (December 2000): 913–28.

Kilmann, Ralph H., Mary J. Saxton, and Roy Serpa. "Issues in Understanding and Changing Culture." *California Management Review* XXVIII, no. 2 (Winter 1986): 88–94.

Klein, Andrew. "Corporate Culture: Its Value as a Resource for Competitive Advantage." *Journal of Business Strategy* 32, no. 2 (March 2011): 21–28.

Klein, Andrew S., Joseph Wallis, and Robert A. Cooke. "The Impact of Leadership Styles on Organizational Culture and Firm Effectiveness: An Empirical Study." *Journal of Management & Organization* 19, no. 3 (December 2013): 241–54.

Klein, Martin Israel. "Corporate Culture and Store Performance: Differences among High Performance and Low Performance Stores." PhD diss., Temple University, 1992.

Knott, Anne Marie. "Is R&D Getting Harder, or Are Companies Just Getting Worse at It?" *Harvard Business Review*, March 21, 2017. https://hbr.org/2017/03/is-rd-getting-harder-or-are-companies-just-getting-worse-at-it.

———. *How Innovation Really Works: Using the Trillion-Dollar R&D Fix to Drive Growth*. New York: McGraw-Hill, 2017.

Kofman, Fred. "Culture: Key to Organizational Success (2.4)." *Huffington Post*, August 24, 2016. https://www.huffingtonpost.com/fred-kofman/culture-key-to-organizati_b_8029134.html.

Kreitner, Robert, and Angelo Kinicki. *Organizational Behavior*. 9th ed. New York: McGraw-Hill, 2010.

Kuhn, Timothy, and Marshall Scott Poole. "Do Conflict Management Styles Affect Group Decision Making? Evidence from a Longitudinal Field Study." *Human Communication Research* 26, no. 4 (2000): 558–90.

Kwantes, Catherine, and Arief Kartolo. "Constructive Organizational Cultures May Reduce Perceived Discrimination in the Workplace." *Constructive Culture* (blog), March 30, 2017. http://constructiveculture.com/constructive-organizational-cultures-may-reduce-perceived-discrimination-workplace/.

Lafferty, J. Clayton, and Associates. *Life Styles Inventory Leader's Guide*. Plymouth, MI: Human Synergistics, 1989.

Lafferty, J. Clayton, and Lorraine F. Lafferty. *Perfectionism: A Sure Cure for Happiness*. Plymouth, MI: Human Synergistics International, 1996.

Lavine, John. "The Readership Key: Are You Ready to Innovate?" Slides presented at the Newspaper Association of America (NAA) Readership Conference, Washington, April 19, 2004. https://slideplayer.com/slide/3003483/.

Lawrence, Paul R., and Jay W. Lorsch. "Differentiation and Integration in Complex Organizations." *Administrative Science Quarterly* 12, no.1 (June 1967): 1–47.

Lee, Jeffrey. "Bishop's Address 2016." Presented at the 179th Annual Convention of the Diocese of Chicago, November 18, 2016. https://www.episcopalchicago.org/our-diocese/bishop/sermons-and-speeches/.

Livingston, J. Sterling. "Pygmalion in Management." *Harvard Business Review*, January 2003 (1969).

Locke, Edwin A., and Gary P. Latham. *A Theory of Goal Setting and Task Performance*. Englewood Cliffs, NJ: Prentice-Hall, 1990.

Mackintosh, James. "What 500 Years of Protestantism Teaches Us about Capitalism's Future." *Wall Street Journal*, November 2, 2017. https://www.wsj.com/articles/what-500-years-of-protestantism-teaches-us-about-capitalisms-future-1509649297.

Mahtani, Shibani, and Douglas Belkin. "How Bad Is the Crisis in Illinois? It Has $14.6 Billion in Unpaid Bills." *Wall Street Journal*, June 27, 2017. https://www.wsj.com/articles/how-bad-is-the-crisis-in-illinois-it-has-14-6-billion-in-unpaid-bills-1498590946.

Maier, Norman R. F. *Problem-Solving Discussions and Conferences: Leadership Methods and Skills*. New York: McGraw-Hill, 1963.

———. "Assets and Liabilities in Group Problem Solving: The Need for an Integrative Function." *Psychological Review* 74, no. 4 (1967): 239–49.

Manjoo, Farhad. "Corporate America Chases the Mythical Millennial." *New York Times*, May 25, 2016.

Manzoni, Jean-François, and Jean-Pierre Baillot. "Changing the Corporate Culture at AXA: The Long and Winding Road." Case Study. Paris: INSEAD, 2013.

Marquardt, Martin, and Dave Bonenberger. "A Personal Touch to Safety Culture." Speech presented at the Human Synergistics 1st Annual *Ultimate* Culture Conference. Chicago, September 29, 2015. Video, 3:22. https://www.humansynergistics.com/resources/videos/content/2016/12/07/a-personal-touch-to-safety-culture.

Marti, Stefan. "Blue Culture: Cultural Development at AXA." Slides presented at the Human Synergistics Summer Conference, Zurich, Switzerland, June 11, 2012. http://st-marti.ch/pdf/Marti_ENG.pdf.

Martin, Karen, and Mike Osterling. *Value Stream Mapping: How to Visualize Work and Align Leadership for Organizational Transformation*. New York: McGraw-Hill, 2013.

Maslow, Abraham H. *Motivation and Personality*. New York: Harper and Row, 1954.

McCarthy, Niall. "The Share of Female CEOs at the World's Biggest Companies Is Greatly Overestimated." Infographic. *Forbes*, March 7, 2018. https://www.forbes.com/sites/niallmccarthy/2018/03/07/the-share-of-female-ceos-at-the-worlds-biggest-companies-is-hugely-overestimated-infographic/#746148cf281d.

McCarthy, Shaun. "The Role of the Board in Managing Organisational Culture." Whitepaper presented at the Australian Human Resources Institute (AHRI) National Conference, Sydney, Australia, August 2, 2017.

McClelland, David C., John W. Atkinson, Russel A. Clark, and Edgar L. Lowell. *The Achievement Motive*. New York: Appleton-Century-Crofts, 1953.

McGrath, Rita Gunther. "15 Years Later, Lessons from the Failed AOL-Time Warner Merger." *Fortune*, January 10, 2015. http://fortune.com/2015/01/10/15-years-later-lessons-from-the-failed-aol-time-warner-merger/.

McGregor, Douglas. *The Human Side of Enterprise*. 25th anniversary ed. New York: McGraw-Hill, 1985.

Meyer, Erin. *The Culture Map: Breaking through the Invisible Barriers of Global Business*. New York: PublicAffairs, 2014.

Michaels, Paul. "Excellent Cultures: Paul Michaels Shares GM Nameplate Success Story." Excellent Cultures, June 14, 2018. Video, 10:58. https://www.youtube.com/watch?v=UgqZ1E255Mk.

Mills, D. Quinn. "The Decline and Rise of IBM." *MIT Sloan Management Review*, Summer 1996. https://sloanreview.mit.edu/article/the-decline-and-rise-of-ibm/.

Minvielle, Etienne, Phillipe Aegerter, Benoit Dervaux, Ariane Boumendil, Aurélia Retbi, Marie Claude Jars-Guincestre, and Bertrand Guidet. "Assessing Organizational Performance in Intensive Care Units: A French Experience." *Journal of Critical Care* 23, no. 2 (July 2008): 236–44.

Mitchell, Sue. "Sanitarium Launches Up&Go into UK Market against Weetbix Rivals." *Australian Financial Review*, January 30, 2015. http://www.afr.com/business/retail/fmcg/sanitarium-launches-upgo-into-ukmarket-against-weetbix-rivals-20150129-131kau.

Mlodzik, Kevin J., and Kenneth P. De Meuse. *A Scholarly Investigation of Generational Workforce Differences: Debunking the Myths*. Los Angeles, CA: Korn/Ferry International, 2009.

Moskowitz, Milton, and Robert Levering. "The Best Employers in the U.S. Say Their Greatest Tool Is Culture." *Fortune*, March 5, 2015. http://fortune.com/2015/03/05/best-companies-greatest-tool-is-culture/.

Murray, Rob. "Boards Need to Measure Their Own Behavior." Slides presented at the Human Synergistics 19th Annual Australian Culture and Leadership Conference, Sydney, Australia, September 2017. https://www.human-synergistics.com.au/docs/default-source/conference/rob-murray---boards-need-to-measure-their-own-culture-and-behaviour.pdf?sfvrsn=2.

Musalem, Alberto G. "Why Focus on Culture?" Speech presented at Towards a New Age of Responsibility in Banking and Finance: Getting the Culture and the Ethics Right, Goethe-Universität Frankfurt am Main, Frankfurt, Germany. Posted by Federal Reserve Bank of New York, November 23, 2015. https://www.newyorkfed.org/newsevents/speeches/2015/mus151123.

National Association of Corporate Directors (NACD). *Culture as a Corporate Asset: 2017 NACS Blue Ribbon Commission Report*. Arlington, VA: National Association of Corporate Directors. https://www.nacdonline.org/culture.

Nesbitt, Mary, and John Lavine. *Reaching New Readers: Revolution Not Evolution*. Readership Institute, July 2004.

Nukić, Ivana Šandrk, and Ivana Načinović Braje. "Considerations of National Culture's Role in Explaining Competitiveness." *Ekonomski Vjesnik: Review of Contemporary Entrepreneurship, Business, and Economic Issues* 30, no. 2 (2017): 383–97. hrcak.srce.hr/ojs/index.php/ekonomski-vjesnik/article/view/5089/3329.

O'Reilly, Charles A., III, and Michael L. Tushman. *Lead and Disrupt: How to Solve the Innovator's Dilemma*. Stanford, CA: Stanford University Press, 2016.

———. "The Ambidextrous Organization." *Harvard Business Review*, April 2004. https://hbr.org/2004/04/the-ambidextrous-organization.

Papanek, Michael, and Liz Alexander. *From Breakdown to Breakthrough: Forging Resilient Business Relationships in the Heat of Change*. New York: Morgan James, 2017.

Peltier, Robert. "Strategic Culture Change Works Wonders." *Power* 148, no. 7 (September 2004): 32–35.

Perme, Catherine M. "Does Culture HAVE to Eat Strategy for Lunch?' *Constructive Culture* (blog), December 4, 2018. https://www.humansynergistics.com/blog/constructive-culture-blog/details/constructive-culture/2018/12/04/does-culture-have-to-eat-strategy-for-lunch.

Pons Bakery. "Moderna Domacica." Pons Bakery Channel. YouTube. Video, 1:32. https://www.youtube.com/watch?v=DYGYnlQjh4A&list=PLyoq7vN_hoA745IIfDZsTHRwuL6E56gOl.

Port of San Diego. "Port President/CEO Announces Retirement." Port of San Diego Press Release, September 17, 2008.

Potter, Richard E., and Pierre A. Balthazard. "Virtual Team Interaction Styles: Assessment and Effects." *International Journal of Human-Computer Studies* 56, no. 4 (April 2002): 423–43.

Potter, Richard E., Robert A. Cooke, and Pierre A. Balthazard. "Virtual Team Interaction: Assessment, Consequences, and Management." *Team Performance Management* 6, no. 7/8 (2000): 131–37.

Powell, Ronald W. "Port District President to Leave at Year's End." *San Diego Union Tribune*, September 17, 2008.

PR Web. "Online Original Design T-Shirt Sales in the US Industry Market Research Report Now Available from IBISWorld." Benzinga, April 2, 2014. http://www.benzinga.com/pressreleases/14/04/p4441150/online-original-design-t-shirt-sales-in-the-us-industry-market-research.

Puranam, Phanish. "Why Even Bad Strategy Is Worth Doing Well." *Insead Knowledge*, January 21, 2014. https://knowledge.insead.edu/strategy/why-even-bad-strategy-is-worth-doing-well-3125.

Quinn, Robert E. *Deep Change: Discovering the Leader Within*. San Francisco: Jossey-Bass, 1996.

Rahim, M. Afzalur. *Managing Conflict in Organizations*. New York: Praeger, 1986.

Ramakrishnan, Sreekanth, and Michael V. Testani. "Leadership's Role in Sustaining a Lean Transformation." SEMS Webinar. IBM Center for Learning and Development, March 16, 2011.

Reader's Digest Australia. "Award: Winner. Category: Breakfast Food." Trusted Brands Australia 2019. http://www.homeoftrustedbrands.com.au/brand-showcase/weet-bix.asp.

Readership Institute. *The Power to Grow Readership: Research from the Impact Study of Newspaper Readership*. Evanston, IL: Readership Institute, Media Management Center at Northwestern University, 2001. http://1e9svy22oh333mryr83l4s02.wpengine.netdna-cdn.com/wp-content/uploads/2007/12/impact-power-grow-readership.pdf.

Reference for Business. "SIC 2043: Cereal Breakfast Foods." *Encyclopedia of American Industries*. Accessed February 26, 2019. http://www.referenceforbusiness.com/industries/Food-Kindred-Products/Cereal-Breakfast-Foods.html.

Reinhardt, Jörg. "Flat Hierarchy: Growing the Culture at Novartis." Interview by Maike Telgheder. *Handelsblatt Today*, June 11, 2015. https://www.handelsblatt.com/today/companies/flat-hierarchy-growing-the-culture-at-novartis/23503718.html.

Riggio, Ronald E. "Pygmalion Leadership: The Power of Positive Expectations." Cutting-Edge Leadership (blog). *Psychology Today*, April 18, 2009. https://www.psychologytoday.com/us/blog/cutting-edge-leadership/200904/pygmalion-leadership-the-power-positive-expectations.

Ringel, Michael, Andrew Taylor, and Hadi Zablit. *The Most Innovative Companies 2015: Four Factors That Differentiate Leaders*. Boston: Boston Consulting Group, 2015. https://media-publications.bcg.com/MIC/BCG-Most-Innovative-Companies-2015.pdf.

Rogers, Everett M. *Diffusion of Innovation*. New York: Free Press of Glencoe, 1962.

Ronen, Simcha, and Oded Shenkar. "Clustering Countries on Attitudinal Dimensions: A Review and Synthesis." *Academy of Management Review* 10, no. 3 (July 1985): 435–54.

Rosenthal, Robert, and Lenore Jacobson. *Pygmalion in the Classroom*. Expanded ed. New York: Irvington, 1992.

Rousseau, Denise M. "Normative Beliefs in Fund-Raising Organizations: Linking Culture to Organizational Performance and Individual Responses." *Group & Organization Management* 15, no. 4 (December 1990): 448–60.

"Safe[t]y Culture Controversy." *Industrial Safety & Hygiene News*, October 2, 2013. https://www.ishn.com/articles/96992-safey-culture-controversy.

Saha, Chanchal, Sarah S. Lam, Sreekanth Ramakrishnan, and Warren Boldrin. "Lean Transformation for Production Planning and Inventory Management of Drawer Configuration." In *Proceedings of the 2015 Industrial and Systems Engineering Research Conference*, edited by S. Cetinkaya and J. Ryan. Nashville, TN, May 2015. https://www.researchgate.net/publication/283732771_Lean_Transformation_for_Production_Planning_and_Inventory_Management_of_Drawer_Configuration.

Sanders, Eric J., and Robert A. Cooke. "Financial Returns from Organizational Culture Improvement: Translating 'Soft' Changes into 'Hard' Dollars." White paper presented at the American Society of Training and Development (ASTD) Expo, Orlando Florida, June 6, 2005. https://www.humansynergistics.com/docs/default-source/default-document-library/financial_returns_from_culture_astd_v-2-0.pdf.

Sanfilippo, Fred, Neeli Bendapudi, Anthony Rucci, and Leonard Schlesinger. "Strong Leadership and Teamwork Drive Culture and Performance Change: Ohio State University Medical Center 2000–2006." *Academic Medicine* 83, no. 9 (September 2008): 845–54.

SaskCentral. *2015 Annual Report*. http://www.saskcentral.com/About-Us/Documents/annual_2015.pdf#search=2015%20annual%20report.

———. "SaskCentral Named One of Canada's Best Workplaces for Women." *Newswire*, March 6, 2017. https://www.newswire.com/news/saskcentral-named-one-of-canadas-best-workplaces-for-women-5915573.

Sasse, Ben. "The Challenge of Our Disruptive Era." *Wall Street Journal*, April 21, 2017.

Saunders, Todd. "Sanitarium—The Perfect Storm." Presented at the 2014 Human Synergistics Australian Conference, Sydney Australia, October 2014. Video, 35:38. https://www.youtube.com/watch?v=CYArE1vC-4Y.

Savage, Grant T., John D. Blair, and Ritch L. Sorenson. "Consider Both Relationships and Substance When Negotiating Strategically." *Academy of Management Executive* 3, no. 3 (February 1989): 37–48.

Schein, Edgar. *The Corporate Culture Survival Guide*. San Francisco: Jossey-Bass, 2009.

———. "Organizational Culture." *American Psychologist* 45, no. 2 (February 1990): 109–119.

———. *Organizational Culture and Leadership*. 4th ed. San Francisco: Jossey-Bass, 2010.

———. "So You Want to Create a Culture?" *Constructive Culture* (blog), November 6, 2015. https://www.humansynergistics.com/blog/constructive-culture-blog/details/constructive-culture/2015/11/06/so-you-want-to-create-a-culture.

Schjonberg, Mary Frances. "Historic Joint Meeting Hears of Effort to Change Church's Culture." *Episcopal News Service*, September 15, 2016. http://episcopaldigitalnetwork.com/ens/2016/09/15/historic-joint-meeting-hears-of-effort-to-change-churchs-culture/.

Schroeder-Saulnier, Deborah. *The Power of Paradox: Harness the Energy of Competing Ideas to Uncover Radically Innovative Solutions*. Pompton Plains, NJ: Career Press, 2014.

Scott, Susan. *Fierce Conversations: Achieving Success at Work and in Life One Conversation at a Time*. New York: Berkley Books, 2004.

Senge, Peter M. *The Fifth Discipline: The Art and Practice of the Learning Organization*. New York: Currency, 1990.

Šešić, Milena Dragićević, with Hristina Mikić and Goran Tomka. "Serbia/ 1. Historical Perspective: Cultural Policies and Instruments." *Compendium of Cultural Policies and Trends*, February 18, 2019. http://www.culturalpolicies.net/web/serbia.php.

Sethia, Nirmal K., and Mary Ann Von Glinow. "Arriving at Four Cultures by Managing the Reward System." In *Gaining Control of the Corporate Culture*, edited by Ralph H. Kilmann, Mary J. Saxton, and Roy Serpa (San Francisco: Jossey-Bass, 1985).

Sharkey, Linda. "GE Capital." In *Best Practices in Leadership Development and Organization Change: How the Best Companies Ensure Meaningful Change and Sustainable Leadership*, edited by Louis Carter, David Ulrich, and Marshall Goldsmith, 161–80. San Francisco: Pfeiffer, 2005.

———. "Leveraging HR: How to Develop Leaders in Real Time." In *Human Resources in the 21st Century*, edited by Marc Effron, Robert Gandossy, and Marshall Goldsmith, 67–77. New York: John Wiley & Sons, 2003.

Sharpe, Richard. "Best Practice Case Study: Improving Leadership Performance at GE Financial." Plymouth, MI: Human Synergistics International, 2011. https://www.humansynergistics.com/docs/default-source/default-document-library/gecasestudy_v-1-1.pdf.

Shortell, Stephen M., Jack E. Zimmerman, Denise M. Rousseau, Robin R. Gillies, Douglas P. Wagner, Elizabeth A. Draper, William A. Knaus, and Joanne Duffy. "The Performance of Intensive Care Units: Does Good Management Make a Difference?" *Medical Care* 32, no. 5 (May 1994): 508–25.

Shyamsunder, Aarti, and Cynthia Emrich. "Win-Win-Win! Constructive Cultures Benefit Women and Men, and Organizations Too." *Constructive Culture* (blog), Human Synergistics International, August 7, 2015. http://constructiveculture.com/win-win-win-constructive-cultures-benefit-women-and-men-and-organizations-too/.

Sichon, Liza. *The Art of Human Resources: An Insider's Guide to Influencing Your Company Culture*. Gold River, CA: Authority Publishing, 2017. Kindle.

Silla, Inmaculada, Joaquin Navajas, and G. Kenneth. Koves. "Organizational Culture and a Safety-Conscious Work Environment: The Mediating Role of Employee Communication Satisfaction." *Journal of Safety Research*, 61 (2017): 121–27. https://www.researchgate.net/publication/314173995_Organizational_culture_and_a_safety-conscious_work_environment_The_mediating_role_of_employee_communication_satisfaction.

Simon, Andrea. "What Type of Culture Do Women Really Want?" *Forbes*, June 1, 2016. https://www.forbes.com/sites/womensmedia/2016/06/01/what-type-of-corporate-culture-do-women-really-want/#59192f7036c7.

Smith, Kevin. "How to Leverage Management/Impact® for Constructive Strategy Execution." *Constructive Culture* (blog), March 18, 2019. https://www.humansynergistics.com/blog/constructive-culture-blog/details/constructive-culture/2019/03/19/how-to-leverage-management-impact-for-constructive-strategy-execution.

Sorenson, Ritch L. "Conflict Management Strategies Used by Successful Family Businesses." *Family Business Review* 12, no. 4 (1999): 325–40.

Sprague, Shawn. "Below Trend: The U.S. Productivity Slowdown since the Great Recession." *Beyond the Numbers* 6, no. 2 (January 2017). https://www.bls.gov/opub/btn/volume-6/below-trend-the-us-productivity-slowdown-since-the-great-recession.htm.

Spain, Everett, and Boris Groysberg. "Making Exit Interviews Count." *Harvard Business Review*, April 2016: 88–95.

Statista. "Revenue of Spreadshirt from 2006 to 2017." Statista. http://www.statista.com/statistics/454899/revenue-spreadshirt/.

StopPress Team. "Sanitarium Takes the Biscuit to Busy People with Weet-Bix Go." *StopPress*. October 27, 2015. http://stoppress.co.nz/news/breakfastbiscuitstory.

Strategy&. "Culture and Culture Change: Why Culture Matters and How It Makes Change Stick." Infographic. Katzenbach Center, PwC, 2013. https://www.strategyand.pwc.com/media/file/Strategyand_Infographic_Why-Culture-Matters-and-How-It-Makes-Change-Stick.pdf.

Straumann. *Annual Report 2012: Stepping into Tomorrow's World*. Basel, Switzerland: Institut Straumann AG. https://www.straumann.com/content/dam/media-center/group/en/documents/annual-report/2012/2012_STMN_AnnualReport.pdf.

———. *Extraordinary Performers: 2015 Annual Report*. Basel, Switzerland: Institut Straumann AG. https://www.straumann.com/content/dam/media-center/group/en/documents/annual-report/2015/STMN_2015AR_final_web.pdf.

———. *We Love What We Do: 2014 Annual Report*. Basel, Switzerland: Institut Straumann AG. https://www.straumann.com/content/dam/internet/xy/resources/corporate/annual-reports/en/STR_Annual_Report_2014_incl_Financial_Report_FINAL.pdf.

Straumann Group. "About the Company: Our Culture." https://www.straumann.com/group/en/home/about/global-straumann-group/our-culture.html.

———. *2016 Annual Report: We Create Opportunities*. Basel, Switzerland: Institut Straumann AG, 2017. https://www.straumann.com/content/dam/media-center/group/en/documents/annual-report/2016/2016%20Annual%20Report.pdf.

———. "2016 Full-Year Results: Conference Presentation for Investors, Analysts, and Media." Slides presented in Basel, Switzerland, February 16, 2017. http://www.straumann.com/content/dam/internet/straumann_com/Resources/investor-relations/annual-report/2017/Straumann-2016-FY-Presentation.pdf.

———. "2017 Nine-Month and Third Quarter Sales: Webcast Presentation for Investors, Analysts and Media." Slides presented in Basel, Switzerland, October 26, 2017. https://www.straumann.com/content/dam/media-center/group/en/documents/presentation/2017/straumann-2017-q3-presentation.pdf.

———. "Straumann Group Posts Revenue Growth of 13% (Organic) with Further Operating-Margin Expansion." Media Release. Basel, Switzerland, 2017. http://www.straumann.com/content/dam/internet/straumann_com/Resources/investor-relations/annual-report/2017/Straumann%202016%20FY%20Media%20Release.pdf.

Sull, Donald, Rebecca Homkes, and Charles Sull. "Why Strategy Execution Unravels—And What to Do about It." *Harvard Business Review*, March 2015. Reprint.

Szumal, Janet L., ed. "The Impact of Leaders and Managers across and within Different Countries." White paper. Plymouth, MI: Human Synergistics International, 2014. https://www.humansynergistics.com/docs/default-source/research-publications/impact_ldr_mgr_across_countries.pdf.

Szumal, Janet L. *An International Study of the Reliability and Validity of Leadership/Impact*. Plymouth, MI: Human Synergistics International, 2002. https://www.humansynergistics.com/docs/default-source/research-publications/livalidity.pdf.

———. *The Reliability and Validity of Management/Impact*. Plymouth, MI: Human Synergistics International, 2012. https://www.humansynergistics.com/docs/default-source/research-publications/szumal-j-l-(2012)-the-reliability-and-validity-of-management-impact-(m-i)-.pdf.

Szumal, Janet L., and Robert A. Cooke. *Management/Impact Confidential Feedback Report*. Plymouth, MI: Human Synergistics International, 2008.

———. *Organizational Culture and Employee Involvement: The Experience of a Transmission Plant*. Plymouth, MI: Human Synergistics, 1991.

Tannenbaum, Arnold S. and Robert A. Cooke. "Control and Participation." *Journal of Contemporary Business* 3, no. 4 (Autumn 1974): 35–46.

Testani, Michael V., and Sreekanth Ramakrishnan. "Sustaining a Transformation through People, Process and Technology Focus." Institute of Industrial Engineers (IIE) Annual Conference and Exposition 2013. Pre-conference Workshop Notes, IBM, 2012. https://www.iise.org/uploadedFiles/Webcasts/PreConferenceWorkshop_Sustaining_Ramakrishnan.pdf.

Thomas, Kenneth W. "Conflict and Conflict Management." In *Handbook of Industrial and Organizational Psychology*, edited by Marvin D. Dunnette, 889–935. Chicago: Rand McNally, 1976.

Thompson, James D. *Organizations in Action: Social Science Bases of Administrative Theory*. New York: Routledge, 2017.

Trist, Eric L., and Kenneth W. Bamforth. "Some Social and Psychological Consequences of the Longwall Method of Coal-Getting." *Human Relations* 4, no. 1 (1951): 3–38.

United Auto Workers, dir. *The Leadership Alliance at Hydra-Matic Toledo*. Detroit, MI: United Auto Workers, 1990. Videocassette (VHS), 36 min.

van Dam, Nick, and Els van der Helm. "The Organizational Cost of Insufficient Sleep." *McKinsey Quarterly*, February 2016. http://www.mckinsey.com/business-functions/organization/our-insights/the-organizational-cost-of-insufficient-sleep.

Wall Street Journal. "Illinois: Land of Leaving." Editorial, December 22, 2016. https://www.wsj.com/articles/illinois-land-of-leaving-1482451561.

Ware, Mark E., Gary K. Leak, and Nancy W. Perry. "*Life Styles Inventory*: Evidence for Its Factor Validity." *Psychological Reports* 56, no. 3 (1985): 963–68.

Wasserman, Noam. *The Founder's Dilemmas: Anticipating and Avoiding the Pitfalls That Can Sink a Startup*. Princeton, NJ: Princeton University Press, 2012.

Weber, Deborah, and Peter Sorenson. "Organizational Culture and TQM Implementation." *Training & Development*, April 1994. Reprint.

Weick, Karl E., and Robert E. Quinn. "Organizational Change and Development." *Annual Review of Psychology* 50 (February 1999): 361–86.

Weidner, C. Ken, II. "Trust and Distrust at Work: Normative and Dyad-Exchange Influences on Individual and Subunit Performance." PhD diss., University of Illinois at Chicago, 1997. https://www.indigo.uic.edu/handle/10027/8765/browse?value=Weidner%2C+C.+Ken%2C+II.&type=author.

Williams, Vickey. *All Eyes Forward: How to Help Your Newsroom Get Where It Wants to Go Faster*. Reston, VA: American Press Institute, 2007.

World Bank. "Small and Medium Enterprises (SMES) Finance: Improving SMEs' Access to Finance and Finding Innovative Solutions to Unlock Sources of Capital." World Bank Group. Accessed February 26, 2019. https://www.worldbank.org/en/topic/smefinance.

WorldCity Staff. "Changing Corporate Culture: Novartis Pharmaceuticals." *World City*, March 14, 2016. https://www.worldcityweb.com/changing-corporate-culture-novartis-pharmaceuticals.

Zanker, Silke, and Richi Gil, "Ultimate Culture Webinar—Tapping into 15 Years of Changing Organizational Cultures around the Globe," October 17, 2018, https://www.axialent.com/webinar/webinar-tapping-into-15-years-changing-organizational-cultures/.

About the Authors

JANET L. SZUMAL is a Senior Research Associate for Human Synergistics Inc. and is the lead author of *Management/Impact* (M/I), the *Organizational Change Challenge™*, and the *Project Management Challenge™*. She received her PhD in Human Resource Management from the University of Illinois at Chicago.

Janet has developed and codeveloped leader's guides and support materials for many Human Synergistics products, including guides for *Leadership/Impact* and the *Cultural Change Situation™*, feedback reports for the *Organizational Culture Inventory* and *Organizational Effectiveness Inventory*, and the OCI® *Interpretation and Development Guide*. Her research on the reliability and validity of Human Synergistics diagnostic tools has appeared in academic journals such as the *Journal of Applied Behavioral Science* and *Psychological Reports*.

Janet's writings on the use and features of Human Synergistics surveys and simulations have appeared in various magazines and books (including the *Team and Organizational Development Sourcebook*), on Human Synergistics' website and the *Constructive Culture* blog, and in workshop manuals for accreditation programs.

ROBERT A. COOKE is CEO and Director of Human Synergistics International and Associate Professor Emeritus of Management at the University of Illinois at Chicago. Rob was previously an Associate Research Scientist at the University of Michigan's Survey Research Center (Institute for Social Research) and a Visiting Scholar at Stanford University. He received his PhD in Organizational Behavior from the Kellogg School of Management,

Northwestern University, where he was a National Defense (Title IV) and Commonwealth Edison Fellow.

Rob specializes in the development and validation of surveys for individual, group, and organization development. His most widely used surveys include the *Organizational Culture Inventory, Organizational Effectiveness Inventory, Leadership/Impact,* and *Group Styles Inventory.* These instruments have been translated into numerous languages and are used throughout the world by consultants and trainers for organizational development and research purposes.

Rob is the author of more than seventy-five articles, chapters, and technical reports. His research has been selected for the William J. Davis Memorial Award for outstanding scholarly research and the Douglas McGregor Memorial Award for Excellence in the Applied Social Sciences. His teaching has been recognized with the MBA Professor of the Year Award and the Alumni Award for Outstanding Teaching at the University of Illinois at Chicago.